DATE DUE		
OCT 0 1 2002		

Economic and Social Progress in Asia

Why Pakistan Did Not Become a Tiger

Economic and Social Progress in Asia

Why Pakistan Did Not Become a Tiger

Omar Noman

Karachi

Oxford University Press

Oxford   New York   Delhi
1997

Oxford University Press, Walton Street, Oxford OX2 6DP

Oxford New York
Athens Auckland Bangkok Bombay
Calcutta Cape Town Dar es Salaam Delhi
Florence Hong Kong Istanbul Karachi
Kuala Lumpur Madras Madrid Melbourne
Mexico City Nairobi Paris Singapore
Taipei Tokyo Toronto

and associated companies in

Berlin Ibadan

Oxford is a trade mark of Oxford University Press

ISBN 0 19 577781 6

Printed in Pakistan at
Mas Printers, Karachi
Published by
Ameena Saiyid, Oxford University Press
5-Bangalore Town, Sharae Faisal
PO Box 13033, Karachi-75350, Pakistan.

Acknowledgements

This book is not the product of a single research project. Accordingly, its acknowledgements of debt are spread wide across institutions and individuals who have either commented on the text or made helpful comments in seminars or lectures where sections of the book were presented. At Oxford University, acknowledgements are due to Professors Robert Cassen, Alex Duncan, Frances Stewart, Samina Ahmed, Gopal Krishna, Neville Maxwell, Gowher Rizvi, Simon Hunt, Martin Rimmer, Roger Hay, and Iftikhar Malik. In the UNDP, Dr Mahbubul Haq, Hans van Sponeck, Inge Kaul, Kees Klein, Neil Buhne, and Fatma Shah supported related work and stimulated many questions. At the Institute of Social Studies at The Hague, Professors Graham Pyatt and Henk Thomas provided valuable comments and the opportunity to get feedback through the presentation of the initial hypothesis at a seminar. In Bangkok, Natsuki Hiratsuka provided stimulating feedback on a number of issues related to Eastern Asia. At the Asian Development Bank, encouragement and feedback were provided by Mr Seki and Dr Hamid. Professor Gus Papanek of Harvard University provided substantive guidance on some of the issues.

The Pakistan Institute of Development Economics provided the important opportunity of presenting a paper based on the book at their annual general meeting. Accordingly, I am grateful to Professors Naqvi, Sarfaraz Qureshi, and Ghaffar Chaudry in particular. Professor Hafeez Pasha of the Applied Economics Research Centre, Karachi University made incisive comments on the paper presented, which were useful for the revisions. Dr Shahrukh Rafi Khan of the Sustainable Development Policy Institute encouraged an excellent debate on some of the issues presented.

At Oxford University Press, the encouragement and support of Ameena Saiyid, Charles Lewis, Zohrain Zafar, and the Yasmin Qureshis is much appreciated.

Omar Noman
Oxford
September 1996

For Bhai, but for whom...

...and in memory of Professor Abdus Salam, whose theory on the fundamental forces is regarded by physicists as one of the landmarks of twentieth century science. Dr Salam, whose work received recognition, inter alia, from the Nobel Prize, passed away in November 1996.

Contents

Tables

Figures

Charts

PART A

ECONOMIC DEVELOPMENT AND SOCIAL CHANGE IN EASTERN ASIA

This world is a children's playground for me;
This spectacle unfolds day and night in front of my
eyes.

A child's play is the throne of Solomon for me;
An ordinary event is the miracle of the Messiah in my
eyes.

Ghalib

Excerpt from *Ghazals of Ghalib,* edited by Aijaz Ahmed, (Oxford University Press, Bombay, 1994)

بازیچهٔ اطفال ہے، دُنیا، مرے آگے
ہوتا ہے شب و روز تماشا مرے آگے
اک کھیل ہے، اورنگِ سلیماں، مرے نزدیک
اک بات ہے، اعجازِ مسیحا، مرے آگے

Inability of those in power to still the voices of their own
conscience is the great force leading to desired changes.

President Kaunda, Zambia

CHAPTER 1

THE EMERGENCE OF TWO CONTINENTS
An Overview of Trends in Asian Development

HISTORICAL PERSPECTIVE

Asia has split into two continents. One part has become a symbol of rapid transformation. The other still conveys the image of a volcano paralysed by poverty and strife. The 'Asian Drama'[1] is now being enacted on two stages. One contains the dynamic East and South East Asia, while the other houses the somewhat plagued South Asia. While East Asia has taken off and in the development literature become a model for countries to emulate, South Asia, along with Africa, has become synonymous with entrenched poverty. Of the 47 countries categorized under low human development by the UN, 6 are in South Asia. Almost all of the others are in Africa.[2] There are none from East Asia or South America.

East Asia represents the first case of post-colonial economic success. One of the most heartening features of the late 20th century has been the rapid increase in incomes in the most populous part of the world. The economic achievements have been phenomenal. No group of countries has developed so rapidly. This sustained increase in incomes has been accompanied, in most countries, by improvements in the distribution of income.[3] This was in marked contrast to the European and American experience, where the inverse relationship provided the basis for the 'Kuznet's Curve', which postulated that income distribution would worsen as income increases, specially in the early stages of development. To a large extent, the difference in outcomes across continents is due to the combined effect of the Chinese revolution and the Meiji restoration, a theme explored in more detail later in the text.

East Asia has also laid the base for the structural transformation of the global economy. The dynamics of change suggest that within five decades China will achieve living standards comparable to the current industrial nations.[4] Thus, if current growth trends are sustained, a quarter of the world's population will have incomes presently enjoyed by a small minority of rich nations. Further, most of East Asia is likely to achieve living standards currently enjoyed in Europe and North America, within the next 20 years.[5]

The dynamism already evident in the region has created many positive externalities, which have helped the poorer countries of the area to grow more rapidly. An illuminating example of this is provided by China. Over 75% of the foreign direct investment (FDI) that has gone into the country, over the last 15 years, has come from Hong Kong, Taiwan, and Japan. Similarly, other countries of the region wishing to emulate economic success, such as Vietnam and Laos, are being assisted not only by FDI from neighbours such as Thailand but also through the demand stimulus provided by the rapid growth in regional incomes.

The reassuring prospect of expanding prosperity for a region which contains half the global population, will do much to alter the abnormal situation created by colonialism. The world's distribution of income has never been as unequal as it has been in the 20th century; at present nearly 80% of the world's income of $23 trillion is generated by a mere 20% of its population. The remaining 80% of the world gets only 20% of its income. This 80/20 perverse symmetry is largely a legacy of a century of debilitating colonialism. The accompanying intellectual enslavement prevented most of the world from participating in the remarkable science and technology revolution which underpins modern economic development. It is, therefore, not surprising that progressive attitudes to technology acquisition and modern education have played such a critical role in the Asian economic revolution (*see* Chapters 2 and 3).

In Asia as a whole, these are exciting times, although troubled in some cases. Independence has entailed the unleashing of change, while trying to manage the frictions released by rapid modernization. These dynamics have been generated after a long period of social stagnation. The social control mechanisms of colonialism tried to ensure that these societies remained frozen in time, since autonomous and internally generated change was disturbing anathema. Change was to be controlled; in South Asia, for example, the overriding purpose of the state was to impose law and order and obstruct change. As a result, society ossified, with the state supporting the most reactionary and conservative sections of society to sustain power. It followed that the state took no responsibility for the development of the mass of illiterate and malnourished citizens.

Independence, on the other hand, has asked searching questions about the direction of change. It has exposed the frailties, injustices, and repressions inherent in many traditional structures. This has involved inevitable conflict with groups who were beneficiaries of frequently coercive mechanisms. Equity of class, ethnicity, race, and gender has generated acute tensions. Independence has meant the freedom to engage in delayed domestic battles.

The process of modernization has entailed asking the larger question of where society should go. Most of Europe was at liberty to ask this question in the 19th and 20th centuries, which led to an era of revolutions, convulsions, conflict, and progress. In Asia, the quest for a new direction has unleashed many similar battles—regarding the place of religion, the traditional elite, and the positive role of many traditional values. This is the struggle over the 'big ideas' which shape societies, since much is at stake. Eastern Asia has been embroiled in many convulsions related to these issues, but has, in general, managed to resolve some, if not all, of the key conflicts. The implications of their success are considerable. As mentioned earlier, the global distributional problem is likely to acquire a different form, if East and South East Asia sustain their development path. There is a grave danger that much of Africa, and parts of South America, may become even more marginalized.

For South Asia, this is a tantalizing moment. All countries of the sub-region are desperately seeking to replicate East Asian success. They are grappling with the positive pressure exerted by this progress. But undertaking the structural reforms required is not easy, partly because it is difficult to redress the errors and change course, while one is battling with mounting difficulties.

Pakistan's economic planners still wistfully recall the 1960s, when Korean technocrats used to visit the country as the model for developing and harnessing an indigenous private sector, with appropriate support and incentives being provided by the state. Since the start of the 1970s, their development paths have diverged dramatically, for reasons explored in the next chapter. During this period, almost all countries in Eastern Asia, including the Muslim majority countries of Eastern Asia, such as Malaysia and Indonesia, have made major advances in both income levels, as well as in social policy.

For India too, East Asia is having an important influence. The rapid and far more equitable development in China is leading to an appreciable gap between the two large countries. Not only has China had much more rapid growth, its human development indicators are far superior. Most of its population is literate, its population growth rate is half that of India, while average life expectancy is 10 years longer. The collapse of India's close ally, the Soviet Union, has also discredited continued adherence to an inward looking central planning model which was pursued in India after independence. The total number of people under the poverty line in India is almost equal to the total population of Africa. As a result of inadequate performance, India is undergoing a major overhaul of economic strategy, which in its essentials, is trying to imitate East Asian policy experience.

Sri Lanka was perhaps better placed than any of the South Asian countries. A relatively small country with high literacy, a reasonable natural resource base, and a good human capital endowment, it was ideally placed for brisk and equitable development. The failure of ethnic accommodation, however, has taken its toll. Sri Lanka has paid a heavy price for the unrelenting civil war, which has consumed the energies of this former showcase. Sri Lanka provides grim evidence of how ethnic conflict, and the resulting lack of social cohesion, arrest development.

Bangladesh has not fared well. It has faced difficulties in coping with the high population density, political turmoil, and lack of strategic significance. Although there have been encouraging signs, such as the success of garment exports and the emergence of some rural credit institutions,[6] Bangladesh continues to lag behind the other major South Asian countries.[7]

The above contrast between East and South Asia should not be viewed as an over-simplistic dichotomy of success and failure. There are many creditable South Asian achievements since independence. Pakistan's growth performance has been impressive and far better than anyone had expected. Its success in supporting entrepreneurial groups in trade and industry, as well as in the 'green revolution' in agriculture, has created significant capacities for future development. Similarly, India has created a substantial technological capacity, reflected in the recent growth of the computer software industry. Several regions have performed creditably. Punjab's agricultural performance, for example, has been robust, as part of a strategy which has ensured a degree of national food security. Regions such as Kerala have also shown a willingness to invest in social development, which was at levels similar to Sri Lanka. The latter's advances in class equity and social liberalism were envied.[8]

While these qualifications are worth bearing in mind, they do not alter the larger picture of a continent being divided into two halves, separated by relative affluence and stability. The differences become evident in the comparison of outcomes which are made in the next section.

This book deals with the grand canvas of economic development and social change. Social change, in this book, is indicated by education, health, and demographic trends; factors which have a strong bearing on equity. This book compares East and South East Asia with Pakistan. After half a century of independence, it is perhaps appropriate to reflect on why outcomes in capitalist economies, pursuing a similar but unfashionable path in the 1950s, have differed. At one level, this book compares different types of capitalism. Was the difference in outcome due to the fact that East Asian nations remained committed to private sector-led development, while Pakistan witnessed a major rupture in direction during the 1970s? Was East Asia able to build on its initial success, consolidate gains and then shift from a necessary initial protective phase to an outward-looking, export-led strategy, while Pakistan vacillated, lost direction and confidence? If so, did this reflect the inability in Pakistan to resolve underlying ethnic tensions?

Another set of questions relates to the difference in equity. Why did Pakistan pursue functional inequality as a policy goal while East Asians succeeded with a more inclusive capitalism? Was the pressure of communism on elites a key part of the explanation? Why was the revival of growth in the 1980s accompanied by social reversals in Pakistan, while there was a positive correlation between economic and social development in Eastern Asia during the same period?

There can be no consensus on these larger issues. At best, one can offer a systematic interpretation of recent Asian development, which tries to explain the available evidence. This is the first objective of the book. The second is an attempt to outline the measures required to create a more cohesive society, and dynamic economy, in Pakistan.

THE OUTCOMES: COMPARING THE ACHIEVEMENTS AND SHORTCOMINGS

For Pakistan it is a back-handed compliment to be compared with the most successful developing economies in the world. For a country that was considered to be a potential economic disaster at creation, it clearly has done far better than expected by some analysts. It is, however, precisely the dynamism that has been evident in patches that raises the question of counter-factual possibilities. Many features of its record suggest that the country could have been far more successful, had it not suffered from crucial economic and social policy reversals.

In order to capture the different dimensions of development, it is useful to compare Eastern Asia and Pakistan at three levels. Accordingly, the review below examines outcomes in terms of income, human development, and economic self-reliance. The latter is referred to not in terms of autarchy but more in relation to a sustainable integration into the global economy. The contrast in results sets the stage for the next chapter which tries to explain the divergence, particularly since the 1970s.

In 1993, the UN rank of countries, according to levels of the human development index, had Japan on top, with all the major East or South East Asian countries in the high or medium human development league (*see* Table 1). Pakistan remains in the low HD category. Its per capita income growth has not been rapid enough; nor have the increases in life expectancy or literacy been of a magnitude which can compare with Eastern Asia.

1. HUMAN DEVELOPMENT INDEX: EAST AND SOUTH ASIA

High Human Development	
Rank (out of 173 countries)	Country
1	Japan
24	Hong Kong
33	Korea
43	Singapore
Medium Human Development	
57	Malaysia
74	Thailand
86	Sri Lanka
92	Philippines
108	Indonesia
Low Human Development	
132	Pakistan
134	India
147	Bangladesh
152	Nepal

A telling overview is provided by Table 2, which compares Pakistan with select East and South East Asian countries. While in 1971, Pakistan's per capita income was nearly double that of Indonesia, it had fallen, in relative terms, to just 60% of Indonesia within two decades. Pakistan was also not far behind Thailand in 1971; two decades later, the per capita income of the latter was 400% higher. A similar pattern of divergence is evident with Malaysia. The most dramatic gap, however, has opened *vis-à-vis* Korea, which was considered more or less at par in the early 1960s, and in some ways faced even worse institutional and socio-political problems than Pakistan. While Korea had reached a level of income which was almost twice as large in 1971, the gap had grown to 16 times by 1991. This is particularly ironic since policy makers in both countries engaged in similar market interventions in the 1950s and 1960s in order to generate high returns to protected capital and create a private sector led industrial structure.

2. COMPARATIVE ECONOMIC DEVELOPMENT
Select data for 1971 and 1991

	Pakistan	Indonesia	Korea	Thailand	Malaysia
GNP per Capita $	170 380	90 630	310 6330	210 1570	410 2520
Exports $ bn.	0.7 6.5	1.2 29.0	1.1 71.1	0.8 28.3	1.7 34.3
GDS, as % of GDP	8.7 11.9	16.8 35.7	14.8 36.5	21.3 31.7	23.9 30.4
GDI, as % of GDP	15.6 18.7	18.4 35.1	25.1 39.1	24.2 38.9	22.4 35.9

Source: *World Development*, various issues.

The gap in per capita income is mirrored in the relative export performance. In 1971, all the five countries were at more or less similar levels. In the next two decades, the Eastern Asians moved from an import substitution phase to greater export orientation. This shift introduced competitive pressures, leading to greater efficiency as well as more extensive technological progress.

The difference in levels of accumulation are also evident in Table 2; while Eastern Asia moved into the virtuous circle of high growth and high levels of savings and investment, policy shocks and insecurities hampered a significant rise in levels of accumulation in Pakistan.

A more detailed comparison of relative performance in income levels is contained in Table 3. This compares the purchasing power of per capita incomes over three decades. This table suggests that the purchasing power of incomes in Pakistan was greater than in Korea in 1960. By the mid 1990s it had, however, become a quarter. Indonesia was also behind Pakistan in 1960, but its per capita income grew by 5.2% annually between 1965-80 as compared to 1.8% in Pakistan. The comparative success of Indonesia, Korea, and Thailand is particularly interesting in view of the large size of their population—the cases of small city states such as Singapore and Hong Kong appear to have far less value due to the difference of scale.

3. LEVEL AND GROWTH OF INCOMES

	Real GDP per capita ($ PPP*)		GNP per capita. Annual growth rate (%)	
	1960	1993	1965-80	1980-93
East & SE Asia				
China	723	2330	4.1	8.2
Japan	n.a.	20660	5.1	3.4
S. Korea	690	9710	7.3	8.2
Hong Kong	2323	21560	6.2	5.4
Malaysia	1783	8360	4.7	3.5
Singapore	2409	19350	8.3	6.1
Thailand	985	6350	4.4	6.4
Philippines	1183	2590	3.2	-0.6
Indonesia	490	3270	5.2	4.2
South Asia				
Pakistan	820	2160	1.8	3.1
India	617	1240	1.5	3.0
Sri Lanka	1389	3030	2.8	2.7
Bangladesh	621	1290	-0.3	2.1

*Purchasing Power Parity.
Sources: UNDP: *Human Development Reports* and the World Bank: *World Development Report 1994, 1995, 1996.*

Table 3 provides further evidence on the growing disparity between India and Pakistan. Average living standards were higher in Pakistan even in 1960, but the gap has grown substantially since then. However, recent policy reforms in India, and current growth trends suggest that the future may well see a reversal in relative performance even in South Asia. Current trends suggest that the Indian economy is likely to accelerate while Pakistan may remain embroiled in domestic disputes and policy inconsistencies, which have an adverse impact on growth.

Two other aspects summarized in Table 3 are worth noting. The first is the remarkable growth in per capita incomes that has been sustained over three decades in Eastern Asia. During 1965-80, the average annual growth of the countries listed, was 5.3%. Between 1980-93, this commendable growth performance fell only slightly, to 4.9%. This was largely accounted for by the Philippines. Most of the larger countries of the region, such as China, Korea, and Thailand, accelerated; China and Korea growing by a phenomenal 8.2% per year over 14 years.

The second feature worth emphasizing is that incomes rose for all the countries of Eastern and South Asia. Only Bangladesh and the Philippines suffered from a period of negative income growth. Had the most populous continent performed anywhere as badly as Africa, or even South America, the strains on the global economy would have been far more intense. As it is, serious distributional problems remain, but the success of large countries in the East bodes well for the structural transformation of the global economy

The sustained and high rates of savings and investment in Eastern Asia are confirmed in Table 4 The average investment rate in 1980, for the nine countries represented in the Table, was 32%; this rose to 34% in 1994. Public investments in infrastructure stimulated private investment in manufacturing, as well as facilitating foreign direct investment. These high investment levels were financed by an average savings rate of 31% in 1980, and 35% in 1994. In some years, countries in Eastern Asia were saving nearly half of their income. The country that was closest to Pakistan was the Philippines. Explanations of Pakistan's reasonable growth performance, in relation to its low investment levels, relate partly to the efficiency of investments, which were policy-induced, and aid inflows. A discussion of how Pakistan's incremental capital output ratio, a measure of efficiency, was affected by policies is contained later in the text

4. RATES OF ACCUMULATION
(% of GDP)

	Gross Domestic Investment		Gross Domestic Saving	
	1980	1994	1980	1984
East and SE Asia				
China	35	42	35	44
Japan	32	30	31	32
S. Korea	32	38	25	39
Hong Kong	35	31	34	33
Malaysia	30	39	33	37
Singapore	46	32	38	51
Thailand	29	40	23	35
Philippines	29	24	24	18
Indonesia	24	29	37	30
South Asia				
Pakistan	18	20	7	17
India	21	23	17	21
Sri Lanka	34	27	11	15
Bangladesh	15	14	2	8

Sources: UNDP: *Human Development Reports* and the World Bank: *World Development Report 1994, 1995, 1996.*

One of the 'fundamentals' to get right is a stable macro-economic environment. A high and volatile price level can cause uncertainty and confusion in markets. This can adversely affect investment levels as well as export markets. It is also difficult for firms to respond to relative price changes to improve efficiency. Bad macroeconomic management has imposed severe costs in parts of the world such as South America. Hyperinflation in the region has contributed to a disappointing performance. Inflationary difficulties also created major difficulties for the revival of the post-Soviet Union economies in recent years.

The advocacy of sound macroeconomic management seems obvious; however, attaining it in practice is difficult under the many pressures faced by governments. In general, Eastern Asia's record in this regard is excellent (*see* Table 5).

5. MACROECONOMIC MANAGEMENT

	Average Annual Rate of Inflation (%)	Budget Deficit/ Surplus	
	1980-93	1980	1993
East & SE Asia			
China	7.0	-2.1	-2.3
Japan	3.8	-7.0	-1.2
S. Korea	6.3	-2.3	0.6
Hong Kong	7.9		
Malaysia	2.2	-6.2	1.7
Singapore	2.5	2.2	12.6
Thailand	4.3	-4.9	2.1
Philippines	13.6	-1.4	-1.5
Indonesia	8.5	-2.3	0.7
South Asia			
Pakistan	7.4	-5.8	-7.4
India	8.7	-6.5	-4.8
Sri Lanka	11.1	-18.4	-6.4
Bangladesh	8.6	-2.5	-4.5

Sources: UNDP: *Human Development Reports* and the World Bank: *World Development Report 1994, 1995, 1996.*

During the 1980s and early 1990s, for example, only the Philippines had an annual inflation rate in excess of a single digit. In this respect, Pakistan's macroeconomic management has generally been sound. In spite of conflicts, natural disasters, and wars, the policy managers maintained a low inflation rate. Except for the post-oil price shocks of the 1970s, Pakistan has retained a relatively low inflation rate. Price stability in the mid 1950s and 1960s was followed by externally-induced acceleration in the 1970s. During the 1980s, the average inflation rate was a reasonable 7.4% (*see* Table 5). This was achieved, however, through extensive borrowing, leading to a mounting debt problem. The unsustainable fiscal deficits led to a stabilization programme, which has contributed to the slackening in growth during the 1990s.

Although problems are accumulating at present, Pakistan's past record of macroeconomic stability has generally matched that of most of the Eastern Asian countries. However, the illustrative data on budget deficits/surpluses does not bode well for the future (see Table 5). In 1993, for example, Pakistan's deficit was higher than that of any of the Eastern Asian, or indeed, South Asian countries. The need, *inter alia*, for far-reaching fiscal reform is urgent if Pakistan is to sustain a stable macroeconomic environment.

The gap between Eastern and South Asia, in direct measures of human development, has grown as rapidly as that in income levels. This is reflected in Tables 6 and 7. Sri Lanka is the only South Asian country with a record comparable to that of Eastern Asia. Pakistan's gains in life expectancy, and infant and maternal mortality have been more or less similar to India's (see Table 6). Pakistan's

6. SOCIO-ECONOMIC INDICATORS

	Life Expectancy		Infant Mortality		Maternal Mortality
	1960	1993	1960	1993	1989-95
			Per 1000 live births		Per 100,000 live births
East & SE Asia					
China	47.1	68.6	150	44	115
Japan	68.9	79.6	11	4	Insignificant
S. Korea	53.9	71.3	85	11	30
Hong Kong	66.2	78.7	44	7	Insignificant
Malaysia	53.9	70.9	73	13	34
Singapore	64.5	74.9	36	6	Insignificant
Thailand	52.3	69.2	103	36	155
Philippines	52.8	66.5	80	43	208
Indonesia	41.2	63.0	139	56	n.a.
South Asia					
Pakistan	43.1	61.8	163	89	420
India	44.0	60.7	165	81	437
Sri Lanka	62.0	72.0	71	17	30
Bangladesh	39.6	55.9	156	106	887

Sources: UNDP: *Human Development Reports* and the World Bank: *World Development Report 1994, 1995, 1996.*

average life expectancy was 43 in 1960, a year less than India's. By 1993, Pakistan and India had increased the life expectancy of their citizens by 43% and 37% respectively. Infant mortality was also virtually halved during this period in both countries. While Pakistan's progress was similar to India's, the gap with Eastern Asia grew. Already there was a noticeable difference by 1960. Life expectancy was, for example, 10 years greater in Eastern Asia, except in China and Indonesia (*see* Table 6). The gap rose further as the East Asian economies 'took off'; while Korea's infant mortality rate was virtually half that of Pakistan's in 1960, the latter's was 8 times higher a few decades later (Table 6).

Most of Eastern Asia also had a lead in literacy by the 1960s as well. But by 1993, the difference in education and demography indicators was enormous (*see* Table 7).

7. LITERACY AND DEMOGRAPHY

	Male Literacy	Female Literacy	Population (Millions)	Population Growth Rate(%)	
	(%)	(%)	1993	60-93	93-2000
East & SE Asia					
China	88.7	70.9	1196.0	1.8	1.0
Japan	99.0	99.0	124.0	0.1	0.1
S. Korea	99.1	96.1	44.1	1.7	0.9
Hong Kong	87.1	95.8	5.8	1.9	0.4
Malaysia	88.2	76.3	19.2	2.6	2.1
Singapore	95.6	85.0	2.8	1.6	0.9
Thailand	95.9	91.4	57.6	2.4	1.0
Philippines	94.6	93.9	64.8	2.6	2.0
Indonesia	89.1	76.9	191.7	2.1	1.5
South Asia					
Pakistan	48.6	23.0	132.9	3.0	2.8
India	64.3	36.0	901.5	2.2	1.8
Sri Lanka	93.1	86.2	17.9	1.8	1.2
Bangladesh	48.3	25.0	115.2	2.5	2.2

Sources: UNDP: *Human Development Reports* and the World Bank: *World Development Report 1994, 1995, 1996.*

Most Eastern Asian countries have achieved virtually universal literacy. The average male literacy rate was 93%, while it was 87% for women by 1993. This contrasts with

23% for Pakistan. The neglect of basic education in general, and female education in particular, has had a serious economic impact. A debilitating population explosion in Pakistan has been partially caused by this neglect. As a result, Pakistan needs to grow by 3% annually just to keep still.

While the average population growth rate in Eastern Asia fell from 1.8% during 1960-93 to a projected 1% in the 1993-2000 period, Pakistan's annual growth rate remains around 3%. These demographic pressures are likely to fuel instability and social upheaval, particularly if the economy continues to stagnate, as it has done in Pakistan during the 1990s.

The balance of economic and social policies in Eastern Asia have helped create the virtuous circle of high growth, extensive literacy, and slow population growth. The imbalance between social and economic policies in Pakistan is leading to a vicious circle, with high illiteracy and demographic pressures generating tensions and conflicts.

The third set of comparative indicators relates to the degree of self-reliance and external orientation achieved. A most heartening feature of Eastern Asia is how almost all countries have graduated out of any dependence on aid (*see* Table). For most countries of the region, aid is an insignificant proportion of GNP. Only in the poor performing Philippines does it exceed 1% of GNP. While Pakistan's 2.5% is not as high as Sri Lanka or Bangladesh, its level suggests that a substantial part of public investment is still dependent on aid.

In Eastern Asia, the corollary to reduced aid is a substantial growth in foreign direct investment. While China is way ahead of the others with FDI of $46 billion in 1994, substantial inflows have gone into Malaysia, Thailand, and Indonesia (*see* Table 8).

An important comparison between Pakistan and Eastern Asia relates to the performance of exports. The countries shared the experience of import substitution industrialization in the initial phase. During the 1970s, there was a major change. As East Asian industrialization expanded outwards, Pakistan suffered serious reversals. During 1970-80 countries such as Korea achieved phenomenal rates of growth in exports (*see* Table 8). While Eastern Asia witnessed annual export growth in the region of 12%, Pakistan achieved a

8. SELF-RELIANCE AND EXTERNAL ORIENTATION

	Exports (millions) 1992	Annual growth rate of exports (%) 1970-80	Annual growth rate of exports (%) 1980-92	Aid inflows (% of GNP) 1994	Net private capital flows ($ million) 1994	Debt servicing* 1980	Debt servicing* 1994	Workers' remittances ($ per capita) 1970	Workers' remittances ($ per capita) 1992
East & SE Asia									
China	84940	8.7	11.9	0.6	46555	4.4	9.3	n.a.	0.2
Japan	339492	9.0	4.6	Donor	Net outflow			****	
S. Korea	76394	23.5	11.9	0.0	8132	20.3	7.0	****	
Hong Kong	31251	9.7	5.0	0.0	Net outflow	6.6	7.9	****	
Malaysia	40705	4.8	11.3	0.1	6661				
Singapore	63386	4.2	9.9	0.0	Net outflow				
Thailand	32473	10.3	14.7	0.4	4138	20.4	16.3		
Philippines	9790	6.0	3.7	1.6	4107	29.3	21.9	n.a.	4.7
Indonesia	33815	7.2	5.6	1.0	7408	13.9	32.4	n.a.	1.0
South Asia									
Pakistan	7264	0.7	11.1	2.5	1657	18.1	35.1	1.0	14.0
India	19795	4.3	5.9	0.8	5497	10.0	26.9	0.1	2.1
Sri Lanka	2487	2.0	6.5	4.6	213	12.4	8.7	0.2	29.0
Bangladesh	1903	3.8	7.6	6.9	47	25.6	15.8	n.a.	7.0

* As % of exports of goods and services.

**** Countries such as these typically import labour and are not net recipients of remittances.

Sources: UNDP: *Human Development Reports* and the World Bank: *World Development Report 1994, 1995, 1996.*

miserly 0.7%. Pakistan's poor performance had much to do with nationalizations, which resulted in a major rupture in development strategy.

Structural reform and policy incentives led to a revival in the 1980s, when Pakistani exports grew by 11.1% annually, a rate comparable to the more successful countries (Table 8). But the country had lost a vital decade.

To a large extent, the country's external sector was bailed out by the export of labour during the 1970s. Migrant remittances to the Middle East had a profound impact on Pakistan. At $14 per capita, this was one of the highest levels in the world. Amongst the Asian countries, only Sri Lanka was higher, as workers fled from the civil strife (*see* Table 8). While remittances eased the balance of payments problems in Pakistan, they disguised the underlying malaise— nationalization and policy shocks in the 1970s had undermined the possible shift towards greater export orientation. As noted earlier, this was the decade when much of Eastern Asia moved from import substitution to export orientation.

In general, external debt servicing has not emerged as a major problem in Asia. It is certainly not of the same magnitude as in parts of Africa or South America. Except for Indonesia (32%) and the Philippines (21%), the debt service ratio remains minor for Eastern Asian economies (Table 8). For Pakistan (35%) and India (26%) the volumes are getting more serious. Pakistan has the highest debt service ratio of the countries listed in the comparative tables; a ratio that has doubled over the past decade.

In sum, over the last half century, Pakistan's comparative economic record is subject to several interpretations. Inevitably, a comparison is made with India. In this, Pakistan does surprisingly well. In many areas, such as rising average incomes, it has done better. In some aspects of human development it has done as well, while in others, such as literacy, its performance is worse. Altogether, this is not a mean achievement, given the circumstances of its birth. Several policies have contributed to this, which are discussed later in the text. A key explanatory factor was the greater role accorded to private enterprise in Pakistan, implying more resource allocation through markets, while the Nehruvian version of planning imposed a severe tax on the economy's growth potential. However, current trends suggest that the relative performance *vis-à-vis* India may change. The latter has undertaken many far-reaching reforms and the growth response is substantial. The human capital base is better and foreign direct investment is also likely to accelerate and reduce some of the infrastructural bottlenecks.

Pakistan's comparison with Eastern Asia is much less favourable. Both started with policy regimes which contained many similarities but began to diverge. There were major differences in social policy, while there was a breakdown in consensus over the leading role for the private sector. The gaps in income, literacy, and health have grown substantially. Pakistan is in the midst of intense demographic pressures and accumulating macroeconomic difficulties, while Eastern Asia is consolidating its gains, deepening its human capital base and moving up the ladder of activities with high productivity. Pakistan is confronted with the difficult dilemma of needing to make major structural changes in order to rectify the mounting problems. It none the less has the benefit of being close to a rapidly growing region, and has a history of dynamic responses which could serve it well.

Before getting embroiled in the detailed explanations of policy choices, which explain the divergence in outcomes, it is worth examining two wider political economy issues. The contentious issues of the impact of religion and democracy on economic development have received frequent comment. Typically, such social fabric explanations of economic performance tend to be vague. The section below tries to disentangle some of the complex issues related to religion, democracy, and development. This brief review cannot do justice to such contentious linkages; the section is principally intended to dismiss excessively simplistic notions of what has produced rapid development in Eastern Asia.

RELIGION, DEMOCRACY AND ECONOMIC DEVELOPMENT

It is inevitable that the process of modern economic development is expected to be accompanied by political and social change. Over the past two centuries, 'modernization' has constituted a complex web of socio-economic change. But interpretations about causality amongst the variables of change differ. One strand of analysts has tended to emphasize the importance of certain cultural values for modern economic development. European sociologists such as Max Weber put forward the hypothesis that the values held by a Christian sect were important explanatory variables for economic growth. Similar views have been expressed in Asia, where the success of the 'tigers' was attributed to Confucian value systems. Arguments which seek a source in traditional values for modern economic development, which is so closely allied to science and technology, are inherently contentious. This is a murky area, which frequently reflects the prejudices of analysts and the target readership.

In this context, it is also worth noting that, globally, monotheistic religions are a minority belief. The majority of the world's population either believes in multiple gods or is secular. The aggregate numbers are, of course, strongly influenced by China and India, but also include a substantial number of East Asian nations, which display a diversity of beliefs. Success and failure in economic development have occurred across several traditional belief systems; thus exaggerated general statements about any religion, and its positive or negative effect on economic development, should be treated with great caution.

In most ideological traditions, it is not difficult to selectively find values which promote accumulation, enterprise, and the acquisition of knowledge. Conflict can arise when modern scientific knowledge is in contention with traditional beliefs. Similarly, it is not difficult to identify customary practices and beliefs which can hamper aspects of development. But identifying whole belief systems as obstacles to development is usually based on some prejudiced views regarding unchanging static societies.

Some analysts view Islam as an obstacle to economic development, attributing low levels of development to religious beliefs. Even a cursory examination of global trends, however, reveals the superficiality of such arguments. For example, out of the 43 countries listed as the least developed in the world, 80% are Christian.[9] Yet no one attributes this failure to Christianity *per se*. Conversely, the predominantly Muslim countries of Eastern Asia, Malaysia, and Indonesia, have fared well economically over the last three decades. Literacy rates of Muslims in these countries are higher than those of Buddhists, Christians, and Hindus in other Asian countries.

All of the above is not to dismiss the effect that certain customs and beliefs can have on progress. In the case of Islamic countries, three issues are worth noting. First, the leading role of the private sector and incentives for accumulation are hardly likely to be hindered by a religion which was started by those actively engaged in trading.[10] The second issue relates to the acquisition of science and technology. This can become an obstacle if clerical groups oppose these ideas as a threat.[11] Islamic countries are not a monolithic block on this issue. Technology acquisition and a shift into higher technology is central to the Malaysian vision.[12] Similar attitudes are evident in Indonesia, whose further economic evolution is based on greater knowledge intensity. At the same time, there are a number of countries which underestimate the importance of, and feel threatened by, the spread of modern science and technology. Similar issues confronted Christianity in Europe, not least when Galileo questioned the scientific accuracy of the Bible.

The third area is social policy. Like Catholic countries, Muslim nations have tended to have high fertility and population growth. Strongly patriarchal systems have also marginalized women. In these areas too, there is no uniform static Muslim society. The diversity is reflected in successful population planning programmes in Egypt, Bangladesh, Turkey, Indonesia, and Malaysia. Some of these campaigns utilized the fact that the Prophet of Islam had one child, a daughter. The conventional role of women is changing in the more liberal states but is static or facing reversals in some of the conservative ones. Social policy is particularly under threat in some Muslim countries which are faced by the rise of puritanism and fascism.

Pakistan's record in each of these categories has been shaped by the composition of the elite and regional ideological currents. The private sector-led strategy did not confront any ideological constraints; on the contrary, the tradition of commerce was useful. As noted elsewhere in the text, Pakistan and East Asia adopted a similar position on state intervention in markets to support and guide the private sector. The reasons for Pakistan's divergence in the 1970s were to do with ethnic and class divisions, not religion. While the neglect of science and technology has been obvious, again its cause has not been obstruction from religious sources. The country has pursued technology selectively—as for example in the pursuit of nuclear technology for security purposes. Similarly, there have been useful economic returns to some of the applied research in agriculture. But the build-up of human capital, as well as technology adoption capacities, were hampered by the neglect of primary education or by an inward-looking industrial structure.

It is arguable that if Pakistan had moved from the import substitution phase towards an outward orientation in the 1970s, the pace of technology adoption may have been accelerated substantially. Adoption of modern technology was critical to the productivity gains and shift in comparative advantage in Eastern Asia but, as the experience of Malaysia and Indonesia suggests, policy responses in these areas were not determined by religion.

In the realm of social policy, however, Pakistan has been affected by ideological currents in the 1980s. While the 1970s witnessed reversals for the private sector, the general tone of social policy was progressive. At the level of rhetoric at least, the policy stance was very much towards the reform of a deeply conservative society, and towards a more progressive role for women. This built on modernizing, through 'top down' measures enacted in the 1960s.[13] This orientation to change was not, alas, supported by the necessary public investments in primary education and health.

In the 1980s, however, the paths of Eastern Asia and Pakistan diverged sharply, as far as social policy was concerned. While economic policies in Pakistan revived the private sector, social policy became the victim of a puritanical religious assault. This resulted in the abandonment of the previous stance of social policy and explicitly reinforced conservative traditional practices, which were detrimental to women. The child-bearing role of women was supported by the regressive patriarchal notions of confining women to home and modest dress (*'chaddar and char diwari'*).[14] Instead of responding urgently to an exponential growth in population and illiteracy, Pakistan lost a decade to religious obscurantism. Through this period, Eastern Asia consolidated its gains and moved decisively forward in terms of the role of women and deepening its human capital.

Thus, at a broad level, there is no simple correlation between the traditional belief systems and economic development. Socio-economic progress inevitably involves a change in many customary relationships. The extent to which societies are able to adapt to these imperatives of modernization helps determine the pace of change. This accommodation does not entail the abandonment of many cherished cultural practices which shape identities. This is clearly evident in cases such as Japan, China, and Korea, where modernization has coexisted with a strong pride in their own cultures. At the same time, there are some ideological trends which can be inimical to socio-economic change. The type of puritanical revisionism which acquired salience in Pakistan during the 1980s did little to promote social reform.[15] The absence of such forces in Eastern Asia is part of the comparison explored later in the text.[16]

Apart from religion, another contentious issue is the relationship between economic and political reform. The majority of countries in Asia are now democracies. Asia already has the highest number of elected female leaders in the world, a trend which is likely to accelerate.[17] Further, the general absence of conflict has clearly been of enormous benefit to the region. None of the high performing East or South East Asian economies have been engaged in an international war in recent decades. This not only released resources for development but also, and perhaps more important, created a physically secure environment for investment in productive assets.

Over the last 50 years, however, democracies were more the exception than the rule. Further, the most successful economies in Asia were under technocratic-authoritarian regimes. Conversely, the country with the uninterrupted experience of democracy, India, had one of the worst records on poverty reduction in Asia. Such comparisons potentially raised discomforting questions about political liberalization and economic development. Proponents of authoritarianism argued for the necessity of such regimes for successful economic transformation, while those seeking political liberalization tried to argue the case that growth would benefit from democracy.[18]

In general, the scale of the political liberalization currently underway in much of Eastern Asia, particularly in countries such as Korea, is impressive. Its importance is underlined by the fact that virtually all of the countries were, until recently, ruled by the military. While extreme fascistic governments have been rare, many regimes were highly authoritarian and intolerant of any organized dissent. Some countries were brutalized politically and economically, such as Cambodia under the Khmer Rouge. Vietnam suffered from a prolonged succession of conflicts, while the Philippines was plundered by the Marcos regime. In a number of cases, there were periods of intense political repression and corruption was common.

In spite of the heartening political liberalization spreading across the continent, many tensions remain. Political liberalization in China and Indonesia appears inevitable in the wake of rapid economic development and opening up to the world, but the pace and direction of change are not easy to predict. Myanmar's harsh military regime continues to ignore the need for change.

In many ways, the major political dilemma across the continent will not be the transition to democratic rule but the problems of governance facing elected regimes. They have to contend with the internal stresses, conflicts and strains associated with rapid change. The diversity of many countries implies potential internal conflicts over ethnicity, religion, and class. Menacing undercurrents are evident in many existing democracies. The rise of an aggressive Hindu party in India, involved in provocative burning of mosques, does not bode well for communal harmony or nuclear non-proliferation in South Asia. The civil war in Kashmir remains a flashpoint, which could continue to absorb energies and resources needed for development. The end to ethnic conflict in Sri Lanka remains elusive, while democratic regimes remain fragile in Bangladesh, Pakistan, and the Philippines. Disturbing levels of elite corruption have undermined faith in democratic institutions in these countries. The danger of racial tension resurfacing remains present in countries such as Malaysia. In brief, managing the problems of governance and minorities in democratic regimes will have a strong bearing on social cohesion and economic development.

The parallels of political liberalization and social cohesion in Europe are interesting. At the time of South Asian independence, Europe was just recovering from the most destructive war in history. Fascists were, or had been, in power in Spain, Germany, and Italy, while the Soviet Union was under the ruthless Stalin. Countries such as Britain, France, Belgium, and the Netherlands had global dictatorships in the form of colonial regimes. But the post-war period has been exceptional, both in terms of rising prosperity and political liberalization. Democratic regimes and the welfare state have collectively reduced internal tensions and created a degree of social cohesion, which is able to absorb severe shocks. A testimony to the efficacy of these institutional changes is the fact that unemployment of over 30 million people in the 1980s has produced minimal social conflict. Further, the establishment of democracies has not hampered economic development in Europe; it should not do so in Asia either.

The threats to development are likely to arise when internal conflicts cannot be managed. In Europe, these challenges are likely to be most acute in the Eastern part of the continent, after the disintegration of the former Soviet Union. Difficulties of governance and social cohesion remain. The last two genocides in Europe have been of Jews and Muslims; other minorities also feel threatened. Avoiding war and sustaining cohesive political and legal systems will test governments in Europe and Asia, in spite of the major recent gains in political liberalization. While both European and Asian experience appears to suggest that economic and political liberalization tend to be correlated, identifying the precise links leads to a number of problems, which are summarized below.

The most prosperous countries in the world are democratic and, as noted earlier, the existence of this democracy has not been an impediment to their recent growth performance. However, there are a number of conceptual problems with the argument that democracy leads unambiguously to better economic performance. We would all like to believe this. Unfortunately, it is simply not true.

There are five issues to contend with. The first is an empirical fact—democracy is neither necessary nor sufficient for a sustained period of economic growth. From this it does not follow that democracy is incompatible with economic development, nor does it imply that authoritarianism is necessary for growth. The reasons for widely differing economic outcomes emerging from similar political systems is largely to do with an excessively simplistic typology of regimes. Not all authoritarian regimes are embodiments of evil, and some have a far more impressive record on human development than democratic regimes, who should not be equated with paragons of virtue simply because they hold elections. There are many examples of wretched elected governments, not to mention the cases of fascists elected to power. 'Authoritarian governments' describe such a wide range of regimes that nothing meaningful can be said about economic performance simply because a regime is democratic or not.

This leads to the second point. The formulation of appropriate economic policies required for a successful structural transformation of developing economies can be, and has been, undertaken effectively by non-elected governments in Asia.

Third, this aspect is not unique to Asia. The major structural transformation of European economies occurred under what we now refer to as authoritarian regimes. The extraordinary science and technology achievements of Europe and North America, including the industrial revolution, have laid the base for mass prosperity. But most of these initial gains transpired under non-democratic regimes—the emergence of elected, representative governments is a far more recent phenomenon.

A fourth conceptual flaw is to imply that particular political regimes will lead to typical economic outcomes, without examining the content of the policies pursued by the political leaders. To take another Asian example, Pakistan's per capita income, in purchasing parity terms, is nearly twice as high as India's. This is not because the latter has been democratic while the former has mainly been ruled by authoritarian regimes. Pakistan has, by and large, pursued economic policies which encouraged rapid growth, while inefficient state controls hampered Indian economic performance. The poor economic outcome had nothing to do with democracy; a different set of policies could have produced higher growth. Further, as recent reforms in India demonstrate, there is no reason why democratic regimes, *per se*, will be incompatible with economic growth in South Asia.

Finally, the lesson from Latin American, Asian, and African experience is not that you need to install a dictator to let the economy rip. What you do need is macroeconomic stability, effective human capital investments, appropriate incentives for accumulation and support for the private sector, and a disciplined state machinery for economic management. Simply having an elected government is no guarantee that you would do any of the above; that is why many people get frustrated and begin advocating an efficient authoritarian alternative, which can raise their standard of living.

In brief, the 'lesson' from global experience is not that governments need to be non-democratic to provide economic growth or that democracies are a peril. As far as the economy is concerned, recent evidence surely suggests that a particular set of policies can have a significant bearing on equitable economic growth, irrespective of whether the government is elected or not.[19]

The important issue for democrats is that a transition to democracy is possible without disrupting growth. The practical problem is to identify how this transition should be managed, to enable economic growth to be sustained and avoid the creation of an excessively rent-seeking or unstable political environment which could adversely affect growth.

In sum, rapid growth has been achieved by countries with diverse belief systems. Secular, Buddhist, Christian, and

Muslim countries have achieved economic success. The key long-term explanation lies in the acquisition of technology to improve productivity, within a framework of incentives which encourage accumulation and equity. The economic and social policy reforms required for successful development are outlined in the next chapter. Focusing on these factors is more important than futile explanations which sustain prejudices.

COVERAGE AND STRUCTURE OF THE BOOK

The future of South Asia may be troubled but not necessarily bleak; this is an important distinction. The sub-region is not a pessimist's dream of an inevitable hurtle into the abyss. Such gloom is understandable in view of current difficulties but there are many possibilities. There is no inevitability and key policy choices will influence direction. The critical objective must be to ensure how these divided societies can be made more cohesive, while the pace of change will inevitably cause strains and frictions. This appears to be stating the obvious but a commitment to such an objective has been notable by its absence in the past. The key to the future direction of Pakistan is what will happen to equity and social cohesion. At a political level, power has to be made more accountable, and judicial reforms are central to this greater accountability. The process would also aid economic development, since a more effective judicial system will facilitate the enforcement of contracts, reduce uncertainty, and thereby contribute to an environment which is more conducive to higher levels of accumulation. The two nations that have emerged in Pakistan—a small privileged elite and a large, discontented mass—need to be brought closer. This process implies major economic and social policy changes. The agenda of equitable development would require the enforcement of measures such as compulsory primary education, effective imposition of income taxes on earnings derived from agriculture, a serious commitment to population planning, and retention of the supremacy of the private sector to sustain the dynamism that has served Pakistan well. The move towards an outward orientation of the economy has to be sustained, but successful exports require resolution of the violence that has debilitated the principal port and largest city, Karachi.

The book is intended as a contribution to the debate on the serious restructuring of economic policies and social institutions that is needed. Such changes can make people share in development and feel that they are participants, not victims. Much of Eastern Asia is well on its way towards this goal; for Pakistan, time may be running out.

The book is divided into three parts. Part A contains four chapters: the first presented an overview of trends and described the recent development experience. Chapter 2 attempts an explanation of comparative performance, incorporating economic policy variables and political economy influences. Chapters 3 and 4 contain country case studies from East and South East Asia respectively. Part B starts with a review of the role of aid in the half century of Pakistan's development. This review also acts as a useful introduction to the detailed case study of the country's socio-economic development since independence, which is contained in Part B. Finally, Part C contains recommendations and a discussion of plausible future scenarios.

NOTES

1. This was the title of Gunnar Myrdal's famous book, published in 1969, which argued that South Asia's 'soft' states were impediments to development. The book also included South East Asia. Most of the book's predictions have not borne up well, although some of the analysis of South Asia remains valid.

2. Apart from African and South Asian countries, the list of low human development nations contains war-affected Afghanistan, Cambodia and Laos, as well as Myanmar.

3. Most countries in East and South East Asia have witnessed an improvement in income distribution, but the process is not universal nor has it happened on the same scale in all countries. Malaysia, for example, has a far more skewed distribution than most countries of the region. This is partially because Malaysia faced another important distributional challenge, which related to racial inequities.

4. For details see the UNDP: *Human Development Report 1996*, (Oxford University Press, New York).

5. Ibid.

6. The most prominent of these is the Grameen Bank, which has had a degree of success with creating a sustainable credit institution for poor borrowers. Bangladesh has also spawned a large NGO community, some of whom have been able to work effectively in different aspects of development.

7. Bangladesh's position is 143, out of a total of 174 countries, in the Human Development Ranking undertaken annually by the UNDP. See end note 4 for the reference. Apart from war-affected countries, only Nepal and Bhutan in Asia rank below Bangladesh.

8. Pakistan's income distribution is by no means worse than all of the Eastern Asian countries. The country's income distribution is better than that of Thailand, Malaysia, or Indonesia. Income distribution is measured by the ratio of the income shares of the richest 20% and the poorest 20% of the population. Comparative income distribution data for the countries concerned is contained in the World Bank's East Asian Miracle report, referred to below.

9. Calculations based on the *Human Development Report 1996,* (UNDP, New York).

10. Maxine Rodinson : *Islam and Capitalism,* (Penguin, London, 1978).

11. See Pervez Hoodbhoy: *Islam and Science,* (Vanguard, Lahore, 1986).

12. This is commonly referred to as Vision 20/20.

13. In the 1960s, measures such as the Muslim Family Law Ordinance, 1962 were aimed at reform of many customs which discriminated against women.

14. For details see, *inter alia*, Khawar Mumtaz and Farida Sher: *Women in Pakistan—One Step Forward, Two Steps Back,* (Progressive Publishers, Lahore, 1989), Qazi, N: The *Women's Movement in Pakistan*, (M. Litt. thesis, Oxford University, 1996).

15. The most extreme cases of puritanical religious orthodoxy are, of course, found in Iran and Saudi Arabia.

16. Both Christianity and Buddhism have had to contend with strong secular influences. Both religions have shared the experience of a communist revolution in one or more countries. Further, secular influences on personal belief have been strong. Recent ideological convulsions in the Muslim world have intensified debate on the role of religion in the public sphere. There has been a spread of puritanical fascism in some countries, while an

ideological civil war is being fought amongst liberal and conservative forces in others.

17. Female Prime Ministers have been elected in Pakistan, Sri Lanka, India, Bangladesh, and the Philippines. Others are likely to emerge in Myanmar and, possibly, Indonesia. The highest proportion of women in the legislature is in China.

18. There is a rich literature on this issue. See, *inter alia*, Olson, M: 'Dictatorship, Democracy and Development', *American Political Science Review*, September 1993; Williamson, J: *The Political Economy of Policy Reform,* (Institute for International Economics, Washington DC, 1994).

19. Comparative research on this issue could be very useful in providing some insight on a difficult dilemma facing many developing economies.

CHAPTER 2

DETERMINANTS OF EAST ASIAN
SUCCESS AND CAUSES OF DIVERGENCE
FROM SOUTH ASIA

*It is enterprise which builds and improves the world's
possessions...if enterprise is afoot, wealth accumulates
whatever may be happening to thrift; and if enterprise is asleep,
wealth decays, whatever thrift may be doing.*

J.M. Keynes
Treatise on Money

SIMILARITIES AND DIVERGENCE

Soon after independence, there were many similarities
between Eastern Asia and Pakistan, as far as development
strategy was concerned. A modernizing elite[1] was in
command, with a technocratic bureaucracy which was as, if
not more, competent than those existing in Eastern Asia at
the time. The state was intervening extensively in markets
and resource allocation, but within the parameters of a private
sector led strategy. Another similarity was the initial pursuit
of import-substituting industrialization, with policy-induced
high rates of return to industrial capital; the rates of return
were as high as 100% for some sectors.[2] This helped convert
merchant-traders into industrialists. The stance of socio-
cultural policy was mildly progressive, with the introduction
of legal provisions which improved women's rights, and the
launch of a family planning programme.

Many features of this strategy have yielded positive results.
Entrepreneurial skills were encouraged and have
subsequently played a vibrant role in industry, trade, and
agriculture. Many state institutions operated with admirable
efficiency, not only dealing with a huge refugee settlement

programme but also ensuring sound macroeconomic management and disciplined intervention in markets. Corruption levels were no different than in Eastern Asia.[3]

The outcomes have, however, diverged substantially, as illustrated in Chapter 1. Three factors in particular account for the difference between the evolution of capitalism in Eastern Asia and in Pakistan.[4] The first was the pursuit of 'functional inequality' as a policy goal in Pakistan. None of the Eastern Asian countries took the view that it was necessary to increase inequalities to raise savings, and that the resulting higher levels of accumulation would generate growth, which would then trickle down. Functional inequality had serious implications for all manner of policies. Asset redistribution, such as land reform, was not pursued. This was particularly ironic because the severe dislocation which led to the creation of Pakistan created conditions which were similar to those which aided land reform in Eastern Asia. Dislocation after war or civil wars helped asset redistribution programmes in Korea, Taiwan, and Japan.[5] While war and internal conflict offer opportunities for restructuring power, it does not follow that the change will be in an equitable direction. While country specifics differ in general, Eastern Asia was faced with intense 'pressures from below', culminating in communist revolutions in some cases. The strength of these regional forces helped shape the direction of change in moments of a post-war political vacuum.

This point is well-illustrated by the case of Pakistan, whose two post-war social dislocations did not force change towards an equitable direction. Arguments for land reform were voiced within the Muslim League and other political forces soon after Pakistan's creation.[6] But there was strong resistance from the landed groups and the proponents of land reform[7] were neither sufficiently organized nor powerful enough to seize this opportunity. The resulting elitist development strategy not only avoided asset distribution but also ignored public expenditures which were vital for inclusive capitalism, such as primary education and primary health. The paucity of public spending on these areas has played an important role in the debilitating population crisis; Pakistan has found out the hard way that while the scale of population does not necessarily affect economic development, its growth rate does. Conversely, early primary education and health investments in Eastern Asia led to the control of quantity, thereby enabling higher per capita expenditures, which have subsequently enhanced the quality of human capital.

The second factor which accounts for the divergence is the breakdown in consensus in Pakistan with regard to the leading role of the private sector. A mix of ethnic and class tensions led to the nationalization of industrial and financial assets in the early 1970s. Nationalization was not confined to large units, spreading as it did to affect even medium and small scale enterprises.[8] 'Left under the Landlords' was a curious political coalition. The former were responding to growing inequities, emerging from the pursuit of 'functional inequality'. They saw in it a betrayal of the equity and opportunity principle that was implicit in the Pakistan movement, i.e. a minority was creating a new nation state in which the mass of the population would have better opportunities. The Left was also wary and suspicious of the private sector.

In Punjab, nationalizations hampered the emerging bourgeoisie, as well as the smaller entrepreneurs. The latter were particularly hard-hit by the 1976 nationalization of small and medium agro-processing units. The private sector viewed these actions as capricious and unreliable, specially after assurances had been given that no nationalization would be undertaken after 1974. Not surprisingly, private capital ceased to invest.

In Sindh province the government, dominated by the landed rural elite, was seen to be using the Left to settle ethnic scores, since rural Sindhis had been marginalized by the industrialization drive in their province. Industrial assets moved from private to public hands, under a state machinery that came increasingly to be dominated by the rural elite. Nationalization was one of the factors which fuelled muhajir antagonism in the 1970s, culminating in the subsequent rise of muhajir 'ethnic' identity and contributing to sustained ethnic conflict in the province during the next two decades.[9] In Punjab and the NWFP, there was no ethnic implication to nationalization but the cost to the development of the private sector was severe. The province of Balochistan was largely unaffected by these economic reforms, consumed as it was by a civil war in the 1970s.

Thus, as opposed to the Left, the landlords had mixed motives for economic reform; ethnicity was clearly a factor. Most of the financial-industrial capital created in the industrial heartland of Karachi was by Muhajirs (refugees from India). It was perhaps no accident that the landlords pressing for nationalization belonged to the ethnic group which had not benefited from the industrialization process. It was also telling that while nationalization of industrial assets went ahead, land reforms were not implemented. Despite much rhetoric, land reforms were subverted.[10] Again, the loss of the 1971 war had created uncertainty and turmoil, with the potential for altering the power structure to reduce the dominance of the rural elite. The power structure was changed, but not in an equitable direction. Indeed, this opportunity for rural asset redistribution was squandered and the landed elite emerged stronger than before.[11]

During this period, none of the comparable countries in East or South East Asia lost the consensus on private sector led development. For example, racial tensions in Malaysia, which erupted with such ferocity at the same time as ethnic difficulties were mounting in Pakistan, did not lead to the nationalization of Chinese industrial assets. The Malays were promoted through state intervention, which used positive discrimination extensively, but private sector led development has remained central. Such a consensus enabled a more confident private sector, with many capacities enhanced through targeted state support. This provided the confidence for the shift from an inward-looking ISI to a greater export orientation. Pakistan's industrial and financial sector, on the other hand, faced enormous insecurities in the 1970s; private accumulation dried up and export performance, relative to Eastern Asia, fell way behind.

The third factor accounting for the divergence was the socio-cultural ideological currents which emerged in the 1980s. During this decade, Pakistan took many steps to revert to the private sector ethos of the earlier period. While it succeeded in this sphere, the country was rocked by a reversal in the direction of socio-cultural policy as noted in

Chapter 1. A country in the midst of a population explosion and with poor literacy needed strong corrective measures in order to rectify past errors. Instead, the Pakistani state was gripped by a menacing ideological puritanism. Instead of progressive reform, in one of the more conservative societies of Asia, this puritanism contained an ideological assault on women. The ethos of 'chaddar and char diwari' reinforced social and private subjugation of women. This puritanism was hardly conducive to the required social policy changes. The contrast with Eastern Asia could not be greater—in virtually all of these societies, women made major gains. They were having far fewer children, were much better educated, were living longer and healthier lives,[12] and increasing their financial independence. By contrast, the 1980s witnessed major reversals for women in Pakistan.

In sum, Pakistan's development path diverged due to the inability to accommodate the ethnic, class, and religious tensions which determined socio-economic policy. These factors had a strong bearing on the economic variables affecting equitable growth—levels of accumulation, efficiency of resource allocation, and the quality of human capital.

As Pakistan approaches its first half-century, it is perhaps worth reflecting on whether many of the conflicts noted above were an inevitable part of forging a nation from such diversity. The 1990s have witnessed a number of positive developments—the puritanical onslaught has been stemmed, embodied partly by the two electoral victories of a female Prime Minister. The efficacy of her regime was limited and it is also arguable that little was achieved to alter the lives of ordinary women. None the less it is an achievement in itself that the state is no longer promoting reprehensible measures against women. The domestic debate on the neglect and reversals suffered by women is more open, particularly through the media and NGOs, such as the Human Rights Commission of Pakistan. While small, such a constituency for progressive change represents a substantial improvement from a period when there was official support for reactionary social measures.[13]

Within Pakistan, a consensus has also been reached on the private sector, with only slight differences in emphasis amongst the different political groups. There is greater emphasis on social policy through mechanisms such as the Social Action Plan, which covers population planning, basic education, and health, as well as rural water and sanitation. At the same time, the progress in the implementation of measures required to address equity and efficiency has been painfully slow. The importance of this critical juncture and the significance of policy choices is stressed later in the text, particularly in Chapter 11.

The rest of this chapter develops a framework which tries to explain the success of Eastern Asia. This is done in two stages—the first examines the wider political economy influences, while the second concentrates on the details of economic policies which stimulated the economic revolution.

THE POLITICAL ECONOMY OF EASTERN ASIA: THE COMBINED IMPACT OF THE MEIJI RESTORATION AND COMMUNISM

Much of the debate about Eastern Asia has revolved around the question of the role of the state, and the extent to which it intervened effectively in markets.[14] However, the question of the importance of particular instruments in leading and directing the market, important as it is, has to be preceded by an examination of why the state was able to play its role so effectively in East Asia, whereas similar interventions have failed miserably in other countries. The core features shaping Eastern Asia can be divided into two categories: (i) the wider political economy influences; (ii) the instrumental role of specific policy interventions.

The political economy of the Asian 'miracle' has been conditioned by two major events: the 19th century Meiji restoration in Japan and the Chinese revolution. Certain key elements of the Meiji restoration created the base for the inclusive capitalism witnessed in much of Eastern Asia. The critical features were the abolition of feudalism, the establishment of a mass education system providing universal primary schooling, a strong science and vocational orientation for higher education,[15] gradual integration with the world economy, and considerable emphasis on the application of modern technology in agriculture and industry.[16]

Particularly important in creating capacities and the opportunity to share in the growth process was the role of the education system. As early as 1872, the spirit of the state's intervention in social investments was evident in government circulars: 'Henceforth throughout the land, without distinctions of class and sex, in no village shall there be a house without learning, in no house an ignorant individual. Every guardian, acting in accordance with this, shall never fail in having them attend school.'[17] The Japanese model, consisting of state support to the private sector and extensive intervention in markets for social services, has exercised considerable influence on the countries of Eastern Asia. Indeed, the Japanese 'model' was evident in much of the pattern of equitable development in the first group of countries to have succeeded—the so-called 'tigers'.[18] The significance of Korea, which more or less replicated Japan,[19] was particularly important in view of its large size and, therefore, the potential for emulation by other countries.[20]

While Japan provided a model of inclusive capitalism, the pressure for structural reform on many societies came from another major political event which has shaped Asia's development. The Chinese revolution in particular, and the threat of communism in general, exerted forceful pressure on elites to create an economic environment in which large sections of the society participated. A serious threat of a communist take-over was faced by most of the Eastern Asian countries. This feature is emphasized in the country case studies of the next chapter. In this environment, divisive development strategies such as the functional inequality pursued in Pakistan, could have run into immediate political constraints in Eastern Asia, invigorating armed struggle for a communist revolution. A central component of the strategy to counter this threat was structural changes such as land reform and universal primary education which paved the path for equitable development. Even when countries did not undertake major asset redistributions, policy measures ensured that there were curbs on excessive consumption by elite groups.

The most well-known cases of extensive land reform are Korea, Japan, and Taiwan, China. It is, however, important to note that in all cases land reforms occurred in a framework which was committed to private sector led development. Thus the landed elite was compensated frequently in terms of equity shares in industrial enterprises.[21] Similarly, technology policy, both in terms of the strong technology orientation of the education system and the openness to joint ventures with foreign firms, was critical to the shaping of growth and sharing from its benefits.[22]

Much of the policy debates and controversies regarding the role of particular policy instruments and institutions in Eastern Asian development have to be viewed in this wider context of economic and political imperatives. The consequent framework for development facilitated the creation of a technocratic and competent public service, which used state institutions to intervene in a disciplined manner. This aspect is recognized as critically important for an effective role of the state.[23] As mentioned earlier, this intervention was selective and subject to criteria which ensured discipline. Selectivity was achieved by concentrating public expenditures in a few areas, such as education and physical infrastructure, while much of the discipline was provided by the adherence to the imperatives of markets.[24]

The pressure of communism on elites was evident across Eastern Asia. The Taiwanese leadership had fled from the Chinese mainland after the communist revolution. Korea was split into two, with the South pursuing a private sector led strategy, and communism across the border. Growing inequities in Thailand led to student uprisings against the military, fuelled partially by the sustained expansion of the Communist Party of Thailand through the 1970s.[25] Shortly after independence, Malaysia was involved in emergency measures against the Communist Party of Malaya.[26] Even in Singapore, Chinese cultural nationalism was mixed with support for communism.[27] Indeed, the most popular political figure in Singapore, Tan Kah Kee, became an official of the Communist Party in mainland China, after his expulsion from Singapore.[28]

Repression was only part of the response. Elites and state managers responded by pursuing inclusive capitalism. This involved extensive intervention by the state, in support of a private sector led development strategy. Widespread access to basic education and health, as well as restraints on conspicuous consumption in favour of accumulation, occurred under these pressures. Progressive social policy, redistribution of assets, and economic management under a disciplined technocracy were part of the modernizing response. The building of technological and managerial capacities at the top, along with broad based skill-oriented education, was reminiscent of Japanese evolution since the Meiji restoration. As noted earlier, Korea in particular, followed a similar mix of market and state but other countries exhibited a broadly analogous pattern as well.

THE ROLE OF ECONOMIC POLICY IN THE DEVELOPMENT OF EASTERN ASIA

The economic success of Eastern Asia has raised important questions about public policy.[29] What constitutes the essential elements of their development strategy? Indeed, is there a distinct strategy? Inevitably, there are many national differences but can certain core elements be discerned? Can these policies be replicated by other countries? The sections below attempt to address the issue of causality, focusing on development strategy as a whole and the instruments used in support of this framework.

There are two outcomes which need to be explained. The first is why these countries achieved an unprecedentedly rapid increase in incomes and living standards. The second is the remarkable improvement in human development indicators that has occurred across the region.

The substantial increase in output has been accompanied by a marked shift from low to high productivity activities. The economies of the region have, typically, diversified from simple agricultural production or mining to sophisticated industrial structures. More complex activities have included the move into internationally competitive services, in areas such as shipping and finance. The increases in output and diversification of activities have required that economies exhibit three capacities: (i) the capacity to absorb technology and build a domestic technological capacity; (ii) the capacity to accumulate physical capital at a rapid rate; (iii) the capacity to allocate resources efficiently.[30]

1. POLICY INFLUENCES ON EAST ASIAN GROWTH

Outcome

Rapid increase in per capita incomes

Intermediate Variables

(i) High levels of investment and savings (ii) Pace of technology acquisition and adaption (iii) Efficiency of resource allocation

Policy Influences

Macroeconomic Management	Social Policy	Industrial Policy	Agricultural Policy	Financial Sector Policy	Trade Policy
Low budget deficits, consistent monetary policy, ensured low inflation and the stability required for efficiency in resource allocation. Competitive exchange rates supported exports.	Education policy emphasized cognitive development and had a strong technology orientation. Health and population policy, along with primary education investments, eased supply side pressures on the labour market.	Active state intervention in markets and supporting infrastructure. Variety of instruments used to direct resource allocation. These included selective use of directed and/or subsidized credit, fiscal incentives for particular sectors, and export subsidies.	Price policy enabled a degree of resource transfer to the industrial sector. None the less prices, select subsidies, and public investment ensured that agriculture was not squeezed excessively. Reasonable rates of return led to good investment levels. Technology and marketing policies in some countries assisted diversification into higher value crops.	Positive real interest rates stimulated savings. Mild financial repression in many countries, through subsidized credit and low deposit rates.	All countries used tariff and non-tariff barriers to protect industries initially. Subsequent liberalization and deregulation central to export led growth.

These intermediate variables are self-evident. Economies cannot grow and diversify so rapidly without accumulating physical and human capital and using these resources efficiently.[31] The key issue is how development strategy stimulated these intermediate variables. A comparison of Eastern Asia suggests that success was based on policy-induced incentives within an agreed structural framework. The latter meant certain 'rules of the game' regarding the market and the state.

By and large, the state did not compete with the private sector in production and trade. Instead, it intervened extensively to build private sector capacities in these activities. Further, state intervention was not restricted to modifications of market signals which influenced resource allocation. Governments played an active role in investments which built physical and human capital and did not leave this aspect of resource allocation to market forces. A mix of market failures, co-ordination problems, and initial lack of private sector capacities shaped the rationale for this role for the state. At the same time, the state's socio-economic policy interventions were structured within the lead role assigned to the private sector. This ensured market discipline and efficiency.

An inter-related web of policy instruments fuelled this structure. The dynamics of change obviously affected the choice of instruments, and the relative significance of each, in different time periods. However, the basic framework is captured in Figures 1 and 2.

Figure 1 is a summary of the collective set of 6 policy influences. On most of the policy issues, there is little disagreement about their efficacy in Eastern Asia.[32] On the first aspect of policy influences, there is no contention about the importance of effective macroeconomic management. In Eastern Asia, this ensured low single digit inflation and thereby a stable environment for price signals to guide resource allocation. Accordingly, these countries avoided the type of macroeconomic instability which has caused such inflationary and debt difficulties in Latin America and parts of Africa. In addition, early adjustment to external shocks has also assisted economic recovery. In Indonesia, for example, rapid adjustment to a terms of trade shock in the 1980s, aided in a relatively quick recovery. The policy debate in this area is not about the desirability of disciplined macroeconomic management but the difficulty in implementing a sound fiscal and monetary policy. Almost universally, Eastern Asian governments maintained an admirable discipline over domestic and external macro-imbalances.

Similarly undisputed is the positive equity impact of social policy in much of Eastern Asia (the second policy area in Figure 1). The benefits of early investments in primary education, basic health and population planning, and in changing the socio-economic status of women, are well-recognized.[33] Their impact on the labour market, on diversification into higher productivity activities, and on direct human development indicators have been documented extensively. Public education investments were concentrated on building a broad primary and secondary base. Public tertiary education was limited and institutions were strongly technology- and management-oriented.[34] The stance of social policy in Eastern Asia was crucial in the expansion of capacities and opportunities, and aided the sense of participation in an 'inclusive capitalism'. It was frequently allied to the dynamics of progressive change in the socio-economic status of women.

The third policy[35] influence is perhaps the most contentious. Industrial policy in Eastern Asia was not a case of *laissez-faire*. A variety of policy instruments were used by the state to affect the structure and pace of industrialization. Directed and subsidized credit, support to chosen sub-sectors, export subsidies, establishment of technology acquisition institutions, and a host of other sector-specific state interventions have affected industrial development. Having acknowledged this role, a World Bank review of East Asian experience[36] came to the astonishing conclusion that these industrial sectors would have developed in this manner even without these extensive interventions. By this logic, if the state intervenes successfully, it is seen to be redundant, while if it intervenes and industrialization does not take off, the policy distortions are to be blamed!

As commentators have pointed out, there is no reason why many of the Eastern Asian states would not have fared worse if the state had not intervened decisively.[37] Many would have remained primary commodity producers or would still be locked into low productivity industrial activities. Eastern Asia provides ample evidence of effective state intervention in support of industrial development. But this efficacy was dependent on a number of conditions—a disciplined institutional capacity within government, with policy targeted at harnessing the domestic private sector, not competing with it.

Industrial policies in Eastern Asia have differed in the scale of intervention in markets and in the use of particular policy instruments. Korean state support created large firms, which had the size and capacity to lead the export drive when Korea shifted from import substitution. Industrial policy also directed credit by size of enterprise, assisting the growth of small and medium enterprises in countries such as Japan, where they have played a vital role in employment. Malaysia's industrial policy is in the process of assisting the shift from a primary producer of basic agricultural commodities to a sophisticated, industrial nation in a short span of time. In short, industrial policy has helped alter dynamic comparative advantage.

Fourth, in the agricultural sector, price and marketing policy did not impose a severe squeeze and ensured a reasonable rate of return on investment. Exchange rate policy did not typically involve an indirect tax on the sector. Grossly overvalued exchange rates have hampered agricultural exports in many parts of the developing world. But countries such as Thailand and Malaysia experienced a substantial diversification of the sector's output composition, which contributed to a robust growth in agricultural exports (see Chapter 4). In addition to ensuring that prices were right, government policy aided diversification through technology acquisition and assistance with export marketing. Countries such as Thailand moved from the production of traditional crops to the growing of sophisticated crops exclusively for the export market. Asparagus, for example, was not eaten domestically at all but Thailand diversified into it, only for exports, on the basis of its comparative advantage for growing the crop. In general, agricultural policies supported productivity improvements and limited the transfer out of agriculture.

In addition to price incentives, export marketing assistance, and technology acquisition, agricultural sector policy also affected asset ownership and equity. As mentioned earlier, countries such as Japan, Taiwan (China), and Korea underwent major land reforms. Rural mobility has also been advanced by social policy, with basic education and health programmes, in particular, responsible for improvements in human development and productivity.

Fifth, the financial sector was aided by policies which encouraged the mobilization of household and corporate savings. Institutions such as post offices and rural savings associations played an important role in several countries. Effective regulation of the banking system built up faith in financial institutions. Interest rates were suppressed in most countries, but by and large remained positive in real terms. In many countries, saving was encouraged by high consumption taxes and fiscal incentives for corporate savings. Luxury consumption was taxed heavily and credit denied for consumer items at different points in time by both Korea and Japan. Singapore and Malaysia instituted mandatory provident fund contributions, which was a form of 'forced' private savings. Savings were also stimulated by pension schemes and public sector surpluses in some cases. Sound fiscal management ensured that private savings were not frittered away in public consumption. Public sector savings were positive in countries such as Singapore and Taiwan (China).

Another feature of the Taiwanese experience was how directed and subsidized credit was used extensively to promote specific sectors. Further, countries such as Korea, Thailand, Japan, and Malaysia, amongst others, stimulated investments through limited financial repression, i.e. interest rates were kept at below market clearing levels. These interventions in financial markets effectively subsidized private firms. However, financial discipline, good management, and control of patrimonial influences prevented the ruin of financial institutions engaged in similar practices elsewhere.

The final area referred to in Figure 1, trade policy, played a crucial role in the diversification of economic structures. The initial phase of industrialization almost universally involved tariff and non-tariff barriers for the protection of emerging domestic firms. This ISI phase was gradually replaced by subsidies, credit, and tax incentives for export as the dominant aspect of trade policy. Some sectors continued to be protected, and a number of export-oriented sub-sectors were also provided protection. But, in general, the shift from ISI to an export-oriented trade policy was vital. The focus of policy became the earning of foreign exchange, rather than measures to limit foreign exchange expenditures. The export drive unleashed dynamic productivity gains through rapid technology acquisition. Competitive pressures and the shift into higher productivity activities sent positive demand signals to the labour market. More skilled and better trained people were needed. This involved investments by the public and private sector in the deepening of human capital.

The dynamic links between the policy areas created positive externalities. For example, basic social policy at the time of import substitution had assisted in the reduction in the rate of growth of the labour force. At the same time, most of the population had become literate. The positive dynamics of change unleashed by the export drive reinforced the need for better quality of manpower. These trade policy-induced demand signals led to appropriate investments in education and training.

In countries such as Taiwan (China), Korea, and Japan, government protection of the domestic market coexisted with export incentives; the latter included duty-free input imports, export credit and targets, and a range of tax incentives for exporters, which raised the returns to capital invested in the desired sectors. South East Asian countries also used export credits and fiscal incentives to raise returns to investment in exports. However direct foreign investment has, typically, played a larger role in their export drives than was the case in East Asia. As relative late-comers, the South East Asians gained, as has China, from the regional availability of FDI.

2. THE INSTITUTIONAL FRAMEWORK: RELATIVE ROLES OF THE PRIVATE AND PUBLIC SECTORS

PUBLIC SECTOR

(a) Institutional Capacity

The institutional capacity of the state to execute its functions aided by an employment policy which did not use government as an 'employer of last resort'. Avoided large scale patronage. Relatively high public sector salaries, particularly for managerial levels, attracted and retained quality technocratic manpower.

(b) Relationship with Private Sector

Public sector typically not competing with the private sector in the production of goods and services, or in marketing.

Extensive state intervention to build up private sector capacity. Collaboration included deliberation councils in some countries, to share information. Public sector involved in the provision of mass basic education and health services as well as physical infrastructure.

(c) Enabling Environment

Reasonable control over law and order, which enhances security and smooth functioning of markets. Enabled enforcement of regulations where necessary which assisted development of the financial sector in particular.

In sum, the six policy areas summarized in Figure 1 interacted to generate structural and dynamic changes in Eastern Asia.[38] These policies led to macroeconomic stability, improvements in human capital, reduction in the pace of labour force growth, diversification of agriculture, and sophisticated industrial development. These achievements required high levels of investment, rapid technology acquisition, and efficiency in resource allocation.

THE INSTITUTIONAL FRAMEWORK

An important aspect of these policies was the institutional framework within which they were implemented. Many policy instruments referred to above have failed to have the desired impact in a number of countries in other regions. The efficacy of particular policy instruments is frequently related to the wider development strategy of which they are a part. The institutional framework which affected development strategy in Eastern Asia is summarized in Figure 2.

There were three aspects to the impact of the state on private sector development. First, most of Eastern Asia invested in the managerial and technical capacities of public agencies. Public sector employment policy was important in this regard. The state was not used as an 'employer of last resort'. Patrimonial influences were curbed. Relatively high public sector salaries, particularly for managerial levels, attracted and retained quality manpower. These technocratic groups were typically insulated from narrow political pressures. This ensured a certain consistency and clarity in decision-making, which built market confidence.

The second institutional aspect of importance for economic development was the relationship with the private sector. As mentioned earlier, the ethos of state intervention was within a framework of supporting and building the private sector, and not competing with it. Private sector capacities were built through several mechanisms. In countries such as Korea, Japan, Thailand, and Malaysia, formal deliberation councils were established. Through these, the public sector reduced the information and transaction costs of private agents. These mechanisms reinforced confidence in policy direction and enabled correction of shortcomings through regular consultations. The state also supported the private sector through direct investments in physical and human capital. These investments were crucial for the launching and sustaining of the export drive. Efficient transport, good ports, and regular electricity stimulated private investment and helped attract foreign direct investment. Similarly, a literate and increasingly skilled labour force was required for the move into higher productivity activities.

Finally, a third indirect role of the state was important in the functioning of domestic markets, as well as attracting foreign private capital. A reasonable law and order environment meant that, *inter alia*, regulations were enforced where required. This was important, for example, in the development of the financial sector. Prudential regulation and supervision played an important role in increasing faith in financial institutions and thereby stimulating savings. In addition, stability provided the security environment which was conducive to foreign direct investment.

In general, non-governmental organizations were not central to the development strategy in Eastern Asia; nor did they play a significant role in poverty alleviation. In some countries, they were engaged in useful poverty relief and social welfare activities. These institutions worked usually at local levels and with communities which were being left out of the mainstream and not benefiting from growth. Similarly, in some countries, NGOs were playing a useful advocacy role. But across the region as a whole, poverty alleviation was addressed by direct government intervention in social policy combined with employment generation by the private sector. The role of NGOs was somewhat peripheral, partly because of the strength of public institutions.

As far as the institutional environment is concerned, the comparison between Eastern Asia and Pakistan shows some initial similarities, followed by a sudden rupture. As mentioned earlier, the consensus regarding the respective roles of the private and public sectors broke down, with the latter competing with, or supplanting, the private sector.

Politicization and the gradual increase in patrimonial influences affected the public sector's efficiency in Pakistan. As a result, the country exhibits many of the characteristics of the 'soft state' feared in Myrdal's *Asian Drama*,[39] although the book's sweeping generalizations have been proved wrong, as noted earlier, particularly in South East Asia. But in Pakistan, an overmanned, poorly paid, and politicized civil service has led to a general deterioration in public institutions. One of the major negative consequences has been the lack of a regulatory framework to enforce contracts in the financial sector. A number of financial scams have gone unpunished, creating uncertainty about the security of savings.[40] In such an institutional environment, savings mobilization suffered. Instead of developing well-regulated postal savings schemes, a weak institutional framework has hampered accumulation.[41]

The law and order conditions have also affected development. To some extent, these were exogenous, due to the inflow of arms after the Afghan conflict. However, internal tensions have also taken their toll. One of the principal economic costs in the 1990s has been to the drive to expand exports and attract foreign direct investment. The violence in Karachi, the principal port and commercial city, has underlined the importance of a stable law and order framework for certain economic activities involving private capital. One of the reasons why authoritarian governments in Eastern Asia did well on economic accumulation was effective control over law and order, which created a conducive environment for private investment.

This chapter has provided an analytical summary of the policy and institutional framework responsible for East Asian development. The next chapter concentrates on one key aspect of these policy influences—the manner in which Eastern Asia acquired science and technology and made the critical human capital investments.

NOTES

1. This was a period when different 'modernization theories' sought to explain the necessity, instruments, and consequences of structural reform. For a review, see Scalpino et al.: op. cit.

2. For details, see Papanek, G: *Social Returns and Private Incentives,* (Boston University Press, Boston, 1972).

3. This is not meant as an excuse for corruption but simply as a statement of fact and a reminder that corruption levels do not explain the difference in outcomes. This view has acquired popular currency but there is no evidence to support the argument that the difference in economic performance is due to higher levels of corruption in South Asia.

4. These issues are explored in greater depth later in the text.

5. See Lipton, M: op. cit.

6. Leading political figures such as Mian Iftikharuddin argued the case for far-reaching land reforms.

7. Similarly, the balance of power post-1971 war was such that rural reform was prevented, a point emphasized below.

8. For analysis of these developments see, *inter alia*, Burki, S.J: *Pakistan under Bhutto*, (Oxford University Press, Karachi, 1980), Hussain, A: *Strategic Choices for Pakistan's Economy*, (Progressive Publishers, Lahore, 1986) and Ahmed and Amjad: *The Management of Pakistan's Economy*, (Oxford University Press, Karachi, 1982).

9. These ethnic tensions persist and have degenerated in many ways.

10. For a review of the land reforms, see Herring, R.J: 'Mr Bhutto's Land Reforms', *Economic and Political Weekly*, July 1978, New Delhi.

11. This point has been captured in a number of excellent analyses. See, for example, Maleeha Lodhi: 'The Pakistan People's Party' (unpublished Ph.D. thesis, London School of Economics, 1981).

12. Japanese women, for example, have the highest life expectancy in the world.

13. It is perhaps in this area that the gap between Eastern Asia and South Asia has been the greatest.

14. The debate has tended to be simplified as one between neoclassical economists who emphasize the role of the private sector and the more institutional economists who emphasize the direction given to the market by the state. For a view of the debate see Little, I: 'Markets and Productivity Growth', (paper presented at the Pakistan Institute of Development Economics, annual conference, Islamabad, 1994).

15. For the relationship between education, economic development, and equity in Japan, see Cummings, W.K: *Education and Equality in Japan*, (Princeton University Press, 1980) and Passin, H: *Society and Education in Japan*, (Columbia University Press, New York, 1965).

16. The main aspects of the Japanese economic evolution and its impact on the region are covered in Myers, R and Peattie, M (eds.): *The Japanese Colonial Empire*, (Princeton University Press, 1984).

17. This oft-quoted paragraph is discussed in Passin, op. cit.

18. The title 'tigers' was given to Taiwan, Korea, Hong Kong, and Singapore.

19. For details of the influence of Japan on Korea's economic development see Kohli, A: 'Where do high growth political economies come from? The Japanese lineage of Korea's developmental state', *World Development*, September, 1994, (Elsevier Science Ltd., Oxford and New York, 1994).

20. Minor city states, such as Singapore and Hong Kong, have always been considered too small and special cases, which had little relevance for other countries.

21. For details see, *inter alia*, Lipton, M: 'Land Reform as Commenced Business', (paper presented at the Program on Comparative Economic Development, Cornell University, 1992); Balassa, B: *Development Strategies in Semi-Industrializing Economies*, (Johns Hopkins University Press, Baltimore, 1982) and *Economic Policies in the Pacific Areas Developing Countries*, (New York University Press, 1991).

22. For a cross country review of education policies see Weiner, M and Noman, O: *The Child and the State in India and Pakistan*, (Oxford University Press, 1995).

23. Those concerned with the replicability of this model worry about how the state can be reformed,when it has become 'soft', i.e. is controlled by rent-seeking groups, who want to use intervention as a mechanism to transfer benefits to a small group in society. In such cases, the move towards a 'hard' state can be extremely complex and is determined by political as well as economic forces. Simplistic institutional reform cannot and does not work in such circumstances.

24. For example, the government would intervene in financial markets to support specific export industries. But, generally, it would not bail out firms which could not survive in international markets. Thus the intervention was not open-ended and was disciplined by market performance.

25. For details see, *inter alia*, Crone, D.K: 'States, Elites and Social Welfare in Southeast Asia' in *World Development*, January, 1993 and Somsakdi, X (ed.): *Government and Politics of Thailand*, (Oxford University Press, New York, 1987).

26. For details see Scalapino, Sato, and Wanandi (eds.): *Asian Political Institutionalization*, (Institute of East Asian Studies, Berkeley, 1986).

27. See, *inter alia*, Huff, W. G: 'The developmental state, government and Singapore's economic development since 1960', *World Development*, August, 1995, (Pergamon, Oxford) and Lee Kuan

Yew: *Social Revolution in Singapore,* address to the British Labour Party Conference, (Government Printing House, Singapore, 1967).

28. For details see Lee Khoon Choy: *On the beat to the hustings,* (Times Books International, Singapore, 1988).

29. There has been an extensive debate about the role of specific policies, as well as the general development strategy. See, *inter alia,* Ito, Takatoshi: *The Japanese Economy,* (MIT Press, Cambridge, 1992); Amsden, A: *Asia's Next Giant: South Korea* and *Late Industrialisation,* (Oxford University Press, Oxford, 1989); Kwon, J (ed.): *Korean Economic Development,* (Greenwood Press, New York, 1990); Streeten, P: 'Markets and States: Against Minimalism', *World Development,* August, 1993, (Pergamon Press, Oxford); Wade, R: *Governing the market: economic theory and the role of government in East Asian industrialisation,* (Princeton University Press, 1990); Lall, S: 'Technological Capacities and Industrialisation', *World Development,* February, 1992, (Pergamon Press, Oxford); The World Bank: *The East Asian Miracle: Economic Growth and Public Policy,* (Oxford University Press, Washington DC, 1993).

30. These points have been emphasized in varying degrees and different forms by all the commentators referred to above. In addition, see Page, J and Petri, P: *Productivity Change and Strategic Growth Policy in the Asian Miracle,* (Policy Research Department, The World Bank, Washington D.C, 1993) and Pack, H and Westphal, L: 'Industrial strategy and technological change: theory versus reality', *Journal of Development Economics,* (Volume 22, 1, 1986).

31. There is a lively debate on the differing productivity performance in the countries of Eastern Asia. See, *inter alia,* Park, S and Kwon, J: *Rapid economic growth with increasing returns to scale and little or no productivity growth,* (Northern Illinois University, Dekalb, 1993); Sengupta, J: 'Growth in NICS in Asia: some tests of new growth theory', *Journal of Development Studies,* (Vol 29, 2, January 1993) and World Bank: op. cit.

32. For a review of the debate on policy, generated by the World Bank's East Asian Miracle study, see Ohno, Izumi: *Beyond the 'East Asian Miracle'—An Asian View,* (Office of Development Studies, UNDP, New York, 1996) and the special section devoted to the report in *World Development's* April 1994 issue, edited by Alice Amsden.

33. Ibid.

34. At the tertiary level, humanities were largely taught at private institutions.

35. With the possible exception of Hong Kong.

36. For details, see the last chapter of the East Asian Miracle study.

37. For a forceful critique of the World Bank's ideological position on industrial policy, see Amsden and Lall's articles in the special issue of *World Development* referred to above.

38. There are a number of differences across countries in each of the policy areas, as one would expect. The summary in the context consists of an aggregation of the essentials of policy. A number of details and differences are omitted.

39. The book also included South East Asia. Almost all of the book's predictions about this region have been wrong.

40. For example, in the Punjab in the early 1990s, there was a series of scandals involving private finance companies, which were unregulated and frequently had the patronage of politically powerful individuals.

41. The need to urgently raise the savings rate is emphasized in the last chapter.

CHAPTER 3

HUMAN CAPITAL, TECHNOLOGY AND ECONOMIC DEVELOPMENT
Virtuous and Vicious Circles

He had read Shakespeare and found him weak in Chemistry
H.G. Wells

OUTCOMES AND INSTRUMENTALITY

In spite of the obvious significance of science and technology to modern economic growth, development economics has tended to struggle with attempts to capture the catalytic role of human capital investments. The problem arose due to two factors: (i) the emphasis of traditional growth theory on the accumulation of physical capital;[1] (ii) the preoccupation of macroeconomics with why output and incomes fluctuate and, relatedly, why a capitalist economy does not produce consistently at full capacity.[2]

The attention given to human capital and technology has been one of the critical determinants of structural change in Eastern Asia. These investments have affected societies in several positive ways, which include directly increasing productivity, improved management capacity, changing the role of women, and reduced population growth. Linking these positive outcomes to specific policies and, even more demandingly, trying to measure these relationships is an extremely difficult undertaking. However, the inability to get precise quantitative measures does not detract from the importance of these investments. The salience of these human capital investments and their multiple benefits are examined in this chapter.

Numerous indicators have been devised to try and measure the quality of human capital In many international comparisons, the Asian countries have emerged on top; a remarkable feat to achieve within a few decades. The result of one such study is summarized in Tables 9 and 10, which are based on a study published in 1996.[3] In the quality of mathematics, an exceptional four out of the top five countries came from Asia: Singapore, South Korea, Japan, and Hong Kong (*see* Table 9). Within the region, two countries had moved ahead of the leading economy, Japan's. In science, three of the top five countries were Singapore, Japan, and South Korea (*see* Table 10). The successful Asian countries have surged ahead of Western Europe and the United States.[4]

An interesting feature of the science ranking is the prominent position acquired by countries such as the Czech Republic. Some of the countries of Eastern and Central Europe are likely to emerge as the next 'tigers'. The relatively successful transition to market economies underway in countries such as the Czech Republic, Hungary, and Poland suggests that a new source of dynamism is likely to emerge after the disintegration of central planning in Europe. Further, some of the Central Asian republics such as Kazakhstan and Uzbekistan may also emerge as emulators of the Asian success stories.

9. COUNTRY RANKING IN ACHIEVEMENTS IN MATHEMATICS

Rank	Country	Score
1	Singapore	643
2	South Korea	607
3	Japan	605
4	Hong Kong	588
5	Belgium	565
13	France	538
23	Germany	509
25	England	506
28	United States	500
37	Portugal	454
38	Iran	428
39	Kuwait	392
40	Colombia	385
41	South Africa	354

Source: *Third International Mathematics and Science Study,* 1996.

10. INTERNATIONAL RANKING OF SCIENCE ACHIEVEMENT

Rank	Country	Score
1	Singapore	607
2	Czech Republic	574
3	Japan	571
4	South Korea	565
5	Bulgaria	554
10	England	552
17	United States	534
18	Germany	531
28	France	498
37	Iran	470
38	Cyprus	463
39	Kuwait	430
40	Colombia	411
41	South Africa	326

Source: *Third International Mathematics and Science Study,* 1996.

In recent years, increasing attention has been paid to the relationship between human capital and structural change in developing economies. There have been two strands to the literature. One strand of analysis has emphasized the instrumentality of human capital for economic development. This has emphasized technology as the key driving force in growth. The term 'technology' is used in the composite sense of constituting products, organization of production processes, institutional research, and extension support. This strand has been reinforced through theoretical work, which made technical change endogenous,[5] and thereby formulated a more sophisticated understanding of the development process than conventional growth theory, in which technical change was an exogenous residual.[6] This theoretical work was built on an historical analysis of the role of technology in economic development.[7]

Along with the theoretical and historical work, emphasizing the instrumental role of technical knowledge in structural change, came the empirical experience of East Asia. The most successful economies in the world, between 1960-90, have been a select band of countries in East and

South East Asia.[8] While numerous factors have contributed to their performance, there is little doubt that their strong technology orientation has played a catalytic role in structural change.[9] The related literature on the NICs has emphasized issues such as the acquisition of technological capability at the firm level as a central explanation for productivity growth and competitiveness. These aspects were summarized effectively by a cross country review:

> For developing countries, one of the most important of the many insights stemming from research into the growth process is that substantial research and development capacity is needed to adapt other people's technology to one's own purpose and to learn how to use it.[10]

The instrumentalists' literature has emphasized the interplay of a mix of factors which lead to structural change in society. This change, which can be viewed as a positive externality associated with a set of modernizing investments, fuels attitudes and processes which are conducive to economic development. These collective factors can be summarized as: (i) technocratic competence in economic management; (ii) effective technology support institutions, for example quality extension services for agriculture and technology transmission centres for industry; (iii) a primary and secondary education system producing students with distinguished cognitive skills, and (iv) creation/nurturing of dynamic entrepreneurial forces, which demand a good human capital base to succeed internationally.

The second strand in the recent human resource literature focuses less on instrumentality and more on human development as the objective of development.[11] Accordingly, attention is paid to using human development indicators as measures of desirable outcome. Quantitative summaries, such as the Human Development Index,[12] aim to capture the benefits of development. The emphasis is not so much on how growth takes place[13] but relatively more on assessing the extent to which basic social investments have accompanied economic growth and thereby benefited the poor directly. The variation between levels of income and average expected outcomes in literacy, life expectancy and so on, is then explained in terms of the pattern of social investments. Related studies have tried to correlate a more equitable pattern of investments with social cohesion.[14]

Conceptually, social policy can influence economic development through four channels, discussed in more detail below. They can help create virtuous and vicious circles which have a deep impact on the dynamics of development. As in many other policy areas, the dynamics of social change are aided or hampered by the creation of these virtuous and vicious circles. A comparison of Eastern Asia and Pakistan is illustrated in Figures 3 and 4.

3. SOCIAL POLICY AND ECONOMIC DEVELOPMENT: EAST ASIA'S VIRTUOUS CIRCLE

(i)   High proportion of public expenditure devoted to primary education, primary health, and population planning.
(ii) Broad-based basic social services, emphasized cognitive development, and technical skill aquisition.
(iii) Increased female participation in paid employment.
(iv) Improvements in quality of human capital as economy grows.

↓

(i)   Universal literacy.
(ii) Sharply reduced fertility and population growth.
(iii) Improved nutrition, particulary of children and mothers.

↓

(i)   Aggregate quantity of people seeking jobs is reduced due to lower population growth.
(ii) Per capita expenditures on social services increase enabling improvements in quality.
(iii) Productivity improves.
(iv) Women's socio-economic status improves.

↓

(i)   High per capita GDP growth.
(ii) Improvement in human development indicators.
(iii) Economic diversification aided by skilled population.

4. SOCIAL POLICY AND ECONOMIC DEVELOPMENT: PAKISTAN'S VICIOUS LINKAGES

(i)   Low spending on basic education and health.
(ii) No serious commitment to population planning.
(iii) Traditional roles of women reinforced by social policies.

(i)   Poor literacy.
(ii) High fertility and population growth.
(iii) Low nutrition levels of children and mothers.

(i)   Explosive demographic pressures are reflected in the labour market. Rapid annual growth in labour force seeking employment.
(ii) High levels of child labour due to lack of basic education facilities.
(iii) Low socio-economic status of girls sustains poor parental interest in their education.
(iv) Lack of skilled manpower.

(i)   Poor human development indicators.
(ii) Lower per capita GDP growth.
(iii) Diversification into higher productivity activities constrained by lack of skills.

HUMAN CAPITAL INVESTMENTS: FOUR SUPPLY SIDE ISSUES

Global experience[15] has emphasized that the key to long-term economic development lies in the capacity to apply science and technology, within a framework of incentives which encourage accumulation and efficient production. Accordingly the capacity to bring in and absorb technology, operate complex machines, diversify from simple to sophisticated processes, and to provide an effective public sector machinery to manage the economy is a function of an effective human resource development strategy. Unfortunately some of the discussion on human capital investment has tended to place exclusive emphasis on quantitative expansion of primary education. The proponents of the expansion of social sectors have frequently argued the case for extending basic education and health as a human right; while there are several economic and non-economic dimensions to this debate,[16] the link between primary social sector investments and economic development is not straightforward. No matter how desirable it may be for social reasons the provision of literacy is no guarantee that incomes will rise.

On the other hand, the growth of incomes does not universally and at the same pace lead to improvements in indicators of quality of life, such as life expectancy, infant mortality, and level of literacy. In general, for any given increase in income the performance of human development indicators depends on the composition and quality of social sector investments and factor market policies which affect the demand for labour.

However, effectively designing an institutional framework for enabling a society such as Pakistan to make the transition from an unskilled to a knowledge-intensive economy involves difficult decisions regarding appropriate sequencing and quality. Attention has to be paid to the evolution of an education system within a context whereby much of the improved labour supply is effectively absorbed. This in turn creates capacities which enable a transition to more complex operations. The sections below contain broad hypotheses regarding the conceptual links between human capital investments and economic development, with particular reference to comparisons between Pakistan and East Asia.

The link between human capital investment and economic development has both supply and demand side dimensions. On the supply side, human capital investment policies can have four forms of impact. The first is the reduction in the quantity of annual increments to the labour force. This eases pressure on the labour market and, *ceteris paribus*, leads to higher per capita incomes. For each country, it is important to specify the mix of instruments required to reduce the rate of population growth. Recent cross country evidence particularly from North East and South East Asia suggests that a mix of an extensive primary education base, particularly for girls, along with expansion of contraceptive supplies and primary health care aimed at reducing infant mortality can effectively reduce the population growth rate in a remarkably short period. There is considerable debate about the relative importance of each instrument in this package, but the aggregate set of measures appear to work because they enable some currently reproductive couples to have better access to contraception, while investments in primary education for girls help alter their social role and delay the age of marriage. A good quality primary education base can also increase participation and retention at the secondary level.

In addition to these measures, the government can provide appropriate direct incentives by penalizing or rewarding the size of the family. The experience of Singapore and China in using such direct incentive mechanisms has been well-documented.

In brief, extensive international evidence supports the view that the component of an HRDS aimed at the poor needs to consist of a co-ordinated policy for different social sector services. The mutually reinforcing character of returns to investments in primary education, primary health, water and sanitation, and population control requires a policy co-ordination which has not always been evident in Pakistan. In principle, the optimal mix of social sector investments should lead to a virtuous circle of higher female education causing greater labour force participation. The latter combined with easier availability of contraception and primary health services should lead to an improved nutritional and health status for women and children.

The reduction in population would not only reduce the supply of the labour force and thereby increase the probability of employment and wage rises, but also curtail pressure on over-stretched government services to provide a reasonable quality of basic education and health, and thereby sustain the virtuous circle. While many developing economies have executed inter-linked social sector programmes effectively[17] and achieved results approximating the virtuous circle outlined above, most have struggled in the ability to provide a convincing and co-ordinated set of social sector interventions.

The second link between human capital investments and economic development relates to the need to have professional management capacity in the public sector. The absence of these skills is most evident in many African countries. Much of East Asia, on the other hand, appears to have invested wisely in building up high quality manpower in the public sector, initially through training programmes overseas and then through building the domestic capacity to reproduce these selective technical and management skills. Indeed, the emergence of a technocratic and highly competent civil service, which enforced disciplined support to the private sector, has been emphasized as one of the critical aspects of East Asian development, in a number of recent studies.

In Pakistan on the other hand, the situation changed in the 1970s when a relatively high quality public sector was replaced by a quantitative expansion of civil servants of dubious quality. Pervasive civil service reforms reduced their autonomy and increased politicization. Civil servants became increasingly subservient to political whims, either of their elected civilian bosses or their military rulers. At the same time, the state started providing an employment subsidy by absorbing excess manpower. Thus the government was caught in another vicious circle. The lack of a population control policy was leading to growing underemployment as the formal sector was employing a small share of the growing labour force. The elected government was absorbing large numbers directly through unproductive employment in the public sector. In the process, the quality of the public sector deteriorated. The increased aggregate wage bill in the public sector meant that skilled manpower was not rewarded adequately. Instead of paying much higher salaries to technically qualified manpower, public sector management suffered from increased patrimonial influences as Pakistan moved more towards a 'soft' state rather than the 'hard' state more common in East Asia. Matters were compounded in the 1980s, as the military regime used the state to extend patronage and the government was monopolized by a few interest groups. Since promotions depended more on personal contacts, there was a further diminution in the rewards for professionalism in the public sector.

The third link between developing human capacity and economic growth relates to the support provided by the state for the creation and maturation of the private sector. In Pakistan, an emergence of an entrepreneurial class was supported by government policies and private sector management skills were enhanced through the availability of skilled management manpower, such as MBAs. In this area, Pakistan's experience did not diverge substantially from much of East Asia's until the 1970s. In the first two decades after independence government policies were geared towards the creation of a substantial entrepreneurial class, as much of the merchant capital that came from India was converted into an industrial bourgeoisie. State support was extensive and included directed credit, trade protection, and public sector investment in selected areas.[18] Further, skilled managerial manpower such as MBAs was being provided by one of the earliest business schools outside of North America, the Institute of Business Administration (IBA) at Karachi. However, after having developed a modern private sector through extensive state support, Pakistan witnessed a major reversal in the 1970s.

While Pakistan went through these convulsions regarding the respective roles of the private and public sectors, North East and South East Asia deepened formal consultative mechanisms for government-private sector collaboration. Market information was shared, credit was subsidized, specific sectors were promoted, and exports were encouraged while selective protection was given against imports.

As noted in earlier chapters the management capacity, confidence, and continuity in both the public and private sectors, suffered due to the policy shocks experienced in the 1970s. Simultaneously, during this period much of East Asia was consolidating the quality of public sector management, thus ensuring that its human capital investments at the top level were leading to good quality economic management. The capacity for independent domestic analysis was created, unlike Pakistan which remains even now largely dependent on international agencies such as the World Bank and the IMF for economic analysis. As far as the private sector was concerned, after pursuing broadly similar policies up to the 1960s the paths of East Asia and Pakistan diverged in the 1970s, as emphasized in Chapter 2. While much of East Asia consolidated the relationship between the state and the private sector, erratic asset redistribution measures in Pakistan had little positive impact on equity while insecurity prevented private sector accumulation of the type and scale evident in many East Asian countries.

Finally, the fourth complex link is between human capital investments, the skill level of the mass of the work force, and economic development. There are a number of issues involved here. In several sectors, the skills required for manual labour may be very basic and simple on-the-job training may be enough. Further, the education system may be providing the wrong skills and creating the wrong ambitions; for example, for clerical office work rather than vocational skills for which there may be a higher demand. An investment in basic skills is not subject to some form of a Say's law in the labour market, i.e. the supply of educated manpower does not imply an automatic demand for that trained labour. In addition, the education system may be biased in favour of the subsidized production of tertiary level social science skills. In such cases, looking at aggregate allocations to education does not tell us very much about the likely impact on economic development. An examination of the composition, the curriculum, and quality of the education sector becomes critical.

In the case of Pakistan, there has been an excessive bias towards the subsidized production of lawyers and doctors. Vocational training institutes build on a poor science and maths base and are frequently removed from the requirements of the market, while at the primary level the quality of the curriculum and the poor physical conditions of schools have hardly been conducive to skill formation which would be useful for economic development. In the 1980s the state seemed far more concerned with ideological control than the provision of technical capacities. Instead of concentrating on a strong maths and science base as much of East Asia was doing, the Pakistani public education system was suffering from endemic institutional decay, including stifling and rigid control over the curriculum.[19] In brief, the ethos of the education system was not geared towards the provision of rigorous science- and technology-oriented education, which was the case in much of East Asia. Neither did the poor quality of the basic education system enable the development of cognitive skills, as it relied more on rote and other mechanical processes. Again, just looking at the aggregate allocation for education would not be a useful guide in judging the impact on economic development. While it is acknowledged that Pakistan was spending too little, this was not the only issue. Had an additional 2% of GDP been spent on this education system it is conceivable that the returns to economic development may have been negligible. In sum, one has to examine the quality and content of the education system rather than simply the quantity of resource allocation.

Further, in Pakistan the state was positively hostile towards population control through most of the 1980s,[20] while the public education system was ruined by ideological imperatives and the desire to exercise political control.[21] However, urban middle class education quality revived as this sector was denationalized; the result was a mushrooming of private English medium schools, concentrating largely on development of skills required by the labour market.

However, while reforms which revived the role of the private sector in the provision of urban educational services have contributed to a significant improvement in quality, there are growing concerns regarding equity. By and large, the corporate sector and the middle class have almost entirely opted out of the public education system. In many areas, the corporate sector has decided that it will not rely on the state and will take care of its human capital needs directly. This is evident in the establishment of private universities,[22] teacher training institutions,[23] technical colleges related to particular sectors of industry,[24] and the mushrooming of private schools.[25]

While the middle and upper classes have opted out and are experimenting with a variety of innovative institutions frequently with external collaboration, the public sector education system remains paralysed. The deficiencies of the public education system are evident in the familiar phenomena of teachers not turning up at primary schools, staff refusing to go to rural areas, poor quality university staff, a stifling intellectual environment, and a high degree of damaging politicization of the student bodies. The problems of the public education system are symptomatic of a deeper malaise: the state in Pakistan is no longer able to function effectively and execute its responsibilities. Thus the government is generally unable to regulate, enforce laws, or manage institutions.

This institutional malaise has been addressed partially over the last decade through a reduction in the role of the state, thus allowing the considerable dynamism displayed by the private sector to flourish. However, there has been little progress in efforts to reform the public sector in order for it to perform effectively the many tasks required of the state, such as regulation of markets, investing in social services and so on. With the exception of a few institutions,[26] much of the public education system is unable to provide even a basic quality of services.[27] The equity consequences of this paralysis are particularly serious at a time when urban middle class education is enjoying a boom and shows every sign of improvement and consolidation of quality. The result is a growing gulf between a relatively high quality English medium private education stream, and a third rate, largely Urdu medium public education system.

One of the important comparative lessons that could be emphasized in the analysis is the manner in which East Asian public sector educational institutions have executed their mandates effectively, while allowing the private sector to flourish in certain areas. In many countries, the state concentrated on providing high quality research and extension support for agriculture and industry, as well as concentrating on the provision of a good primary education base. Considerable innovation was allowed on the direct provision of services by the domestic and international private sector with effective regulation by the state. In Pakistan, there has been an intense debate on the needed reform for public sector institutions[28] but relatively little progress.

By the 1990s, the accumulation of past neglect has begun to bite. A 3.2% annual growth in labour force is accompanied by a sharp contraction in the Middle Eastern labour market. At the same time, a structural adjustment programme has, as one of its concerns, a reduction of the role of the state in production and trade. While the direction of the reforms regarding the changing role of the state may be justified, there are transitional problems regarding absorption of excess public sector employees at a time of increasing under- and unemployment. Thus, while future policies must concentrate on stimulating the growth of manufacturing exports in particular, they have to be accompanied by major efforts at population control and human capital formation. This is where one needs to pay careful attention to the composition and quality of the education system as well as accompanying health and direct population control measures.

HUMAN CAPITAL: DEMAND SIDE CONCERNS

The discussion above examined four aspects regarding the supply side of human capital investments. Although there were some references to demand it is important to summarize the demand side issues separately. Growth in demand for labour is derived from the growth in output. Thus, policies which stimulate the growth of commodity production are necessary complements to human capital investments; otherwise one gets into a situation such as Tanzania's or that of much of the former Eastern bloc, where the supply side human capital measures are not matched by appropriate stimulatory policies for growth. However, the degree to which the labour force has to be absorbed depends on social sector investments which determine the rate of growth of population. Over the long run, for any given growth rate of income the difference between demand and supply in the labour market is thus partly determined by social investments. This has obvious implications for wages and per capita income growth.

Demand side concerns, other than the rate of growth, include a public sector which rewards and retains professional skills. If these skills are not demanded and appreciated, then the returns to concentrating on the supply side through the provision of trained, skilled manpower, will be limited. In such circumstances, increased supply of qualitative manpower will result in a drain overseas—the familiar sight of technical manpower migrating. The impact of demand side policies on determining effective returns to education investments are highlighted by international comparisons. For example, while sub-Saharan African countries invest proportionately more on education—4.1% of GDP on average compared to 3.7% in East Asia—the latter set of countries absorb the labour force more effectively due to strong labour market demand. The poor growth performance of sub-Saharan African countries, on the other hand, has meant high unemployment for the educated manpower, thereby devaluing the returns to investment in education.

In the case of Pakistan the growth performance has in general been impressive, leading to fairly strong demand in the labour market. However, as mentioned earlier, weak policies on the supply side have meant that under- and unemployment have grown faster than they would have, had more concerted attention been paid to population planning and investments in primary education and health.

In sum, there are two dimensions to a human resource development strategy (HRDS). One aspect is the somewhat passive one of providing basic social services to enable the poor to take advantage of employment opportunities. By building their basic educational and health capacities, these social investments assist individuals in becoming more employable, while social returns may take the form of reduction in the rate of growth of labour supply. The second aspect of an HRDS is more dynamic in the sense of building the capacity to create, initiate, and manage economically productive activities. This refers to the technical capacity to manage the economy, diversify the production base, and absorb technology. Human capacity for these functions involves: (i) the creation and retention of indigenous management skills in the public sector; (ii) skilled research and extension manpower in support of the commodity-producing sectors; (iii) the provision of incentives and institutional support to entrepreneurs.

These dynamic human capital issues have been emphasized in a number of studies which have noted that the critical requirement for a strategic diversification of Pakistan's economy is human capital in the form of an improved applied research and related extension service, consolidation of the private sector-state relationship to provide a more stable environment for entrepreneurial activity, and investments in population planning and basic education/health facilities. These measures have to be accompanied by incentive reforms for accelerating the growth in labour demand, in areas such as labour-intensive manufacturing exports.

The next two chapters contain short case studies of East and South East Asian countries, within the context of the conceptual issues raised in Chapters 2 and 3. These country reviews are followed by a more lengthy examination of Pakistan's socio-economic evolution.

NOTES

1. For a review of growth theories, see Rostow, W: *Theories of Economic Growth from David Hume to the Present,* (Oxford University Press, 1990).

2. This was the primary motivation for the work of Keynes and the resulting 'Keynesian revolution' in macroeconomic theory.

3. The *Third International Mathematics and Science Study* was based on a survey of 50 000 students in 45 countries. The number of schools participating was 15 000. The survey focused on the capacity of 13 year olds in science and maths. In addition, it examined the quality of the teachers, an area in which Japan excelled. While the survey gives a limited picture of maths and science achievement and the quality of students and teachers, it is a good proxy for the technical intellectual capacities being created at an early age.

4. The results of such studies do not imply that the countries lead the frontiers of science. The work of path-breaking research institutes is not reflected in studies such as these, which aim only to capture the capabilities of young students and the quality of teaching of science and mathematics.

5. For theoretical work on endogenous growth see Romer, P: 'Increasing Returns and Long Run Growth', *Journal of Political Economy*, 1994, pp.1002-37; Romer, P: 'The Origins of Endogenous Growth', *Journal of Economic Perspectives*, 20, 1993; and Nelson, R and Winter, S: *An Evolutionary Theory of Economic Change,* (Cambridge, Harvard University Press, 1982).

6. For a recent analysis of the impact of technology on growth globally see, *inter alia*, Lipsey, R: 'Notes on Globalisation and Technological Change', (Canadian Institute for Advanced Research, Programme in Economic Growth and Policy, Working Paper # 8); Madison, A: *Dynamic Forces in Capitalist Development,* (Oxford University Press, New York, 1991) and Lipsey, R: 'Markets, Technological Change and Economic Growth', (Paper presented at the 10th annual general meeting of the Pakistan Institute of Development Economics, Islamabad, 1994).

7. Pioneering work in this area has been done by Nathan Rosenberg. See *Inside the Black Box—Technology and Economics,* (Cambridge University Press, 1982), and Rosenberg and Birdzell, L: *How the West Grew Rich,* (Basic Books, New York, 1986).

8. These regional developments have been summarized in the World Bank: *The East Asian Miracle,* (OUP, Washington, 1993).

9. On the technological aspect of East Asian development see Dahlman, C: 'Technology Strategy in the Economy of Taiwan: Exploiting Foreign Linkages and Investing in Local Capability' and Brimble, P and Dahlman, C: 'Technology Strategy and Policy for Industrial Competitiveness: A Case Study of Thailand' (both papers published by the World Bank, Private Sector Development Programme, 1990).

10. United Nations: *Globalisation and Developing Countries: Investment, Trade and Technology Linkages in the 1990s,* (New York, UN Department of Economic and Social Affairs, 1992).

11. An example of attempts to capture the wider benefits of development is represented in the launch of the annual *Human Development Report* by the UNDP in 1990.

12. There has been a considerable debate about the value of composite indicators of economic welfare. For a flavour of the debate see, Anand, S and Sen, A: *Human Development Index: Methodology and Measurement,* (UNDP, Human Development Report Office, New York, 1994); Pyatt, G: 'Measuring Welfare,

Poverty and Inequality', *Economic Journal*, Volume 97, 1987; Pyatt, G: *There is nothing wrong with the HDI but...*, mimeo, (Department of Economics, University of Warwick, 1992); McGillivray, M: 'The human development index: yet another redundant composite development indicator?' *World Development*, Volume 19, # 10, 1991.

13. This omission is however addressed in the 1996 *Human Development Report*, (UNDP, New York).

14. See, for example, UNDP: *Sustainable Human Development*, (New York, 1994).

15. For details of the conceptual links and empirical evidence see, *inter alia*, Psacharopoulos, G: *The contribution of education to economic growth-international comparisons*, (Ballinger Publishing, Cambridge, 1984); Harbison and Myers, *Education Manpower* and *Economic Growth*, (McGraw Hill, New York, 1964); Kim, Y.B.: *Education* and *Economic Growth*, (Korean Educational Development Institute, Seoul, 1980), and Mace, J: *Themes, Concepts and Assumptions in Economics and Education Policy*, (The Open University Press, London, 1979).

16. For a summary of the recent debate on human development, poverty alleviation policies, and economic growth see three articles by Paul Streeten, Paul Isenman et al., and Srinivasan in *The American Economic Review, Annual Proceedings*, (May, 1994).

17. Well known examples are Sri Lanka, Thailand, Malaysia, Indonesia, and Korea. Useful comparative information is contained in Papanek, Noman et al.: *Assessing the impact of sectoral and macroeconomic reform on the poor in South Asia*, (Asian Development Bank, Manila, 1994).

18. In some cases, the public sector invested in particular firms to overcome risk aversion, and then handed over these units to the private sector.

19. Similarly, professionals undertaking the public service examinations had to respond to an increased dose of questions on religion, reflecting an underlying shift in official attitudes, which was also reflected in the introduction of compulsory Arabic.

20. This point has been made in both chapters 1 and 2.

21. The measures taken to establish a rigid political control over the campuses was partly a reaction to the 1960s, when student

revolts contributed to the downfall of Ayub's military regime in 1968. Subsequent governments have been wary of political mobilization on campuses.

22. Three large private universities have been established over the last decade: the Lahore University of Management Sciences, the Aga Khan Medical University and the Hamdard University. In addition, approximately 50 private colleges have been established while British, American, and Canadian universities have either established campuses within Pakistan, or have entered into twinning arrangements with private educational establishments. Two more private universities are proposed.

23. Private teacher training institutions are increasingly catering to the demands of the mushrooming private school sector. Prominent amongst these are the Ali Institute in Lahore and the Aga Khan Teacher Training Centre at Karachi.

24. For example, in the largest industrial group, textiles, the private sector is funding the establishment of two technology institutes. The textile industry used to have private institutes in the 1960s, but these were nationalized in the 1970s. Similarly, there have been proposals to privatize or substantially reform the poorly functioning public technology development centres, such as the Metal Industries Development Centre at Sialkot.

25. During the 1980s, there was a major reversal of education sector policies to allow the revival of the private sector. The supply response was substantial, with a large number of schools and colleges covering the urban landscape.

26. Such as the HEJ Chemistry Institute at Karachi University, the Solid State Physics Centre at Punjab University, the Institute of Business Administration at Karachi, and the recently established GIK Institute of Science and Technology, near Islamabad.

27. This is evident in high failure and drop out rates, as well as problems of governance, such as inability to control widespread cheating.

28. See, for example, L.Hayes: *Pakistan's Education System*, and several papers by Pervez Hoodbhoy on the reform needed in the science, technology, and maths orientation of the education system.

CHAPTER 4

COUNTRY BRIEFS: EASTERN ASIA

The history of things that didn't happen has never been written.
Henry Kissinger

1. Japan
2. China
3. Korea
4. Taiwan (China)

INTRODUCTION

The collective influence of the Meiji restoration and communism, particularly the Chinese revolution, have had a profound impact on the modern evolution of Eastern Asia. In the second half of the 19th century, Japan was one of the few Asian countries which were still free. The rest had been colonized. A free Japan was able to engage in a major modernization of society during the Meiji restoration, which started in the 1860s. In the process, Japan became a participant in the science and technology revolution that was sweeping across Europe. Military conquest prevented the other great Asian nations, such as India and China, from the possibility of active participation in the widespread acquisition of modern technical knowledge.[1]

At the time of Japan's modernization, India was under the rule of a single country while China was suffering from territorial seizures from a variety of nations. The Opium War against Britain (1839-42) was followed by the Anglo-French occupation of Beijing and a series of unequal treaties, including the ceding of Hong Kong and Kowloon to Britain. Conflicts with Japan and Russia led to further reversals. By contrast, the acquisition of modern knowledge as well as

Japan's defeat of Russia at the turn of the century instilled a degree of self confidence in Japan's military and technical capacity.[2] Ironically, in some ways, Japan's technological catch-up during the Meiji period was similar to that undertaken by Peter the Great in Russia, who launched a major modernization drive. Japan's modernization was to subsequently influence the economic development of neighbouring countries. Japan became an inspiring model from within the region for those envious of its success and wishing to emulate it.

At the same time, revolutions of another kind were to exert an enormous influence on equity. The success of the Chinese revolution as well as communist struggles in other countries generated intense pressures on elites. Those countries which continued to pursue a capitalist development path typically responded in two ways: repression to control communist insurgencies or movements, combined with policies which extended the benefits of development to a wide constituency.

These wider political economy influences affected modernization-and equity in Eastern Asia. The specifics of socio-economic development in each country were shaped by institutional and policy measures, which are explored in the remainder of this chapter. The sections below provide a cursory summary of a few East Asian countries: Japan, China, Korea, and Taiwan. The next chapter documents the cases of Malaysia, Thailand, and Indonesia, the South East Asian countries which are in the process of emulating East Asian economic success. The case of the Philippines is also considered, as a South East Asian country having several parallels with Pakistan.

JAPAN

After centuries of virtual isolation, Japan was engulfed by a wide ranging domestic transformation in the 19th century. The process of modernization was led by a few young provincial leaders who had orchestrated the downfall of the Tokugawa shogunate.[3] The modernization was motivated by the Japanese elite's desire to come to terms with the advances in science and technology, which were transforming Europe and America. Socio-educational reforms played a critical role. Under the renowned 'Rescript on Education' issued by the emperor, Japan established an impressive network of schools, technical colleges, and universities. The opening up to the world and the acquisition of these technical capacities coincided with the restoration of the monarchy under the young emperor Meiji; effective power, however, lay with the provincial military chiefs. The net result of the Meiji modernization was that the one major free country in Asia had acquired the nucleus of modern technical knowledge essential for economic development.

Japan's metamorphosis[4] from a feudal society to an industrial nation was spectacular. Between the Meiji restoration, which commenced in 1868, and the outbreak of the Second World War in 1939, Japan had one of the fastest growing economies in the world, sustaining an annual per capita growth rate of 3% over six decades. One of the interesting counter factuals of history is the extent to which Asian modernization would have resembled the pattern of Japan if the continent had been free in the late 19th century. Inevitably, some of the other major countries in Asia would have caught up technologically with the rest of the world during the 19th century.

The First World War had provided a major stimulus to the Japanese economy as demand from the allied powers enabled the expansion of Japan's factories, foundries, and shipyards. The next wave of global destruction during the Second World War proved even more decisive in the evolution of modern Japan. Defeat and subsequent occupation by the US forces was followed by a number of structural reforms. These included a major land reform, through which a large class of disgruntled tenant farmers acquired land and a stake in society. Educational opportunities were extended further and institutional reforms created a corporate structure which built a consensual social contract with labour.

While war and social dislocation provide opportunities for equitable social reform, there is nothing inevitable about the direction that such reforms can take. Partition, war, and social dislocation in South Asia offered many similar potential opportunities but the major progressive direction of reform was typically thwarted by the lack of organized political pressure from 'below', as exerted in much of Eastern Asia by communism. Other cleavages, of ethnicity and religion in particular, dominated and therefore diluted the pressure for social reform on elites.

A number of equity-enhancing reforms, of which land reform was a central component, were imposed under the administration of General Douglas MacArthur of the United States. The direction and content of these reforms were heavily influenced by developments in China and domestic political strains. The likelihood of Mao's victory in China led to the reassessment by the US of Japan as a powerful anti-communist ally. The threat of communism was emerging not only in China and other countries of the region but also within the peasantry in Japan. Land reform was part of the response which played an important role in curbing the growth of rural support for Japan's left wing parties.[5] Subsequently, except for a brief period, Japan's socialists have not been in power and the country has been ruled by a liberal-democrat alliance, which has governed the country through much of its post-war economic success.[6]

Japan's post-war capitalism has been shaped by a set of institutional and policy mechanisms which have exercised considerable influence in recent East Asian success. Two aspects of the institutional framework deserve particular mention. The first was the balance between the market and the state. While there was a social consensus on the leading role to be played by markets in resource allocation, equally important was the role assigned to the state in building capacities, directing resource allocation, and stimulating investment. Activities in each area were guided by the principle of supporting the private sector, not competing with it.

State intervention was exemplified by the role played by the Economic Planning Agency (EPA) and the Ministry of International Trade and Industry (MITI). The EPA prepared five year plans, which provided important guidelines and principles to the private sector. These plans did not specify details of inputs needed to achieve certain targets. The role of the EPA was more in line with identifying bottlenecks and providing a coherent policy direction. MITI on the other hand played a major role in guiding the shape of the industrial structure. The financial sector was also heavily regulated. Effective regulatory capacity and disciplined public institutions ensured that the role assigned to the state was executed effectively. Interventions in each sector were typically the outcome of consultation with the private sector. The state also played a major role in the provision of education and health services. In sum, Japan's economic success was not the result of *laissez-faire* but was shaped by a judicious division of the market and the public sector.

The other institutional aspect worth noting is the framework which has governed the labour market. The larger corporations entered into agreements with enterprise-based trade unions on employment and wages, which have served Japan well. The high level of unemployment immediately after the war was reduced through the rapid growth in output. Employment levels have tended, however, not to fluctuate with the vagaries of the business cycle as much as in many other countries. Firms have retained workers and adjusted wage levels during difficult periods, which has enhanced corporate loyalty and helped sustain a non-adversarial relationship between management and labour. Some firms introduced lifelong employment guarantees. Such institutional arrangements, within the context of rapid growth and expansion of the social sectors, created an environment of an inclusive capitalism.

Post-war Japanese growth was aided by rates of savings and investment which were in the region of 25% of GNP. The postal savings institutions played a significant role in resource mobilization. In addition, the pace of technology adoption accelerated due to joint venture and licensing agreements with US firms. Investments by Japanese firms in R & D, as well as public spending on education and training, enhanced the adoption of new industrial techniques.

Within this framework, specific sectoral policies influenced growth. Japan's industrial sector, contributing nearly 40% of GNP, is the second largest in the world after the United States. A country that has very few natural resources has, within a century, built a complex industrial structure based on chemicals, steel, transport equipment, and electric and general machinery. Japan has gradually moved up the productivity scale and away from relatively simple manufacturing activities in areas such as textiles. Before the war, silk and cotton production dominated the industrial structure. Even in 1950, half of Japan's export earnings were accounted for by textiles. By the mid-1990s, their share was less than 2%, reflecting the remarkable transformation of Japan's industry in the last four decades. The industrial sector has adjusted well to shocks and changing comparative advantage. During the 1970s for example, the combination of the oil price shock and increased competition from the emerging East Asian economies produced a strategic response. The MITI helped guide the shift from labour- and energy-intensive activities to those with higher productivity. Some sub-sectors were declared structurally depressed, while others such as electronics, vehicle production, and machine production received targeted support.

The financial sector has undergone major liberalization since the 1980s. Interest rates have been deregulated, financial futures markets introduced, and easier access allowed to foreign firms to operate in the Japanese market. The liberalization and deregulation reflect the changing needs and increased sophistication of the financial sector. For long periods, it was heavily regulated in support of industrial policy. Credit was directed to specific sectors and interest rates, though positive, were below market rates. This was effectively a transfer from households to the corporate sector. Japan grew rapidly during a period of regulated exchange and interest rates and central bank influence on resource allocation. However, at present the imperatives of globalization are leading to a major overhaul of the financial sector and greater integration with the global financial systems. Japan's policy makers no longer face the dilemma of creating the conditions appropriate for accelerating development. They are now engaged in reforms which maintain the competitiveness and efficiency of an advanced post-industrial economy.

The agricultural sector is now a relatively insignificant part of the Japanese economy. Post-war rural unrest was potentially damaging for the general political stability that has assisted Japan's economic development. A land reform limited holdings to 1 hectare, while absentee landlords were not allowed to own land. Land reform was followed by an aggressive industrialization, in which many of the former landlords participated. Within the agricultural sector the most important crop is rice. This has enjoyed very heavy protection through import bans. Numerous price and marketing interventions guarantee high returns to rice production. As in many other areas, the rice policy is also undergoing change. Japan imported rice for the first time in 1994 and the liberalization of the rice trade has been the subject of pressure under the new World Trade Organization.

Macroeconomic management has been sound throughout the post-war period. Fiscal deficits have been low or the government account was in surplus. Total government spending has been rather low, at 16% of GNP, partly on account of negligible defence spending after demilitarization. But Japan's economic modernization predates the Second World War and was underway even during the period of relatively high defence expenditures. Disciplined monetary policy adjustments have ensured low inflation, while exchange rate management has stimulated exports. However, the continuing trade surplus has exerted upward pressure on the exchange rate. This in turn has provided incentives for Japanese firms to invest abroad. Japanese FDI has consequently played a critical role in some countries of the region, particularly in South East Asia.

In brief, Japan's economic development has been shaped by the mix of policies and institutional arrangements outlined in Chapter 2. Consensus over private sector led development, strong state intervention to influence resource allocation and equity, emphasis on technology acquisition to improve productivity, shift from ISI to export led industrialization, and sound macroeconomic management collectively constituted a successful development strategy. The use of specific policy instruments was eclectic and pragmatic, changing with the requirements of an increasingly complex economy.

The outcomes have been exceptional. The Japanese live longer than anyone else. Women have the longest life expectancy in the world: 82 years. The average life expectancy of men is 76. Per capita income is the third highest in the world, at over $US 20 000 in purchasing parity terms. The unemployment rate is the lowest in the industrial world, 3.1%. One of the most successful trading economies has emerged from a nation with virtually no natural resources to speak of. Japan's export of goods now exceeds $350 billion, as the country has shifted from exporting tea, textiles, and toys to high productivity industrial products. It is not surprising that the success of Japan has had such a positive impact on other East Asian countries seeking to modernize and accelerate their pace of development. Rapid regional development offers more economic opportunities than threats. In 1993, for example, Japan's trade surplus with Asia of $56 billion exceeded that with the United States. Japan's direct investment in Eastern Asia is also booming.

Like all advanced industrial nations, Japan faces numerous competitive pressures and policy challenges. During the 1990s, it has suffered from a recession. But the country is well placed to make the adjustments. Inevitably, the economic success and military influence of China is altering the regional picture, causing some alarm in Japan. While current trends suggest that Japan will lose its pre-eminence in the region, it will gain more than lose from the dynamism of an increasingly prosperous zone.

CHINA

After more than a century of turmoil, subjugation, and civil war, the 1949 revolution created a radical and unified political structure in command of China. The success of Mao's revolution sent shock waves across Eastern Asia. Japan was particularly troubled by its implication, as was a United States entering into a 'cold war' with the Soviet Union. The loser of the Chinese revolution, the deposed Chiang Kai-shek, migrated and ruled over Taiwan with extensive support from the United States. The regional impact of the largest country in the world having a communist revolution was immense. For those countries of the region that wished to pursue private sector led development, the warning was clear. If the development strategy was too elitist and the benefits of growth were not widespread, there was a threat of communist revolt. Any such ferment could be expected to get support from the Soviet Union and/or the People's Republic of China. This set the stage for the type of 'inclusive capitalism' which was pursued in Eastern Asia.

China's socio-economic development after the revolution followed a path familiar to that experienced by the Soviet Union under central planning. There were major gains in human development indicators. Literacy became virtually universal a few decades after the introduction of compulsory primary education; major improvements in health and population planning were also achieved. In the rural areas, private property rights were replaced by communal farms and the industrialization drive was to revolve around basic heavy industries.

Within three decades, the economy ran into major constraints. After initial increases in real wages for two decades after the revolution, incomes were stagnating. Central planning was running into co-ordination problems as the economy became more complex. The system of administrative prices provided inappropriate signals of scarcity. At the same time, the lack of private incentives was adversely affecting efficiency and effort. In spite of reasonably high savings and investment levels, the efficiency of investments was poor. Technology acquisition was also inadequate due to the lack of international trade and contact.

Further, in a reversal of recent history, developments in Eastern Asia began to affect the economic evolution of China. By the mid-1970s, the 'tigers', including the ethnically Chinese-dominated Taiwan and Singapore, had emerged as examples of the economic success of inclusive capitalism. The process was expanding to South East Asia. In many countries, groups of Chinese descent were leading the entrepreneurial drive. In subsequent years these groups were to play an important role in the revitalizing of the mainland Chinese economy after it had opened out. It was somewhat ironic that these smaller successful economies were driving change in a huge, centrally planned country.

By the mid-1970s, the inefficiencies of central planning and the success of neighbouring economies led to mounting pressures on China for reform. Similar problems were afflicting the Soviet Union, although the history of central planning there went back to the 1920s and the economy was far more industrialized than that of China. But while the Soviet Union vacillated and was paralysed by the inability to agree on a direction for reform, China moved swiftly. Under Deng Xiaoping, China commenced property and price reforms in agriculture, which provided the incentives for investment and growth in rural areas. As a result, a substantial group of beneficiaries and a constituency for reform were created.

In the industrial sector public investment in physical infrastructure, foreign exchange and trade liberalization, the availability of an educated and competitive work force, as well as a stable law and order environment collectively contributed to a successful transformation. Foreign direct investment has played a significant role in China's recent industrialization. The country has been attracting annual capital inflows in the region of $58 billion in 1992 and $100 billion in 1993, more than any other country in the world. These volumes are substantial and have increased dramatically after the disappointments encountered in attracting foreign capital in the 1980s.

The composition of these capital flows reflects the dynamics of East Asian growth. Most of the capital has come from within the Eastern Asian region. Capital from Hong Kong and Taiwan has not only provided an important stimulus but has also testified to the utility of having a substantial body of entrepreneurs in the Chinese diaspora.[7] They have responded to the economic incentives provided by China to relocate production in the coastal zones. In recent years, Japan has increased its presence but still lags behind Hong Kong and Taiwan. The United States is the major trading partner amongst the western economies.

As in any other country, FDI is attracted only when the domestic house is in order. China created a hospitable infrastructure and incentive regime for foreign capital. This built on an initial phase of domestic industrial reform which had accompanied the liberalization of the agricultural sector. In the early 1980s, approximately 100 enterprises were allowed to operate under a more liberal incentive structure.

These firms were concentrated in the Sichuan province. The success of the experiment led to the expansion of the new rules to 1200 enterprises across the nation. This approach reflected the pragmatism practised by the Chinese economic reformers.

As in other areas of policy, reform was initiated on a small scale and provided the learning curve for the next stage. This has led to various anomalies, such as the 'dual price' system, wherein some commodities have controlled as well as free market prices. These inefficiencies will require resolution but the reformers prefer selective changes and build on success rather than address all anomalies simultaneously.

Macroeconomic policy has managed to control inflation at reasonable levels. However, price stability has been threatened by excessive monetary expansion by local authorities. But monetary, fiscal, and external sector policies have managed to keep inflation within reasonable bounds for such a rapidly growing economy. Fiscal deficits have stayed within prudent limits, while real exchange rate adjustments have maintained competitiveness of exports. During the 1980s, China effectively had three exchange rates: the official rate, the official 'swap rate' to encourage exports and the 'black market' rate. In 1994, the official and swap rates were unified, which effectively devalued the currency by 50%.

Growing inflationary pressures are being addressed through the wide-ranging financial and fiscal reforms being implemented in the 1990s. Improving the regulatory framework for the banking system and controlling the growth of the money supply are important, not only for inflationary control, but also for efficient enterprise reform. Similarly, expanding the tax base, particularly the introduction of new indirect taxes, is important for generating revenues needed to redistribute the benefits of development from the rich provinces to those being left behind. Fiscal and monetary reforms are attempting to address the macroeconomic problems which are emerging with rapid growth. The success of these reforms is important in order for the economy to sustain this growth.

Export-led, foreign capital financed industrialization and agricultural incentive reforms were central to the adjustment that China has made to the limitations of central planning. A greater role for internal and external markets while the state concentrates on the provision of physical infrastructure and the upgrading of human capital has unleashed the dynamics which are producing high growth.

The results have been exceptional. China has achieved per capita growth rates of income which are unparalleled and if the country is able to sustain this pace for another four decades or so, global poverty would be reduced substantially and the world economy would undergo a major structural change.

The rapid pace of recent development is, however, causing a number of strains. Regional and income inequalities have worsened while the pace of political change lags far behind socio-economic liberalization. Addressing these inequalities and political demands will pose difficult challenges for the regime. The agenda for political liberalization is vast. Since 1949, China has suffered from the violent excesses of the cultural revolution and has also sustained political controls in many areas. Much of the future of East Asia will be determined by the manner in which China can liberalize politically, while sustaining its economic dynamism without the feared descent into anarchy.

In sum, China has exercised an immense influence in the shaping of East Asian development. The Chinese revolution helped create the political pressure to address equity issues within regional development strategies. Developments in China affected the nature and extent of the United States' support to Japan. The success of inclusive capitalism has, in turn, shaped developments in China. The country's adjustment to the shortcomings of central planning has been aided considerably by foreign direct investment provided largely by the successful market economies of the region.

KOREA

Korea suffered a partition as traumatic as that of South Asia, a partition which created two countries and led to an international war. The division was ideological, but not on religious lines. Japan's defeat in the Second World War ended three decades of its colonial rule over Korea; the territory of Korea was divided into a communist-dominated north and a US-supported south.[8] Attempts by the United Nations to create a unified Korea did not bear fruit. While the communists dominated the north, they also had considerable influence in the south. In the late 1940s, communist and left wing organizations were a powerful force and a source of intense political friction.[9] The military vacuum created by the withdrawal of the United States forces from the south in 1949 led to an invasion from the north. The result was a three year internationalized conflict. Apart from the two combatants, the United States, the Soviet Union, China, and 14 other countries as part of the troops supplied by the United Nations, were involved in the Korean war. The end of the war in 1953 formalized the creation of two countries.[10]

South Korea and South Asia shared many similarities other than partition. South Korea failed, like Pakistan, to establish a democratic system in the 1950s; in 1961 the military *coup* led by Major-General Chung Hee Park was similar to Ayub Khan's *coup* three years earlier. The civilian administration under Prime Minister Chang was as ineffectual as Pakistan's civilian regimes of the 1950s. The regimes before Chang's were also beset by numerous political and social challenges which had produced insecurity and uncertainty regarding Korea's future direction. The political system in Korea was also intensely corrupt, an aspect that has persisted over the years as the recent trials of former presidents have demonstrated.[11] Recent Presidents have apologized publicly and some have sought repentance and forgiveness by retreating to monasteries.[12] As in Pakistan, the political system has remained unstable. In the 1970s, South Korea experienced political assassinations, student unrest, and violent struggles for the restoration of democracy. Recourse to political repression, censorship, and the important role played by students in rebellion are among the other common features.

Further, President Park created an electoral college for presidential elections in 1973, which was reminiscent of Ayub's basic democracies. In other aspects too, the political paths have been similar. Electoral democracy was reinstalled in Korea in 1988, the same year as in Pakistan. Both countries had spent the 1980s under military rule.

Internal political turmoil, and the security situation *vis-à-vis* North Korea, has entailed high defence expenditures. Nearly 25% of government spending is on defence; defence expenditure typically exceeds the joint spending on education and health. These high defence expenditures are not dissimilar to Pakistan, although not quite as high in proportion to income. However, as evident from the cases of countries such as Israel and Korea, high defence spending *per se* does not explain poor economic performance. Korea's economic record has been exceptional.

In the economic arena, Korea has played an exceptional role in the transformation of Eastern Asia. With a population of 44 million, its achievements as one of the four 'tigers' are much more substantive than that of city states such as Hong Kong and Singapore. One of the nations which have managed the transition to high human development countries, Koreans have witnessed a substantial rise in their standard of living. Much of the 1950s in Korea were spent in post-war repairing of physical infrastructure. Aid inflows played an important role in creating the transport and other physical infrastructure. A similar role was played by aid in Pakistan (*see* Chapter 6). During the 1950s, both Korea and Pakistan had low growth or stagnation in per capita incomes. Korea began to grow rapidly in the 1960s, as did Pakistan. There was a sharp divergence in the 1970s, however, as Korea stepped up its rate of growth and Pakistan stagnated, in exports as well as in income. Korea moved into more and more sophisticated areas while Pakistan concentrated on relatively simple manufacturing. The 1990s have witnessed positive but slower growth in Korea, while Pakistan has suffered a fall in per capita incomes in some years. From the late 1960s till the early 1980s, the growth rate in GNP diverged considerably, as Pakistan was initially affected by a civil war and dismemberment, followed by nationalization of industrial and financial sectors. During this period, the economic gap with Korea widened substantially.

Rapid growth followed in all of the six five year plans enacted since 1962. Indeed, in each plan period except the fourth, the actual growth rate was faster than the planned rate, (*see* Table 11).

11. ANNUAL GNP GROWTH

Plan Period	Target Rate of Growth (%)	Actual Rate of Growth (%)
1962-6	7.1	7.8
1967-71	7.0	9.6
1972-6	8.6	9.7
1977-81	9.2	5.8
1982-6	7.5	8.6
1987-91	8.2	10.0

Explaining Korea's economic success and the key policies which contributed to it provides an interesting comparison with Pakistan. Three core aspects of policy are noted below:

(i) The state's role in resource allocation and building private sector capacities

The extensive role of the state has been central to Korea's capitalist development. The government has used a wide array of instruments to affect market prices, direct resources, and gradually shift the country's comparative advantage. Since 1962, five year plans have played a strong role in defining strategic economic objectives and guiding the private sector accordingly.

Private capacities have been built up by the state providing information, reducing transaction costs, and supporting infrastructure. State intervention has been guided by the important principle that the government should not compete with the private sector, but should build private capacity where it is inadequate. Institutional mechanisms such as deliberation councils were established to provide a forum for private sector and government co-ordination. The state also helped create large enterprises called '*cheobels*'.

In this aspect of policy there were few differences between

Korea and Pakistan in the 1950s and 1960s. In the latter too, the state intervened in financial markets and industry to build an indigenous bourgeoisie in the first two decades after partition. But, as noted earlier, the paths diverged in the 1970s. Pakistan's debilitating civil war and dismemberment in 1971 was followed by nationalization of industry and finance. In 1971, Pakistan had lost one of its poorer regions, and Bangladesh had come into being. After a brief period, the economy recovered as did exports. Subsequent nationalization, however, altered the consensus over private sector led growth. In Korea, on the other hand, the state deepened its support for the private sector. Having helped create capacities, government policy concentrated on providing the necessary support for the shift from import substitution to export led growth. Public investments in physical infrastructure combined with macroeconomic management which ensured low inflation and a competitive exchange rate, assisted the export drive. In addition, tax incentives were provided to increase the profits of exporters, who also received privileged access to credit and tax rebates on imported inputs. In brief, industrial policy encouraged exports by raising profitability of capital invested through price interventions, subsidies, and supporting investments.

(ii) Technology acquisition and human capital

One of the most impressive features of Korean development has been the swift movement up the productivity ladder. From a basic agricultural society, the country has gradually moved into textiles and light industry, and then into sophisticated engineering and electronic production. Korea has the largest ship building industry in the world and is the third largest producer of electronic parts.[13] South Korea is one of the world leaders in semiconductors. While textiles remain a major export earning in excess of $15 billion annually, the country's largest export earnings are provided by electronic products ($22 billion).

The move into higher productivity activities has been led by the private sector, but within the framework of a technology policy that has been shaped by the government.

Three aspects of policy have assisted technological acquisition. First, the export-oriented strategy outlined in the first plan (1962-6) created a framework for joint ventures, licensing arrangements, and competitive exposure to new technology. Second, government policy built on this outward orientation by providing generous tax concessions as well as institutional support for private firms to spend on Research & Development. Finally, education and training policy has helped create the managerial and technical orientation. This has built capacities and a conducive environment for the acquisition and upgradation of technology.

Pakistan's industrial technology acquisition was aided by sector specific institutes, such as the Metal Industries Development Centre in Sialkot and textile colleges in Karachi. Some managerial capacities were created for the corporate sector quite early in the country's evolution, through the Institute of Business Administration in Karachi and later, a similar institution in Lahore. An advanced nuclear technological capacity has been established, although it has little or no economic benefit. A few centres of excellence have emerged in chemistry and physics. But in general, the efforts are patchy and inconsistent. There has been no significant export drive to provide the impetus. Private sector R & D expenditure is virtually non-existent. There is a general lack of educated manpower, particularly those with technical skills. As with other areas, once the economic gap with Korea started growing, the divergence in technological capacity grew also. An outward-looking, dynamic Korea built skills and rewarded professional development; many of the most educated Pakistanis also had an outward orientation—they left the country.

(iii) Property reforms and social policy affecting equity

Like Japan, South Korea's equity-enhancing reforms were influenced by the pressure of communism. The Land Reform Acts of 1947 and 1948 were enacted at a time of internal turmoil and responded to demands for greater equity. These Land Reform Acts provided the basis for the owner-operated farms which supported the regime. Since then, agriculture has received considerable tariff and quantitative protection and price supports for the main crops such as rice. The country also grows potatoes, wheat, beans, and barley. But Korea's is not a particularly productive agriculture. The focus of policy has been on industrial development. As the share of agriculture has fallen and domestic incomes have risen, Korea has emerged as the sixth largest importer of agricultural products, with imports exceeding $7 billion annually. Korea's early land reform has ensured that large rural interests have not emerged as a constraint to industrialization or as regressive forces in control of the state apparatus.

Korea's social policy was based on the education structure built by the Japanese. A relatively high literacy rate of 50% was an asset and further investments in basic education have ensured virtually universal literacy. Literacy and health improvements, coupled with a rapid increase in female participation in the labour force, have led to major human development gains as well as an effective control on the demographic growth rate. This in turn has reduced pressures on the labour market, and has further enhanced per capita expenditures on education. This sustains quality improvements, which help both productivity and healthier life styles: the virtuous circle described in Chapter 3.

While Pakistan suffered a similar social dislocation as Korea at the time of partition, no land reforms were implemented. Another opportunity arose after the war in 1971. In neither case was land reform implemented seriously, and after five decades, the rural elite retained a vital role in the national political structure. In 1996, for example, Pakistan's cabinet had a higher proportion of landlords than that of any other Asian country. The picture is not static and 'feudalism' in Pakistan has changed a great deal since independence, as the final chapter points out. However, the scale of the change has been far more rapid in countries such as Korea.

Both Korea and Pakistan received generous aid support from the United States. Yet the same donors pushed for land reform and progressive social policy in Eastern Asia but not in Pakistan. Perhaps the critical difference lay in the domestic power structure and the equity pressures exerted on it.

Korea has 'taken off'. Its future evolution will be shaped by internal and regional dynamics. It is probable that the two Koreas will unify,[14] along the path of Vietnam and Germany. The possibility of unification has never left the political agenda and talks continue although as one would expect, a number of problems remain, particularly the difference in levels of development and the distribution of power after unification. South Korea's economy has matured and joined the ranks of the OECD as one of the most sophisticated industrial structures. It seems almost inconceivable that Pakistan and Korea were in a similar economic league just a few decades back. There is plenty there for the pessimist. For the optimist, it is a useful reminder that economies can be transformed in just four decades.

TAIWAN (CHINA)

As in the case of South Korea and Pakistan, Taiwan is the product of a partition. All three partitions had an ideological base. While the partitions of China and Korea were determined by communism, South Asia split along communal lines. Politically severed from mainland China by the Japanese after the Sino-Japanese conflict in 1895, the islands comprising modern Taiwan reverted to Chinese rule in the early 20th century.[15] Shortly after the end of the Second World War, and Japan's defeat therein, Taiwan became a province of China, which was then ruled by General Chiang Kai-shek's Nationalist Party (the Kuomintang). The success of the revolutionary forces under Mao in 1949 led to the fleeing of Chiang Kai-shek to Taiwan, where the defeated nationalist forces established an independent government.[16]

Taiwan has since then been ruled by the migrant elite who did not have a physical base in the newly-created state. The status of these migrants was somewhat similar to that of Pakistan's muhajir elite who led its independence movement and then migrated to a land where they had not resided previously. The nationalists who fled from mainland China have ruled Taiwan since 1949, under martial law for most of the period. By the mid-1990s, Taiwan, like Korea, had made the transition to democracy. But for most of the post-revolution period, Taiwan was governed by a rigid and authoritarian regime. Its record on economic development and poverty reduction has, however, been exceptional.

Indicators of success

Taiwan's success in socio-economic development is reflected in indicators of living standards. Life expectancy has increased by nearly 30%, from 58 years in 1950 to 75 years by 1995. Indications of prosperity are illustrated by the growth of ownership of consumer durables: the number of television sets per 100 households increased from 1.3 in 1963 to 118 in 1991, while the number of automobiles per 1000 persons rose from 1 to 163 during the same period.

Incomes have not only risen but are more equitably distributed. In 1950, the top 20% of all households had 15 times as much income as the bottom 20%. These extremes have narrowed considerably since then. By 1994, the top 20% had 5 times as much income as the bottom 20%. The figure had fallen even further in the 1980s but in spite of the slight worsening in the 1990s, the trend over the past four decades has been towards a sharp reduction in inequalities during a period when aggregate incomes have grown.

Taiwan's living standards are comparable to those of many West European states and better than those in most of Central and Eastern Europe. Per capita income is nearly $US 11 000. Unemployment has remained extremely low since 1960. Rapid and sustained labour intensive growth over the past four decades has been central to the elimination of poverty. The move from import substituting industrialization to export led growth has played a major role in generating the demand for jobs. The export drive was led by the private sector, while the state made substantial investments in infrastructure to overcome the bottlenecks to a successful export drive.

These public investments have been facilitated by high levels of savings. The savings rate was nearly 30% by 1995, with nearly a third provided through public savings. The savings rate has increased in every one of the past three decades, due to the development of a financial sector which mobilized resources effectively, as well as fiscal measures which encouraged savings.

The efficiency of resource use has been aided by the judicious balance between the market and the state. Countries with equivalent levels of the savings rate have performed less well due to the inefficiency of the resources invested.

Taiwan has undergone a demographic transition, as fertility rates have declined sharply. Virtually universal education for women, and high female labour force participation, have led to a rapid decline in the population growth rate. By the mid-1990s, the population growth rate had fallen to 0.9% from 3.3% in the 1950s. This has enabled Taiwan to sustain a virtuous circle, as more per capita expenditures on education and health improve the quality of human capital, and enable the move into higher productivity activities. This leads to higher incomes and greater prosperity, which provide the resources for further development of human capacities.

The political economy influences on equitable development

The economic policies which were responsible for such equitable growth are summarized below. Before a discussion of these policy influences, it is worth noting the wider political economy pressures within which Taiwan was operating. Many of the equity-inducing pressures related, not surprisingly, to the success of the Chinese revolution on the mainland. In 1949, a communist rebellion in Taiwan led to a massacre which cost nearly 20 000 lives. Such pressures from 'below' were to exert an important influence on the development strategy, forcing a series of measures which ensured that a form of inclusive capitalism was pursued to mitigate threats of rebellion.

At the same time, the economy remained firmly in the hands of the private sector, with the state avoiding a competing role. The modernization of Taiwan followed a path which was similar to that followed by Japan after the Meiji restoration. The openness to technology acquisition, the emphasis on a strong supportive state, and progressive social policy were elements which were similar to the Japanese modernization process.

Japanese colonization of Korea and Taiwan was relatively brief and soon after their independence, these countries were to pursue a modernization strategy which was similar to Japan's. In addition, the resources and markets provided by the United States, as part of the Pacific strategy to contain communism, assisted countries such as Taiwan. These aid resources helped lay the initial physical infrastructure that was necessary for the development of agriculture and industry.

A number of key policy measures were shaped by these regional political economy influences. These included a widespread land reform and the move from ISI to labour-intensive, export-led growth, which emulated the Japanese experience. A strong state enforcing equity-oriented reforms and effectively directing the economy within a private sector led development strategy produced the framework for Taiwan's inclusive capitalism.

Economic policy and equitable growth

The economic policy determinants of Taiwan's success can be divided into four areas.[17] The first is the disciplined monetary and fiscal policies enacted by the Kuomintang soon after they came to power. The new government had seen the catastrophic effects of hyper-inflation on society on mainland China before the revolution. Subsequent fiscal restraint and cautious monetary policy have created the stability that markets have required. By the 1960s, the Central Bank had 'conquered' inflation. Throughout the 1960s, the average annual rate of inflation was less than 5%. In the following decade, in spite of the two oil shocks, average inflation did not rise above single digits, with the decade as a whole having an annual average of 8.7%. The sharp appreciation of the Taiwan dollar assisted inflationary control during the 1980s and the pattern of low inflation, less than 3% in many years, has persisted during the 1990s. Continued and sustained macroeconomic stability has not only facilitated the development of markets and the transmission of relative price signals for resource allocation but has also played an important role in retaining a competitive position in export markets.

Second, public expenditure priorities have played a significant role in promoting equity and supporting the private sector. In spite of high defence spending which in the early years absorbed nearly 50% of government spending and accounted for nearly 14% by the 1990s, public expenditures have been well targeted to specific socio-economic goals. As far as social expenditures are concerned, the first two decades emphasized basic education and health. These expenditures, as elsewhere in Eastern Asia, were critical for the reduction of population pressures in the labour market, provided virtually universal literacy, and improved basic health conditions.

Subsequently, relatively more resources were devoted to the acquisition of increasingly sophisticated technological skills as the economy moved into higher productivity activities. At the same time, public sector management capacity was built through education and training abroad, an area which was facilitated by aid resources.

It is worth noting that both Taiwan and Korea incurred substantial military spending but managed to sustain high growth.

In addition to basic social spending, fiscal policy concentrated on relieving physical infrastructure bottlenecks. This was most evident in the 1970s, when infrastructure bottlenecks were constraining growth. As a result, the government launched ten major construction projects. These and other projects helped relieve shortages of energy and transport. Three nuclear plants were established for electricity generation, two new ports and airports were constructed, new electric railway lines were built while the old ones were modernized, and there was a major improvement in the quality and quantity of roads for freight.

The provision of social and physical infrastructure through the state played a significant role in supporting private sector led development. The state's role was not confined to this supportive role; it also intervened extensively in agricultural and industrial sectors, in order to shape the pace and nature of development in these areas.

The third important determinant was the type of agricultural policy pursued. The government not only shaped asset distribution in rural areas but also subsequently supported efficient sectoral development through price, marketing, and technology policies. The structure of rural society was heavily influenced by the elimination of absentee landlords through a land reform programme between 1949 and 1953. However, the design of the land reform programme was such that it facilitated the emergence of a dynamic freehold farming class, as well as aiding the growth of entrepreneurial forces in industry. The compensation given to landlords provided the capital for their shift into industry and finance. At the same time, the establishment of a land bank enabled the smaller farming groups to purchase land, which led to most tenant farmers ending up as owners of their land.

The dynamic expansion of industry and the relative relegation in the importance of agriculture provided the context for the second structural reform of agriculture which took place in the 1970s. Starting from the mid-1970s, the government began to consolidate irrigated areas into larger landholdings. These larger holdings were more suitable for mechanized farming, which was more appropriate in view of the growing scarcity of labour.

The first land reform was followed by a series of measures which modernized agriculture and increased its efficiency. These built on the extensive investments in irrigation infrastructure which had been made in the 1920s and 1930s. A technically competent farm extension service and an efficient input distribution network had enabled the adoption of productivity-enhancing chemical fertilizers and pesticides. By the early 1990s, farmers were applying high doses of chemical inputs: over 1 ton per hectare of chemical fertilizers on rice and sugar-cane land. The use of machinery had also increased in keeping with the developments in factor markets and the increasing relative price of labour. Output price policies have ensured that the returns to farming have been good and the transfer from agriculture to industry has not been to the extent that it would seriously hamper the development of the former.

Accordingly, crop production has diversified into more productive areas. Traditionally, the main crops were rice, groundnuts, sugar-cane, and sweet potatoes. Gradually the land devoted to other crops has risen. Horticultural production has grown substantially, particularly around more expensive urban areas. The growth of livestock production, specially poultry and pigs, has been matched by expansion in feed crops such as maize and soya beans. In brief, a diversified, reasonably equitable, and dynamic agricultural sector has emerged through policy measures which have affected asset and income distribution, while providing the incentives for yield improvements.

Fourth, in the industrial sector, Taiwan's shift from a producer of textiles and basic chemicals to a manufacturer of sophisticated products was assisted considerably by the shift from import substitution to export led growth. The initial phase of ISI helped build the capacity and provided the protective environment for creating domestic entrepreneurial skills. From the mid-1960s onwards, deregulation and liberalization of the trade regime substantially altered incentives. Production for the domestic market was no longer favoured through protective measures.

The removal of this protective framework was accompanied by the establishment of export zones. In 1965, the Ministry of Industries created an export zone at Kaohsiung which was followed by two other sites within the next decade. These export zones assisted the shift away from import substitution, attracting nearly 300 firms, which provided a nucleus of exporting firms. The diversification of the industrial structure received similar support when the government created an Industrial Science Park at Hsinchu in 1980. Tax incentives for firms to undertake R & D and a favourable policy regime for exports have contributed to the upward shift in the industrial structure. Sophisticated research-based companies have subsequently played a major role in export growth.

Industrial policy in Taiwan has thus accelerated the diversification of the industrial structure and facilitated technology acquisition through an open trading regime and fiscal incentives which encouraged research and development spending in export-oriented firms. Like Korea, Taiwan's dynamic comparative advantage was altered by an activist industrial policy. Commentators who maintain that in spite of its success, industrial policy was merely 'market conforming' and that the market would have produced a similar result, appear to be guided by ideological considerations.[18]

Finally, it is worth noting the role of external resources in Taiwan's development. The changing role reflects the success of the economy. In the first two decades, aid, particularly that provided bilaterally by the United States, was utilized to create the physical infrastructure, assist in macroeconomic stabilization, and reduce the balance of payments constraint to growth. By 1970, aid had come to an end and was replaced by foreign direct investment (FDI) as the major external resource stimulus to growth. The lead in FDI was taken by Japanese firms, who invested substantially in electronic production; in terms of volume Japanese firms were closely followed by those from the US. European firms also played an important role in FDI, although not as prominently as Japanese and American corporations.

In recent years, Taiwan has entered a third phase with regard to the role of international capital transfers. After ending dependence on aid inflows, and 'graduating' into the category of countries which receive substantial amounts of FDI, Taiwan has become a major exporter of capital. Taiwanese firms have played a key role in the growth of FDI in mainland China since the late 1980s. By 1995, Taiwanese firms had invested over $5 billion in mainland China. Ironically, China's FDI drive has been led by the two nations which are expected to rejoin China as part of a single nation-state. The other major contributor to Chinese FDI is Hong Kong, whose future status is somewhat clearer than that of Taiwan.

Future directions

Taiwan's economic success was achieved under a politically authoritarian regime. Indeed, through most of the period martial law was in force. However, as in Korea, the 1990s have witnessed a shift towards democratic government. Parliamentary elections in 1996 have reinforced the emergence of groups who were not refugees from mainland

China. China views Taiwan (Formosa) as a province which ought to revert to a position within the mainland's sovereignty. While political relations remain delicate, the degree of economic integration has been intensive. The enormous scale of Taiwanese capital inflow into China has been a useful indicator of such integration.

Taiwan's own economy faces challenges which are more similar to those faced by mature industrial economies than typical 'developing countries'. Regional comparative advantage is continuously shifting, as countries with abundant labour supply and a good human capital base provide stiff competition to various sectors of the Taiwanese economy. Firms have adjusted by moving into higher productivity and knowledge-intensive activities, as well as by shifting production overseas in order to maintain competitiveness. Taiwan's FDI into China has taken advantage of the overseas market access provided to that country through the most favoured nation status. In addition, Taiwanese firms have maintained competitiveness by utilizing factor services at prices below those prevalent in Taiwan. Political liberalization, 'integration' with China, and problems of prosperity confront Taiwan in the near future. Being one of the leading economies in a booming and dynamic region is likely to provide many opportunities to Taiwan in the next phase of its economic evolution.

This chapter has summarized the development experience of some of the East Asian states, to add flesh to the analytical bones sketched in Chapters 2 and 3. The next chapter considers the expansion of success into South East Asia, where many countries are emulating the success of the countries described above.

NOTES

1. Which countries would have acquired technology and participated most. actively in the world trading system is an interesting counter factual. One would have expected some of the Asian countries to have flourished in the absence of conquest, while others may not have been able to do as well.

2. For details of Japan's evolution see, *inter alia*, Storry, R: *A History of Modern Japan*, (London, Penguin, 1970) and *Japan and the Decline of the West in Asia, 1894–1943*, (Macmillan, London, 1979); Nakayama, S: *Science, Technology and Society in Japan*, (Kegan Paul International, London and New York, 1992); and Yoshida, S: *Japan's Decisive Century*, (Praeger, New York, 1967).

3. For details see Storry and Yoshida: op. cit.

4. At the same time Japan retained its cultural identity while undergoing major change.

5. For details see Kataoka, T (ed.): *Creating Single Party Democracy— Japan's Post-war Political System*, (Hoover Institution Press, Stanford, 1993) and Kyogoku, J: *The Political Dynamics of Modern Japan*, (University of Tokyo Press, Tokyo, 1987).

6. The Liberal Democratic Party ruled from 1955 to 1993, and returned to power as part of a coalition in 1994. For details see Kataoka and Kyogoku.

7. Russia, on the other hand, did not have a substantive body of overseas Russian entrepreneurs; in any case, conditions were remarkably different there. The Soviet Union had disintegrated and the resulting instability was not conducive to foreign direct investment.

8. For details see, *inter alia*, Han, Woo Keun: *A History of Korea*, (Eulyoo Publishing Company, Seoul, 1972); Hulbert, Homer: *A History of Korea*, (Routledge, London, 1952); and Cho, Soo Sung: *Korea in World Politics, 1940-50*, (University of California Press, Los Angeles, 1967).

9. Ibid.

10. Economically, Pakistan benefited from the Korean war-generated commodity boom. It provided a stimulus for the emerging private sector.

11. The return to democracy in the 1990s was followed by the arrest of, and charges against, two former Presidents. They were accused of widespread corruption in league with the major business houses, as well as being held responsible for massacres of civilians.

12. President Chun made a televized apology in 1989, returned his accumulated wealth in property, and went into a Buddhist monastery with his wife.

13. After Japan and the USA.

14. The discussions on unification have been chequered and have stalled through various provocative actions, such as the submarine incident in 1996. As a response to this action by the North, which involved loss of life, South Korea broke off talks on unification.

15. For interpretations and analyses of Chinese history see, *inter alia*, Fairbanks, J.K: *The Cambridge History of China*, (12 Volumes, Cambridge University Press, 1986) and *China: A New History*, (Harvard University Press, 1992).

16. The origins of Taiwan explain the sensitivity of its status. China continues to regard Taiwan as a province, which will eventually become reunited with the mainland. The Taiwanese constitution, at the same time, maintains the fiction that its government is the legal authority over all of China.

17. For analysis and reviews of Taiwan's development experience see, *inter alia*, Chang Han-yu and Myers, R: 'Japanese colonial development policy in Taiwan, 1895-1906; A case of bureaucratic entrepreneurship', *The Journal of Modern Asian Studies*, Volume XXII, 4, 1963; Kou, S: *The Taiwan Economy in Transition*, (Westview Press, Boulder,1983); Galenson, W: *Economic growth and structural change in Taiwan*, (Cornell University Press, Ithaca, NY, 1979) and Europa Publications: *The Far East and Australasia 1995*, (26th edition, London).

18. The debate on the effectiveness of industrial policy in East Asia was referred to in Chapter 2.

CHAPTER 5

COUNTRY BRIEFS: SOUTH EAST ASIA

Asia has become modernized, not westernized, and the process of modernization has taken place on the basis of their own traditional culture, just as it happened in the West, with the same sort of resulting contrasts and strains.

E. Reischauer, Harvard University

1. Malaysia
2. Thailand
3. Indonesia
4. The Philippines

This chapter contains empirical summaries of three economic success stories in South East Asia: Malaysia, Thailand, and Indonesia. In addition, there is a discussion of the Philippines as the South East Asian country which appears to be beset by many problems similar to those of Pakistan.

MALAYSIA

Malaysia's independent development has had to contend simultaneously with a triad of inherited difficulties. The first was the legacy of racial division and segregation. The second was the scale of inequalities between households within racial and ethnic divisions. The third was the need to transform an economy which concentrated on primary commodity production, principally rubber.

Malaysia's political economy has been shaped by these parameters.[1] Coalitions between the Chinese, Indians, and the local Bumiputra populations have dominated Malaysian politics. Even before independence in 1957, the electoral coalition between the United Malays National Organization

(UNMO), the Malayan Chinese Association (MCA), and the Malayan Indian Congress (MIC) provided the racial cement to a diverse society. UNMO has retained political leadership since independence. The President of UNMO, Tunku Abdul Rahman, was the first Prime Minister; the current Prime Minister Dr Mahathir is also the leader of UNMO. Perhaps significantly, Dr Mahathir and the heir apparent Mr Anwar Ibrahim are part of the technocratic, not the landed Malay elite. Indeed, UNMO has frequently been in conflict with the hereditary rulers of provinces, the sultans.

Issues of racial balance have shaped the boundaries of Malaysia. The predominantly Chinese Singapore was expelled from the Malayan federation in 1965. Similarly, racial links between Malay and Indonesian groups had earlier caused territorial difficulties between Malaysia and Indonesia. Even in the islands which have constituted Malaysia since 1963, racial tensions have proved explosive. The race riots in the late 1960s were particularly serious and threatened to undermine the integrity of the country. The political response to these eruptions was swift and well-considered. It has resulted in a social contract between the principal racial groups which has persisted through the last three decades.

Along with racial integration, Malaysia's other equity challenge has been the skewed income distribution among different classes. The gross inequities of income along with the organized power of the Communist Party of Malaysia (CPM) led to a communist insurrection in Malaya in 1949, the year of the Chinese revolution.[2] The CPM, which was formed in 1930, was led principally by Chinese peasants working on foreign-owned plantations. Somewhat ironically, in view of subsequent developments, the most entrenched left wing groups were based in Singapore, whose politics remained quite radical even in the 1950s. The communist insurgency was put down by the colonial authorities and radical politics in both Singapore and Malaysia was subsequently contained by a mix of repression and accommodation.

Malaysia has maintained a democracy since independence, except for the period of emergency after the race riots. While electoral practices have been sustained, various curbs have been in place for a variety of reasons, some more valid than others.

Rapid economic development has been central to the response to problems of racial and household inequalities. Malaysia too has maintained the sound balance between the market and the state referred to in the last chapter. In its case, the demands were perhaps even more onerous than those faced by less diverse societies. Malaysia pursued a market-oriented development strategy primarily led by the Chinese and, to a lesser extent, Indian private sector. State interventions were focused not only on technology, physical infrastructure, and human capital support, but were also used to explicitly promote the local Malay population. These positive discrimination policies, however, occurred within a policy framework which stimulated rapid growth. Not surprisingly, tensions over relative shares have been muted while the size of the pie has been growing rapidly. It is also worth noting that much of the asset redistribution has been through transfers of assets from foreign ownership to the Bumiputras. The redistribution has not been from the Chinese to the indigenous population. The capacity to transfer assets from foreigners to the Bumiputras provided a 'windfall gain' in the sense that it avoided redistribution amongst domestic groups.

Rapid economic development and poverty reduction: the indicators of success

Malaysia's success in reducing poverty has been admirable.[3] In 1970 the majority of households, 52%, were poor. This absolute level of poverty was reduced to considerably less than a quarter by 1995, with only 15% of households remaining in poverty. Primary education is free, universally available, and compulsory for nine years. Total female school enrollment is to the ratio of 77% which is slightly higher than the male rate (75%). By the mid-1990s, Malaysia enjoyed full employment and was importing an estimated 1 million workers.

Malaysia's dynamic economy has had the fastest rate of growth in South East Asia in recent years. Since 1988, the average annual per capita rate of growth has been nearly

7%. This exceeds the 1970s achievement of a GDP growth rate of 6.8% per year. A per capita income of $US 2700 places Malaysia firmly in the ranks of medium income countries, with the prospect that over the next few decades, the country will sustain its 'take off' and become one of the major industrial economies. Within a few decades after independence, Malaysia has transformed itself from a foreign-owned plantation economy to a vigorous and vibrant industrial nation.

Malaysia is the world's largest exporter of palm oil, as well as a substantial contributor to the rubber, tin, and tropical hardwood trade. In addition, the country has notable natural gas and petroleum reserves. An abundance of natural resources is, of course, not a guarantee of economic success. Malaysia has, however, utilized its natural resource base well and has diversified into manufacturing exports. Indeed, by the late 1980s, the value of Malaysia's manufacturing exports exceeded the revenues earned from primary products. Malaysia has a highly open economy, with an export-GDP ratio of 82%.

Positive discrimination to alter the racial share in economic success has partially yielded the desired results. The share of Bumiputras in corporate equity ownership, for example, has risen from 2.3% in 1970 to 21% by 1994. Interestingly enough, the share of Chinese and Indian ownership has risen from 31% to 46% over the same period. Thus, asset redistribution has been achieved by reducing the share of assets held by foreigners from 65% to 25%. The primary beneficiaries have been the Bumiputras, but the Chinese and Indians have also gained.

While inter-racial asset distribution has improved and poverty reduced rapidly, progress in inter-household equality has not been achieved. Malaysia's Gini Co-efficient, particularly amongst the Bumiputra, is worse than in most Asian countries. While in many Eastern Asian countries income distribution has improved considerably, this has not been the case in Malaysia. Income distribution tensions have not mounted due to the complexities of the situation; as mentioned earlier, poverty has been reduced substantially while access to basic social services is virtually universal.

Collectively, these have increased the stake of the majority of the population in the economic system. At the same time, inter-racial equity pressures have such political salience that progress in this area appears to effectively 'compensate' for static or worsening household income distribution.

The role of policy in Malaysia's economic success

As in East Asia, Malaysian policy-makers have had a strong influence on the nature and pace of development. Four aspects of public policy have been instrumental in stimulating growth and in poverty reduction. The first have been policies which create incentives for producers. While governments intervened periodically in price setting, by and large the price system was allowed to perform in a manner that generated profitable returns to investment. For example, agricultural policy did not generally tax farmers so heavily through the price system as to reduce the incentives to increase crop production. Eastern Asian policy regimes in general, and Malaysian policies in particular, did not squeeze agriculture to the detriment evident in some parts of the world. In addition to prices, the other important incentive for accumulation was stable property rights.

The second role of public policy was to increase productivity by enabling the acquisition of technological and managerial knowledge. This took several dimensions depending on the stage of economic evolution. In agriculture, the first stage was typically to improve productivity of traditional crops through productivity-enhancing chemical inputs. Subsequently, diversification into higher value products was again assisted by the introduction of technical knowledge. Similarly, in the industrial sector, the move into higher productivity areas requires the acquisition of technological knowledge. As we saw in the case of Taiwan, such upgradation was facilitated by public policy through the creation of science industry parks and related tax incentives for firms to engage in R & D. In the early stages of industrialization, the knowledge acquisition process is relatively simple.

An area of policy which has aided technological catch-up in Eastern Asia is export-led growth. This openness to the world led to a number of contractual arrangements which facilitated the transmission of technical and modern managerial processes. Technical orientation can also be enhanced by the capacities created by an education system. An illiterate workforce is unlikely to be able to come to terms even with relatively simple technological upgradation. Thus, individual capacities created through the education system, allied to open trading regimes created dynamic knowledge gains in much of Eastern Asia, which in turn, enabled the move into higher productivity areas. Even in the area of services the development of a sophisticated financial sector for example, requires acquisition of complex managerial and technical capacities, as Malaysia is discovering at present.

The third aspect of the development strategy is how to facilitate productive activities. Private farmers and industrial producers typically require support of two types—physical infrastructure and credit. As we saw in the last chapter, Taiwan's export drive was facilitated considerably by the public investments in energy, transport, and telecommunications. Similarly, as documented later in this chapter, Malaysia's investments in infrastructure as well as the development of its financial sector have played a major role in easing the credit and infrastructure constraints to development. As the economy grew, the financial sector aided savings mobilization. The larger savings further sustained the growth momentum. These high levels of savings have enabled substantial investments in needed infrastructure.

Finally, public policy can affect distribution of income and assets. The distributional pressures in a diverse country such as Malaysia were both horizontal and vertical. The relative shares in society were influenced by a number of measures such as taxes, transfer mechanisms, social policy investments, and asset redistribution policies.

In sum, economic growth and poverty reduction are affected by a mix of (i) incentives, (ii) technology acquisition, (iii) investment and saving levels, and (iv) distribution mechanisms. This quartet of influences is determined by a wide array of policies. Much of East Asian, South East Asian, and Malaysian success is due to getting this complex balance right. The precise instruments have depended on the stage of each economy. The success of the region has been based on effective policy interventions in each of the four areas. The emphasis on specific areas has changed with circumstances.

The balance between these four policy dimensions for Malaysia's economic development has been evident in the broad frameworks outlined in the New Economic Policy (1971) and the New Development Policy (1991).[4] The NEP formed the base for the Outline Perspective Plan (1971-90), which was then operationalized in five year plans and annual budgets. A similar policy planning exercise was pursued subsequently when the NDP's announcement was followed by a 1991-2000 Outline Perspective Plan. From the NDP has emerged the popular political slogan of 'Vision 20/20', associated closely with the Prime Minister, envisaging the aim of becoming a developed industrial economy by the year 2020.

Agricultural policy

An indication of the diversification of Malaysia's economy is provided by the share of rubber in export earnings. At the time of independence, rubber exports provided over 50% of export earnings; this share fell to a mere 2% by the mid-1990s. Apart from manufactures, the other natural resource-based exports have grown in prominence. Petroleum, palm oil, and timber exports each earn more than twice the amount that rubber does. In recent years, curbs have been put on timber exports as part of a sustainable forestry management policy. The Forest Research Institute has taken the lead in responding to international criticisms about Malaysia's timber exports, which are now in closer accord with international guidelines.[5]

Poverty in rubber plantations has been partially addressed through direct support for small holders and estate labourers. Government assistance has taken the form of chemical fertilizer subsidies, technical extension support for small holders to improve their productivity, and selective assistance in marketing.

The first phase of crop diversification involved palm oil, which grew at annual rates of 20% during the 1970s and 10% during the 1980s. As a result, Malaysia alone produces more palm oil than all of Africa put together, whereas its 1970 output was less than Nigeria's. In addition to the provision of price incentives, diversification into palm oil has been assisted considerably by the knowledge provided to producers by public and private sector organizations. The Palm Oil Research Institute of Malaysia along with the Malaysian Palm Oil Promotional Council has helped increased productivity and provided valuable marketing support. Research into fertilization procedures, mechanization of harvesting, and increasing post-harvest transportation efficiency have supported the knowledge base and therefore the productivity of the industry.

A similar mix of technology support and price incentives is promoting diversification into other crops. Recent growth in cocoa and livestock testifies to the vibrancy of the agricultural sector. Introduction of good quality seeds, hybrid varieties, modern management techniques, and export marketing regulations have combined to make Malaysia the fourth largest producer of cocoa and led to accelerated growth in livestock, including aquaculture and deep sea fishing.

Industrial policy

The three stages of Malaysian industrial development have followed a pattern that was evident in Eastern Asia. The first phase was simple industrialization, based largely on agro-processing and the production of essential consumer goods for the domestic market. A protective policy regime created the framework for import substituting industrialization (ISI). The second phase involved deregulation and liberalization of the trade regime, as the country moved into the export of manufactures in the 1970s. The initial manufacturing export drive was led by relatively labour-intensive sectors such as textiles and basic electronics, which is a common pattern in the early stages of manufacturing exports. The third stage of industrialization has involved a move up the productivity ladder in line with changing factor endowments. As labour has become increasingly scarce and expensive relative to neighbouring competitors, Malaysia has sought to move into higher productivity capital-intensive manufacturing exports.

At the same time, a heavy industry base has also been established. As a result, Malaysia has built car and steel industries, sophisticated home electronic products, and computers. Some of the basic 'strategic' or 'prestige' industries were initially under public ownership but have been or are being privatized. The next phase of industrialization is emphasizing knowledge-based sectors such as semiconductors. In order to keep pace with the human capital requirements for these sophisticated sectors, education and training policy is focusing increasingly on the development of the tertiary sector.

Industrial policy in Malaysia has also followed the pattern evident in much of Eastern Asia. The state intervened extensively through the Malaysian Industrial Development Authority and the Heavy Industries Corporation. By and large, industrial policy has tended to concentrate on making the policy changes and infrastructure facilitation required by the private sector. Joint ventures with foreign firms, particularly Japanese, have also been an important source of technology and management skill acquisition. In some areas, the state itself took the lead but with mixed success. As a result, some of these state-owned enterprises are being privatized. At the same time, the government has formed Khazanah Nasional in 1994, which is similar to Singapore's state run investment agency, with a view to encouraging investments in major strategic industries considered important in determining the future shape of the industrial structure.

The development of directly productive services is also contributing to Malaysia's economic transformation. From the late 1980s onwards, there has been a major boom in tourism, the scale of which seems to have surprised the government. The country has also undergone a substantial diversification in other services. For example, Malaysia already has a reasonably well-developed financial sector, servicing the credit and savings requirements of industry. The government is also trying hard to establish Malaysia's presence in the global financial markets, as another important regional centre.

Considerable attention at present is being paid within the public sector investment programme to facilitate the further development of industry and services through investments in physical infrastructure. Sizeable investments in new ports, airports, roads, and railways are planned to meet the emerging infrastructural requirements. The dynamics of high savings and investment, frequently over 30% of GDP, are sustaining a high growth rate.

Future directions

Malaysia has managed to enjoy a period of sustained growth and poverty reduction, while racial tensions have been addressed by a social contract whereby each of the main parties has stood to gain. Will Malaysia march onwards at this furious and breathtaking pace or will an integration success story come asunder, as some fear, like in Yugoslavia? On balance, fears of strife undermining Malaysia appear to be too pessimistic. While the strains of diversity and needed political liberalization are likely to be felt, the possibility that Malaysia's economic prosperity will deepen appear to be bright.

THAILAND

Political instability and economic development

Thailand's recent political evolution has been shaped by a continuous and bitter struggle over the supremacy of military or civilian power. Since the 1980s, the transition to civilian rule has been marked by reversals and uncertainty over the military's intentions.

The seven phases of Thailand's civil-military relations since the Second World War bear an uncanny resemblance to those of Pakistan. The first, between 1948-57, contained somewhat weak and diverse sources of authority within a bureaucracy-dominated government, which formed an economic alliance with the Chinese entrepreneurial elite. The country played an important strategic role in the cold war for the United States, as part of the South East Asian Treaty Organization (SEATO), providing a military base in anti-communist activities.

The phase of uncertain and timid regimes was followed by a *coup* by General Sarit, who used the SEATO General Secretary as the initial Prime Minister, and then took power himself. The elections which were proposed for 1958 were cancelled. The timing and manner were similar to Ayub Khan's 1958 *coup*, when Iskander Mirza was gradually dispensed with and Ayub took over control. Those elections, planned for 1958, were also cancelled.

The third phase witnessed rapid economic growth under an authoritarian military government, with a 'modernizing' ethos. This technocratic elite operated without an electoral mandate. This phase lasted till 1972, similar to the end of the Ayub-Yahya phase. The fourth phase, of civilian democratic rule, also lasted till 1977, more or less as long as the Zulfikar Ali Bhutto period. The civilian government was paralysed by struggles between factions as well as by extra-parliamentary pressures from political forces seeking systemic change, such as the communists and the military, which was seeking to re-establish its authority.

The fifth phase witnessed the emergence of a severe military regime which was aided indirectly by the poor state of the neighbouring communist regimes in Laos, Cambodia, and Vietnam. The Cambodian conflict split the Thai communist movement and China's difficulties were also becoming apparent. The likelihood of the communist movement succeeding in Thailand receded. Partly as a result, Japanese firms accelerated economic development through FDI in a country with a reasonable infrastructure and educated, competitive labour. The US military and infrastructure assistance also accelerated during this period. At the political level, the military was divided and made frequent *coup* attempts. There was a revival of the process of civilian 'power sharing', as civilian leaders were inducted into government as junior partners to the military. This process resembled the civilian power sharing arrangement initiated by General Zia in 1985.

The sixth phase of Thai politics involving the resumption of elected government started in 1988, the same year as Benazir Bhutto came to power through elections. This period was short-lived in Thailand as disillusionment increased against a civilian regime viewed as inept, corrupt, and unable to address the growing inequalities. Consequently, the *coup* which replaced the civilian regime of Chatichai in 1991 did not lead to any popular protest. Again, somewhat similar to the situation in Pakistan, the military made it clear that ultimate authority rested with it, while its intervention compounded uncertainty and gave conflicting signals about the direction of the political system. Similar interventions ended the tenure of Bhutto's and Sharif's elected regimes in Pakistan.

The current seventh phase of Thai politics involves the resumption of elected government. However, problems of governance and instability continue to cast shadows over the political system but it is generally expected that civilian rule is likely to become more entrenched.

Through these tribulations, the monarchy has played a significant role in the accommodation of different factions competing for power. The monarchy's role in the transition to civilian government is somewhat similar to that played by Juan Carlos in Spain after the end of Franco's rule, i.e. a stable institution using its symbolic authority to guide squabbling political groupings and thereby contributing to national integration.

The social base and conflict over civil-military relations is symbolized by developments under Phibun during the 1930s. The militaristic Phibun, impressed by Japan's modernization, had developed extensive political relations with the Japanese colonial regime and was responsible for Thailand siding with Japan during the Second World War. Under Phibun, Thailand's traditional historic name, Siam, was changed as part of a somewhat distorted conception of the modernization of a monarchical society. The strong military-bureaucratic factions present during the different phases of Phibun's rule continued to participate in subsequent struggles between the military and elected civilian leadership. Indeed, these factional struggles have echoed through recent tribulations.

As in Malaysia, Thailand also has to deal with integrating major racial/ethnic groups. There have been periods when nationalistic Thai antagonism against the Chinese entrepreneurs has surfaced, as under Phibun in the 1930s.

But subsequently, there has been a relatively harmonious integration. The initial wealth of many entrepreneurs was built around the rice trade and concentrated in Bangkok, a regional concentration that persists to this day.

It is quite evident from the above that Thailand's political system has been far from stable. There has been an unrelenting struggle amongst different military-bureaucratic factions, between the elected civilian leadership and the military, as well as incessant pressure from different components of civil society. Thailand has not been a case of an uninterrupted authoritarian regime driving economic development and seeking legitimacy from its success. Indeed, through much of the trials and tribulations of political contests, the Thai economy has performed reasonably well. South Eastern states do not provide some monolithic example of ruthless political authoritarianism producing rapid economic growth. The interplay between economics and politics has been far more complex and, in many cases, economic success has been based on a consensus over some core economic policies, rather than due to a coercive authoritarian regime *per se.*

In more recent decades in particular, the Thai economy has performed exceptionally well and demonstrated the type of dynamism evident in East Asia. The process of economic development has, to a degree, insulated itself from periodic political instability. Somewhat similar to Italy, economic dynamism in Thailand has coexisted with political uncertainty. The economic achievements and their causes are discussed in the sections below.

Indicators of economic success

Average living standards in Thailand have increased substantially over the past four decades. Per capita income in purchasing parity terms is $US 7000, which is higher than in the richer countries of East Europe, such as Hungary and Slovenia, as well as Brazil and South Africa. In the decade between 1985 and 1995, Thailand was one of the fastest-growing economies in the world, averaging 8.5% per year. Only two other countries grew faster. The economic boom has been led by labour-intensive manufacturing exports. This has accelerated the structural transformation of the economy as manufacturing became the single most important sector, overtaking agriculture both in terms of share in GDP and exports. In fact, manufacturing exports now account for nearly 80% of export earnings. An indicator of export-led growth in the 1980s is provided by the fact that the trade-GNP ratio rose from 40% in 1980 to nearly 70% in 1995, indicating increased openness of the economy.

The boom since the mid-1980s has been qualitatively different from that experienced during the 1960s, when the economy also grew at an annual average in excess of 8%. The impressive growth in this period was, however, largely concentrated in the agricultural sector. Its narrow base led to subsequent difficulties when a fall in the terms of trade of Thailand's commodity exports led to major difficulties in balance of payments and debt servicing. These shortcomings became evident towards the late 1970s. After a decade during which the rate of growth had slackened from the hectic pace of the 1960s but was still a very respectable 7% per annum, Thailand was confronted with supply side structural problems. Exclusive reliance on agriculture in export markets proved a bottleneck when the world commodity markets crumbled in the wake of the oil shocks, particularly after the 1979 rise. A short period of adjustment during the early 1980s partially succeeded in reducing an inflation rate that was high in comparison to neighbouring countries. Following this, the Thai economy diversified and expanded at a spectacular pace. This resurgence was due to a mix of price reforms and the regional relocation of industry, which fuelled FDI into Thailand.

The improvements in income have been accompanied by the spread of basic education and health services. Literacy is virtually universal; primary education is compulsory and free for the first nine years. Average life expectancy at birth is 70 years, which is consistent with the average expected at this level of income.

While the growth of incomes has been rapid, and many basic social services have been extended almost universally across society, a number of entrenched inequalities persist.

Although attempts are under way to spread development beyond Bangkok, substantial regional inequities remain. At the same time, a Gini Co-efficient index of 0.46 suggests that income inequality has not improved much. In other areas, such as infant mortality, the progress is admirable but an agenda of improvement still remains; the national average infant mortality is 36 per 1000 live births. While infant mortality dropped by 30% during the 1980s, it remains relatively high in some of the poorer regions.

Thus, while the majority of the population is clearly much better off, their relative position has not necessarily improved. However, as long as the increases in absolute levels of income were reasonable and sustained and the reach of education and health services was widespread, the process of economic development yielded tangible benefits and increased the stake in society for the majority of the population.

The causes of economic success

Three factors account for the recent economic boom. The first has to do with incentive reforms. In the early 1980s, exchange rate devaluation sharply improved the competitiveness of Thailand's exports. Second, the country benefited considerably from the regional relocation of industry. Labour-intensive processes were becoming increasingly uncompetitive in countries such as Japan, Taiwan, and Korea. Firms from many of these countries were adjusting to the change in factor prices by seeking to locate production overseas. As a result, Thailand was a beneficiary of a substantial inflow of foreign direct investment. The initial conditions which made Thailand a good location for FDI was the third factor responsible for the boom. This related to the availability of educated, competitive labour which was the result of substantial investments in basic education. In addition to the quality and competitive price of human capital was the availability of reasonable physical infrastructure. Changes in political regimes did not affect these fundamentals and were therefore not a factor which adversely affected the FDI inflows.

Somewhat ironically, the boom of the mid-1980s started the year after the World Bank and IMF had withdrawn resources from Thailand on the grounds of slow progress with desired economic reforms. The scale of the FDI inflow and the positive impact of exchange rate adjustment overwhelmed impediments in the reform process.

A testimony to the self-sustaining vibrancy of Eastern Asia, and the benefits generated by being in a successful region is provided by the fact that virtually all of Thailand's FDI came from within Asia. Between 1985-95, over 80% of the FDI came from Japan and the East Asian NICS. The United States and Europe were, however, a major market for the manufacturing exports based in Thailand. The success of manufacturing was illustrated in the shift in relative sectoral shares. Till 1980, agricultural exports accounted for 70% of the income earned; this fell to 12% by 1995, as the FDI-led manufacturing export boom accounted for over 80% of earnings by 1994.

Getting the exchange rate price 'right', attracting FDI related to shifting regional comparative advantage, and building on past investments in human and physical capital explains a large part of the recent success. However, the earlier phases of development, and the economic and social policies contributing to these need to be examined to explain the progress that has been maintained, and the shortcomings which prevail.

Agricultural development

While the buoyancy in the manufacturing sector and its growing relative importance has attracted attention, it is worth noting the important role played by agriculture in Thailand's success, not least in the growth of agro-industry. Thailand is one of two net food exporters in Asia.[6] The country plays an important and sometimes dominant role in the global trade markets of cassava, rice, rubber, and sugar. This export success has, however, been achieved largely through expansion of cultivated land and not so much by yield improvements. Indeed, somewhat ironically, yield levels of major crops such as rice and sugar-cane are low, particularly in relation to the rest of Asia. Rice yields are virtually the lowest in Asia.

These low yields have one positive implication for future development. In the foreseeable future, Thailand's crop sector could be a source of rapid productivity gains in a context where manufacturing exports are booming. This provides the potential for achieving very high growth.

Agricultural policy has played a critical role in the diversification of the agricultural sector. Price and tax incentives, excellent research and extension support, and a well-developed marketing infrastructure facilitated the two phases of crop diversification. During the 1960s, the first phase of crop diversification involved a shift from rice, as lands ill-suited to its production were utilized for diversification into simple crops such as maize and cassava. The policy for diversification was, however, extremely export-oriented, building on Thailand's tradition of rice exports. Cassava and maize were introduced and grown almost entirely for export.

The second phase of agricultural policy provided price incentives, infrastructure investment, and technical support and targeted credit for a more sophisticated diversification. The sector shifted into intensive livestock farming exports, particularly frozen chicken, in which Thailand has become one of the leading exporters in the world. Also encouraged in the second wave of diversification were sophisticated horticulture and aquaculture. Thus Thailand has undergone two successful phases of crop diversification, led by the private sector but supported by policy-induced incentives and technological support.

Thailand's service sector is a major source of foreign exchange earning; indeed, tourism revenues are the single largest source, an inheritance from the days when Thailand became a 'rest and recreation' centre for US troops. The tourism sector has since then, however, become far more sophisticated and is geared increasingly towards attracting a wide assortment of tourists, including the 'quality' end of the market. While competition from other countries of the region such as Malaysia and Indo-China is intensifying, Thailand's openness, convenience, and experience are likely to ensure that tourism remains a major revenue-earner. The rate of growth may have peaked but the level should remain high.

Future directions

Thailand's future development challenges contain a mix of opportunities and difficulties. The good prospects relate to the possibilities of productivity gain in agriculture and the opportunities for Thai firms, raised by the opening of Indo-China. There seem to be a number of opportunities in forestry as well as manufacturing exports. Thailand is also well-placed to move into the next stage of more complex manufacturing. As the economy matures and exploits these prospects, other difficulties remain. The country faces tough competition from countries such as China as far as attracting FDI is concerned. Challenges to environmental management are also growing as soil degradation, forest depletion, and rampant pollution take a toll on both efficiency and the quality of life. A larger share of incomes, generated from the high growth, would need to be allocated to address these environmental problems.

INDONESIA

Indonesia is perhaps the only Muslim majority country where a communist take-over has been a real possibility. Indonesia is one of the largest countries in the world, and also one of the more diverse.[7] After independence, this geographically dispersed and highly diverse mix of Buddhists, Hindus, Christians, and Muslims was led by President Sukarno. One of the towering figures of the non-aligned movement, Sukarno, along with Nehru and Nasser, played a visible role on the international stage in the immediate aftermath of the success of independence movements. Their international stature as symbols of the reassertion of suppressed identities earned a certain respect and prestige. But each had to contend with a daunting domestic agenda for creating a political nation, reviving cultural pride, and establishing a viable economy from the debris of colonialism.

Nasser, Nehru, and Sukarno shared another similarity: their broad approach to economic development was one in which the state was to play a leading role. The extent of the state's dominance was not as extensive as that under central planning, but much of the resource allocation process was directly determined by government controls. In none of the three countries did the economy do particularly well. India's low growth period ended only with the dismantling of much of Nehru's economic inheritance. Similarly, the Egyptian economy has underperformed, even though it has been assisted by large inflows of aid. The Indonesian case was perhaps the worst. By the mid-1960s, the economy was in desperate straits. Economic stagnation and related poverty problems had led to acute social tensions, which were contributing to the growing popular base of the Communist Party.

Indonesia's political system broke down under the weight of expectations, factional struggles, and the numerous challenges to national integration from regional mutinies. The parliamentary phase was replaced by martial law in 1957, a common period for the termination of the initial experiment with representative governments. The presidential system which subsequently prevailed under Sukarno's 'guided democracy', relied substantially on the organizational efficiency and extensive mass support base of the Indonesian Communist Party (PKI—Partai Komunis Indonesia). Towards the mid-1960s, the battle for succession after Sukarno was being fought, with the expectation in some quarters that the PKI would emerge as a dominant force. The power struggle was won by the army, which reinforced its authority by an effective *coup* under Suharto in 1965.[8] In the subsequent repression, a significant proportion of the PKI's cadre was physically eliminated and the party was banned.

A major shift in policy orientation occurred under Suharto, as Indonesia moved towards a mixed economy. A more prominent role was to be played by the private sector, while the state concentrated more on the provision of basic social services and the creation of physical infrastructure. The development of some sectors of industry, particularly those involving substantial capital and high technology, continued to be undertaken by the public sector. The changes in the policy environment were generally targeted at creating an environment which encouraged markets. Suharto's regime sought to counteract widespread discontent and create a popular support base through measures which would accelerate growth and reduce abject poverty.

Economic performance indicators

After her dismal performance until the 1970s, Indonesia's entry into the countries classified as middle income testifies to her subsequent recovery. An average per capita income of $3600 in purchasing power parity terms provides an indicator of the growth achieved over the past 25 years. Primary education was made compulsory in 1986 and each Indonesian child has a right to 9 years of free basic education. The population under the absolute poverty line has been reduced dramatically: from 65% in 1960 to 16% by 1995. Social investments and an active population policy have also succeeded in bringing down the population growth rate to 1.5% per annum, thus avoiding the scale of the demographic crisis engulfing some of the South Asian states. Except for far-flung regions, access to basic social services is quite widespread.

A major part of the recent economic success has been due to oil and gas revenues. The existence of natural resources has not, however, led to automatic increases in living standards in other cases. Many countries such as Nigeria have squandered these resources. Indonesia's economic planners have used them reasonably well to diversify the economic base and create the capacities for sustained development.

Indonesia provides an interesting example of recovery from economic collapse. The policy framework of a mixed economy has contained both extensive protection for high technology industries and more competitive labour-intensive exports. While the wisdom of promoting the particular industrial sub-sectors is open to question, there is little doubt that Indonesia has built a substantial technological capacity while simultaneously reducing poverty at a rapid speed. A competent managerial technocratic group has been given strong support by the political elite for the effective management of the economy. This they have done well, particularly in relation to the challenges that Indonesia has had to confront.

The policy framework

In terms of substance, Indonesian policy instruments were similar to those described in earlier country briefs and need not be repeated. The initial restoration efforts in the late 1960s revolved around the need to control inflation and develop a sound financial system as part of the measures required for macroeconomic stability. The announcement of balanced budgets from 1966 onwards became a symbol of the new macroeconomic discipline, which succeeded in creating the conditions for supply side incentive reforms to work.

The policy reforms were elaborated through an indicative planning process, which was instituted in 1970. The first five year plan was strongly directed at reviving agricultural production. Price reforms reduced the severe implicit tax that had been imposed on the sector which had led to supply shortages of staple food, specially rice. Price reforms were accompanied by major investments in infrastructure, particularly irrigation. In addition, improved marketing of high yielding seeds, fertilizer, and pesticides as well as subsidies on their use led to a sharp response in rice production. Indeed, by 1985, Indonesia had become self-sufficient in rice production.

The 1970s were a period of brisk expansion in rice production and an oil boom. Indonesia's oil output tripled between 1968 and 1978, with the aid of FDI, as the oil price rise of 1974 proved a bonanza for the country. The FDI was aided by changes in policies with regard to FDI, with relaxation of restrictions on profit repatriation and a number of guarantees regarding security of assets. A more conducive policy environment to FDI was embodied in the 1967 Foreign Investment Law.[9]

The next decade witnessed another mix of mining and crop successes, although the composition of commodities changed somewhat. In addition to petroleum and rice expansion, the 1980s saw the success of policies for wider crop diversification and the commercial exploitation of natural gas resources, mainly in off-shore locations in the South China Sea. Increased efficiency and diversification of both cash crops and non-rice food crops was aided by a mix of incentives, knowledge support, and subsidized input supplies.

Subsidized credit and chemical inputs accompanied by an effective extension service led to a healthy supply response in crops such as sugar, tobacco, maize, and cassava. In many cases, the increased incomes were of particular benefit to the poor as much of this activity was carried out by both small landholders and on commercial large plantations. Improved inputs and techniques supported through the Ministry of Agriculture's project management units helped increase small holder incomes in a number of cash crops, thereby playing an important role in raising primary incomes of the poor.

The pressure to diversify the economic base away from excessive reliance on hydrocarbon exports has intensified after the fall in petroleum prices since the mid-1980s. These low levels are likely to persist with the increased supply emanating from the successor states of the former Soviet Union, such as Kazakhstan and Azerbaijan. In many ways, the government policy has responded well to the needs for diversification. By 1991, industry superseded agriculture as the most important sector for the first time. This structural shift has been delayed in Indonesia due to a slow start. The country's relatively late industrialization has been due partly to the initial failure of transition when foreign-owned enterprises were replaced by civil servant managers without the necessary commercial discipline or experience. As a result, even the existing small industrial sector went into decline rather than expansion, and industry accounted for less than 10% of GNP after two decades of independence.

A shift in industrial policy largely came into effect in the late 1960s. Under the new industrial policy a number of high technology industries as well as several intermediate goods industries, remained the preserve of the public sector. The choice of industrial sectors chosen for protection and the level of technology pursued in relation to factor endowments have been a subject of considerable controversy in Indonesia. In some areas, the inefficiencies of the final product sector which was being protected were compounded by the protection needed for the intermediate industries which were linked to it. Until the mid-1980s, the basic contours of industrial policy encouraged a mix of public sector-owned high technology and intermediate industries, and a growing private-owned component of consumer goods industries and basic agro-industries.

During the late 1980s, partially in response to the problems with declining petroleum revenues, industrial policy underwent another change to reduce the scale of the transfers from mining to the capital intensive industrial sub-sectors. The process of deregulation and removal of controls has widened the industrial sector further. There has been a rapid growth of joint ventures in various simple as well as more complex consumer goods sub-sectors. Motor vehicle production, electronics, textiles, food and beverage processing units, and a number of other agro-industries have mushroomed. As a result, Indonesia has a complex and less inefficient industrial sector combining petrochemicals, ship building, telecommunication, and aerospace at one end of the technology spectrum to numerous agro-processing units at the other.

Future directions

Indonesia remains politically fragile and tensions could mount. Whether the battle for succession after Suharto affects the economy depends on the scale of the disturbances. Struggles for a more open and accommodating political system should not, in principle, adversely affect the next stage of Indonesia's economic evolution.[10] Diversification of manufacturing activities, and increasing the competitiveness of the protected high technology sub-sectors are immediate challenges in the industrial sector. Planned infrastructure investments in support of the growth of labour-intensive manufacturing exports are likely to provide the stimulus for sustaining the growth momentum.

THE PHILIPPINES

The Philippines, the only Christian country in Asia, has one of the most disappointing development records in the eastern region. It has squandered the fortuitous position which it enjoyed in the 1950s. The Philippines had many characteristics which should have made it into one of the leading countries of Eastern Asia. Far from fulfilling its promise, the country has been embroiled in endemic political and economic crises.

Its economic development potential has been stifled, as discussed below, by an excessively long period of capital-intensive import substitution. This was accompanied by extensive rent-seeking, which created economic distortions and ruined many public sector institutions. At the same time, the resistance to needed equity-enhancing structural changes, particularly land reform, has prevented the development of a form of inclusive capitalism evident elsewhere in Eastern Asia.

Political evolution

The political evolution of the Philippines has been shaped by three features:

The first is the difficulty of national integration in a society where communal and communist movements have threatened dissolution. The Muslim separatist movement in the Mindanao region has been sustained through several decades. Along with the Muslim struggle has been a communist insurgency, seeking to militarily topple a power structure controlled by a few families.

Second, the Philippines has had a persistent battle between civilian and military groups regarding supremacy of authority. A long period of martial law under President Marcos, followed by periodic *coup* attempts against the elected government of Cory Aquino, reflected the underlying conflicts over authority.

Thirdly, the rural elite, having prevented reform in a highly inequitable society, has consolidated its position through private militias. Nearly 600 private militias are under their control, creating a civil society with organized personal security capacities. The Philippines has yet to resolve the tensions generated by each of these three sources of division and friction.[11]

The Marcos era sustained a network of power alliances, many of which were built during the periods of the Spanish and the American rule. The phrase 'crony capitalism', used to describe developments under Marcos, reflected the sense of a small elite controlling power and resources. The end of the Marcos era, which lasted for two decades starting from

1965, left a legacy of a corrupt, demoralized, and narrow elite besieged by communal and communist threats.

The failure of the internationally visible Cory Aquino government to implement many of the reforms expected of it reflected the difficulties of change, specially from a regime which contained many elements resistant to those reforms. The internal contradictions of the Aquino government prevented any strong sense of direction, specially in the economic field. In the political arena, her government was constantly under the threat of a military *coup*, several of which were attempted. The current regime under President Ramos appears to be better placed to undertake some of the needed reforms. The regime enjoys a more secure power base and lower popular expectations to pursue the settlement of insurgencies and implement structural economic reforms.

Thwarted economic development

By the late 1950s, the Philippines had the most advanced industrial structure in South East Asia, contributing nearly a quarter of GDP. At the same time, the access to the US market for its agricultural exports, particularly of sugar, suggested that the country would emerge as the leading economy in South East Asia. While the economy has not been stagnant and grew quite rapidly in the 1970s, it has not been able to sustain a long period of increasing per capita incomes. The pattern of growth has been characterized by fits and starts. Consequently, growth has not been rapid enough to produce a major reduction in poverty. Partly due to this the pressures on distributional shares have mounted, demands to which the elite have been reluctant to concede.

The explanations for the missed opportunity of the Philippines abound. A mix of five factors accounts for the poor growth and distributional performance, namely:

i) The period of import substitution industrialization persisted for too long. A policy regime of high protective tariffs, interest rate subsidies, and dual exchange rate for capital imports created a highly favourable environment for manufacturing for the domestic market. These incentives were successful in creating a capital-intensive, protected industrial structure. This policy framework was, however, retained for too long, sustaining major inefficiencies and generating little employment per unit of value added in manufacturing. The move from the ISI phase to an external orientation was delayed to the detriment of export competitiveness and employment generation.

ii) Competitive pressures in markets were mitigated by rent-seeking monopolies, which emerged through access to the state. The inefficiencies of these enterprises were exposed in the 1980s, when a number of financial and industrial firms collapsed. The rewards of 'rent-seeking', particularly in the Marcos era, led to a highly inefficient institutional framework. Patrimonial public sector institutions and inefficient firms thrived in a protected environment. During this period, the Philippines' decline in comparison to East and South East Asian countries was accelerated.

iii) Agricultural dynamism was thwarted by low producer prices, export taxes, and marketing monopolies.

iv) Little was done to address the problems of distribution in a highly inequitable society. The issue of asset distribution, particularly of rural land, has long been an issue of contention in Filipino society. Land reform remains part of the political agenda. There is a long history of failure to seriously implement land reform, as has been the case in Pakistan. In the Philippines, the demand for land reform was central to the growth of the communist movement in the 1930s and had led to the launching of a programme of social justice by the then President Quezon. This was largely unimplemented, as were the half-hearted attempts launched by President Marcos in 1972. The issue of land reform surfaced again under President Aquino, who launched a wide-ranging Comprehensive Agrarian Reform Programme (CARP). This, too, has been blocked and has fallen far short of expectations. Thus, the Philippines has perhaps been unique in Eastern Asia. Whereas most other countries have undertaken equity-oriented reforms in the face of communist pressure, the Filipino elite appears to have resisted.

v) Social policy has failed to curb the rate of population growth effectively. For much of the period, population growth has remained in the region of 3% annually. This has created intense pressures in the labour market, particularly when policy distortions were encouraging capital intensity. Migration and remittances have mitigated pressures, but the opportunities for migration may not be so favourable in the near future.

Future directions

The agenda for policy reform in many areas is self-evident. Towards the mid-1980s, the policy debate revolved around the need to dismantle the network of rent-seeking monopolies, devalue the currency, reduce tariffs and non-tariff barriers, and remove price distortions favouring capital intensity. In recent years, the Ramos government appears to be willing to implement many of these changes, to reduce the type and extent of state control, and to encourage more labour-intensive manufacturing exports. Privatization of state-owned enterprises has been accelerated, telecommunications monopolies broken up, and reforms enacted to attract FDI. Along with measures to reduce the infrastructure bottlenecks, this collective set of actions constitutes the central elements of a Vision 2000, aimed at enabling the Philippines to catch up with the regional NICS.

In principle, the prospects for the Philippines being able to turn things around are reasonably good. It is surrounded by a fast growing dynamic region, and has a reasonably good human capital base. Years of underperformance have created a domestic constituency for a concerted direction towards a more open and dynamic economy. In addition to the incentive and facilitative reforms referred to earlier, a few more intractable problems remain. The question of asset distribution, particularly land reform, remains part of the agenda. Further, more aggressive social policy measures to reduce the population growth rate need to be sustained. In brief, while many challenges remain, it is conceivable that the next stage of the Philippines' development will be far more productive than that suggested by recent experience.

This brief review of some of the national experiences of South East Asian development suggests that many of the positive features of East Asia are being replicated. Many countries of the region have not only profited from the dynamism unleashed by East Asia but have also directly benefited through the regional shifts in comparative advantage. For example, as Thailand's case study showed, the country's export drive was fuelled by East Asian capital. Many countries of the region have 'taken off' and their degree of self-reliance is indicated by the gradual withdrawal of aid. As many countries graduate, some in Indo-China and others such as the Philippines, offer new prospects. In the near future they will require aid resources particularly to build the physical and social infrastructure.

Finally, the explanation that Eastern Asian development has been eased by homogeneity and continuous authoritarian regimes is seen to be too simplistic. Almost all the countries of South East Asia have had to contend with racial, ethnic, and religious diversity. Their political systems have struggled with a daunting agenda for national integration and prevention of internal and regional conflicts. Political turmoil and uncertainties have been inevitable, but through them all, the economic development record has by and large been impressive and uplifting.

NOTES

1. For details see, *inter alia*, Osman-Rani, H and Fisk, E (eds.): *The Political Economy of Malaysia*, (Oxford University Press, Kuala Lumpur, 1982).

2. For details see Short, A: *The Communist Insurrection in Malaya,1948-1960*, (Friedrich Muller, London, 1975).

3. For analysis of Malaysian economic development see Cho, G: *The Malaysian Economy*, (Routledge, London, 1990); Kanapathy, V: *The Malaysian Economy Problems and Prospects*, (Asia Pacific Press, Singapore, 1990); and Mehmet, O: *Development in Malaysia Poverty, Wealth and Trusteeship*, (Croom Helm, London, 1986). A data summary is contained in Europa Publications: *The Far East and Australasia*, (London, 1994).

4. This has formed the base for Dr Mahathir's famous '20/20 Vision', which summarizes the direction articulated in the NDP.

5. These are established by the International Tropical Timber Organization.

6. The other is Vietnam.

7. By 1995, Indonesia's population had grown to 190 million, making it the fourth largest country in the world by size of population.

8. Sukarno was eased out gradually by Suharto and then kept under house arrest until his death in 1970. His life was spared, unlike that of Bhutto, who was a great admirer of Sukarno's nationalism and international prestige.

9. FDI laws were liberalized further in the late 1980s.

10. Conflict in East Timor, however, could prove to be more intractable to resolve.

11. The obvious parallels with the unresolved problems of governance in Pakistan are explored in the last chapter.

PART B

ECONOMIC DEVELOPMENT
AND SOCIAL CHANGE IN PAKISTAN

These countries, although they do not belong to the socialist world, can draw on its achievements in building an independent national economy and in raising their people's living standards. Today they need not go begging to their former oppressors for modern equipment. They can get it in the socialist countries, free from any political or military obligation.

Nikita Khrushchev
First Secretary of the Communist Party, 1956

Aid should be given not in order to contain the spread of communism, not because other nations are doing it, but because it is right.

John F. Kennedy
US President, 1961

CHAPTER 6

THE ROLE OF AID IN PAKISTAN'S ECONOMIC DEVELOPMENT

OVERVIEW

Aid has been a twin-edged sword. It has facilitated and hindered development. It has been influential when the country was taking one step forward but it was also frequently supportive of measures when the nation took two steps back. It is this duality and inconsistency which confounds any simplistic analysis of the impact of aid. As the sections below demonstrate, aid donors have played a surprisingly diverse role in project finance and policy change. The fiftieth anniversary of independence provides an opportune moment to reflect on a relationship that is undergoing fundamental change.

A number of issues emerge. Is there a connection between substantial aid inflows and the low domestic savings rate? Has the debt acquired been justified by the investments made and the income gained through aid? By the mid-1990s, does the absence of a political imperative to give aid combined with the growing importance of private capital flows signify the end of aid? What measures need to be taken to prepare the country for the end of aid?

In the economic arena, aid has played a significant role in physical capital formation, and in providing balance of payments support, particularly for industrial development. Donors have made an increasingly important contribution to policy reforms. The macroeconomic framework is frequently formulated by the Bretton Woods institutions. Policy-based conditionality provides the tool for the adoption of a wide range of macro- and microeconomic reforms. Principle donors have also been enthusiastic supporters of private sector led development. Accordingly, they have helped institutions and financial structures in order to support the development of the private sector.

Aid has enabled Pakistan to borrow resources at very favourable interest rates. The average rate of interest on external public debt is 4%, which is considerably below what the country would have had to pay in the market. Apart from these economic benefits, some aid donors have widened their coverage in the 1980s to support a few civil society institutions, like the Human Rights Commission and NGOs working on issues such as women's rights and the environment.

However, the inequities of Pakistan's development have also been shaped by donors. The doctrine of 'functional inequality' was formulated in collaboration with donors. Similarly, aid has neglected key education and health investments, partly due to the short term horizon of donors. For most of the fifty year period, donors have neither supported such key investments directly nor have they felt it important to address these through policy conditionality. Donors have not been shy to impose needed policy conditionality. But none have linked their lending to mandatory primary education, for example.[1] As a result, huge aid resources have been poured into a country which remains largely illiterate after half a century of independence.

Part of the explanation lies in the political role of aid. External resources have tended to ebb and flow in line with the state of US-Pakistan relations. The aid channels were principally bilateral during the 1950s and 1960s, while they became more multilateral largely through the World Bank during the 1980s. The political imperative has been strong and has frequently overridden serious consideration of desirable socio-economic reform.

While much of the dynamism and strength of the donor economies lie in technology and education, their aid advisers have chosen to neglect, until recently, an emphasis on investments in human capital. Virtually none of the needed structural reforms vital for equitable development was given serious and concerted support by aid donors.

There have been notable exceptions and the role of donors has not been static. Many had emphasized required reforms by the late 1980s. By this time, the consequences of past neglect of social investments had become far too obvious. By the late 1980s, some agencies such as the UNDP were analysing the policy requirements to address unbalanced development.[2] Similarly, the World Bank was advocating changes in socio-economic policy, including the need for introducing taxation of agricultural incomes. Agencies such as UNICEF had a history of project involvement but they too began to emphasize the need for policy changes for more equitable development.

This emphasis is welcome but perhaps it should have come far earlier. The course of equitable development in Pakistan would have been very different had similar views influenced policy in the early years after independence. Alas, donor policy advice at that time reinforced domestic inequities and helped create many of the problems which donors were rightly complaining about by the 1980s. The principle responsibility for these measures, of course, lay within the country and the political economy of these choices was referred to in Chapter 1. The sections below examine the role of aid in different sub-periods.

IMPACT OF AID: 1947-58

Immediately after partition aid resources were targeted, not surprisingly, towards relief work. The primary focus on disaster relief and infrastructure rehabilitation is reflected in resource allocation. Approximately 75% of the initial $133 million given by the United States during 1951-4 went into disaster relief.

The aid programme was dominated by bilateral assistance. The United States contributed 80% of aid inflows. The terms of aid reflected the nature of assistance to non-income generating activities. Most aid came in the form of grants (85%). US aid inflows were part of a larger political relationship, particularly the anti-communist security alliance into which America was inducting Pakistan.

The development impact of aid was hampered by policy indecision. The US administration had mixed views about the efficacy of aid to the third world in general. This hesitancy was reflected in the rather dismissive and hostile attitude to aid adopted by the Randall Commission on Foreign Economic Policy (Washington, 1954) and the Mutual Security Act 1953. Thus, until the mid-fifties, Pakistan's receipt of aid grants was conditioned by its disaster relief needs as well as lack of belief in development assistance in the major donor country.

USAID development strategy towards Pakistan began to emerge near the beginning of the First Five Year Plan. The Mutual Security Act 1954 signalled a shift towards the importance given to aid efficiency by the United States and the end of policy indecision regarding aid strategy to Pakistan. The main plank of the USAID programme became the development of infrastructure to lay the base for agricultural and industrial growth. Closely attached to project aid were 50 technical assistance projects. Part of the objective of the latter was to support institution building as the second pillar on which to base economic growth. During 1954-8, the total aid commitment rose to approximately $700 million; the grant element in aid also began to decline with the shift away from disaster relief.

The aggregate growth performance of the economy was disappointing, particularly in the agricultural sector where there was a decline in per capita incomes. Aid resources were neither large nor well-targeted enough to have any substantive impact on raising the growth rate. The primary contribution of aid was to assist in laying the infrastructural and institutional base for growth. The dividends of these inputs were manifest in the high growth performance of the sixties, when additional aid resources built upon the modest beginnings of an aid strategy in the fifties.

Aid financed over 50% of the total public sector development expenditure in the First Plan. Although aggregate investment was not large enough to meet plan growth targets, aid resources helped in achieving modest developmental gains. Commodity aid, which comprised approximately 33% of total capital inflow, was particularly useful for sustaining import requirements of the rapid industrialization programme. Non-PL-480 commodity assistance provided a mixture of raw materials, semi-finished products, chemicals, and machinery for the industrial sector.

Pressure on the balance of payments was being exerted, as mentioned above, by the neglect of the agricultural sector. Aid helped relieve part of the foreign exchange constraint by financing nearly 33% of imports in the First Plan period. In the absence of aid, the development strategy of the fifties would have run into a much more stringent balance of payments constraint. Nearly 40% of aid to Pakistan during this period was accounted for by PL-480. The provision of US agricultural surpluses under this programme enabled easy import of grain.

The PL-480 programme provided valuable assistance to the government's pursuit of import substitution industrialization at the expense of agriculture. An investible surplus was extracted from agriculture, as PL-480 assisted in moving the terms of trade against the sector.

The neglect of agriculture had three adverse consequences. First, the decline in per capita rural incomes was particularly inequitable since the bulk of the poor were concentrated in the agricultural sector. To this extent, PL-480 resources helped in the transfer of income from the rural poor to the relatively affluent urban areas. The second adverse consequence was also distributional. Jute was the primary source of foreign exchange in the first decade. Jute revenues, emanating from East Pakistan, were being transferred to the industrialization programme concentrated in West Pakistan.

The third adverse impact of agricultural neglect was the constraint on the balance of payments imposed by the necessity to import food. Not only did these imports require PL-480 assistance, they also 'crowded out' foreign exchange for the industrial sector. Thus, the availability of PL-480 may well have helped sustain an unbalanced growth strategy which needed drastic revision in the next decade. Effectively, low producer price incentives were being compensated for through food imports.

The United States' bilateral aid programme dominated external capital inflows. This is reflected in the accompanying charts. Charts 2 and 3 give an idea of magnitude in relation to the economy. US aid was financing 38% of development expenditure and 27% of imports. The emphasis on commodity and food aid to ease balance of payments constraints is reflected in Chart 1, which shows that 75% of aid was in the form of quick disbursing programme aid.

1. US BILATERAL AID COMMITMENT TO PAKISTAN: 1951-8 (% of total)

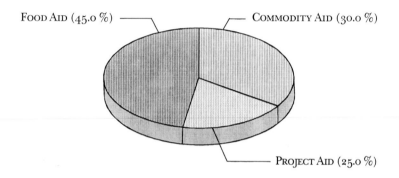

FOOD AID (45.0 %) — COMMODITY AID (30.0 %)

PROJECT AID (25.0 %)

IMPACT OF AID: 1959-70

The Ayub Khan era represented the high point of consortium influence on Pakistan's economy. With the formation of the Aid-to-Pakistan consortium in 1960, there was a shift away from the virtually exclusive bilateral influence of the fifties. Although the United States remained the most important single donor, multilateral institutions such as the World Bank acquired greater prominence.

One of the most important contributions of aid in this period was in the field of policy formation. This was the era of the legendary Harvard group, who were closely involved with macro-policy formation.

Foreign capital provided the additional investment resources vitally needed to achieve the very high growth targets of the Second and Third Five Year Plans. Aid-financed investment in water, power, and transport strengthened the

2. US AID COMMITMENTS TO PAKISTAN: 1951-8
(as shares (%) of various economic indicators)

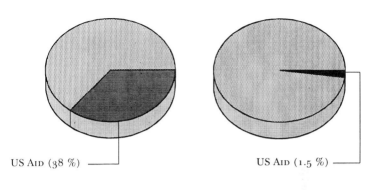

US AID (38 %) ——

GOP DEVELOPMENT EXPENDITURES

US AID (1.5 %) ——

GDP

3. US AID COMMITMENTS TO PAKISTAN: 1951-8
(as shares (%) of various economic indicators)

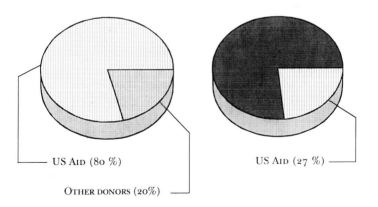

—— US AID (80 %)

OTHER DONORS (20%) ——

US AID (27 %) ——

TOTAL AID

TOTAL IMPORTS

infrastructural base. Aid resources were an important component in the construction of the Tarbela and Mangla dams and other such irrigation-related infrastructural development.

The industrial sector was the largest recipient of project aid during the Second Plan (1960-5). External resource financed nearly 40% of the Second Plan's development programme. The magnitude and growth of aid is reflected in Table 12. Aid as a percentage of GNP rose from 0.02% in 1952 to 5.8% in 1970. As a proportion of development expenditure, aid's share went up from a mere 0.5% to a high 34%. Indeed, the centrality of aid was only too evident in the mid-sixties, when there was a sharp cut in external resource inflows. Aggregate investment suffered and trade liberalization was reversed.

Programme aid tried to address the structural balance of payments difficulties. From 1960 onwards, aid resources were made available for gradual import liberalization. One of the major balance of payments constraints on the growth process was the shortage of foreign exchange for the import of industrial raw materials. This had led to considerable excess capacity in the industrial sector. Aid-backed import liberalization in 1964 led to a sharp increase in capacity utilization and effectively lowered the capital-output ratio. The effect on growth was the same as would be the case if the savings rate went up or if there was a decline in capital intensity of investment decisions.

The aid-underwritten import liberalization came to a grinding halt in 1965 as the United States withdrew resources to Pakistan because of the war with India. This suspension had a profound impact on the Pakistani bureaucracy's attitude to aid. The political fluctuations of aid have, since then, created a relationship of insecurity and long-run unreliability. These perceptions have been strengthened further by periodic, politically motivated suspensions of US aid in the seventies and eighties. The stability which was so apparent in the aid relationship of the early to mid-sixties has never been re-established. The vicissitudes of the US-Pakistan relationship have been mirrored in an attitude to aid which is more wary, pragmatic, and cynical. The termination of

USAID after the Soviet withdrawal from Afghanistan has reinforced scepticism.

12. FOREIGN AID COMPARED WITH INCOME, DEVELOPMENT EXPENDITURE, AND IMPORTS
Select Fiscal Years

Item	1952	1956	1960	1967	1968	1970
Foreign aid (Rs million)	5.0	472	1068	3105	3334	3570
Proportion of gross national product (%)	0.02	2.1	3.4	7.5	5.7	5.8
Proportion of development expenditure (%)	0.5	34.8	38.1	42.2	37.7	34.0
Proportion of imports (%)	0.1	18.6	31.1	55.8	47.0	49.8

Source: Pakistan Planning Commission.

In the latter part of the sixties, the main contribution of aid shifted from the industrial to the agricultural sector. PL-480 grain imports were used to stabilize wheat prices after decontrol, thus partly rectifying the disincentive effect of PL-480 in the fifties. Better price incentives and the adoption of the seed-water fertilizer package made a decisive contribution to the growth of the agricultural sector. Thus, in conjunction with assistance to the industrial sector in the early sixties, aid helped in basic structural reform of the commodity-producing sectors.

The shortcomings of aid in this period were closely related to the deficiencies of the overall development strategy. Approximately 85% of aid resources went to West Pakistan, thus accentuating regional tensions. Similarly, there was serious neglect of social sectors and poverty issues. The crisis which erupted in Pakistan was primarily political. None the less, the inequalities of power were often buttressed by uneven allocation of economic resources. Economic policy did little to mitigate sensitive distributional issues. To the extent that aid donors were involved in economic policy formulation, they must share responsibility for the failures of the sixties.

The financial costs of repayment commitments began to be felt as the debt service ratio rose sharply from 3.6% in

1961 to nearly 18% by the end of the decade. As aid repayments absorbed increasingly larger slices of foreign exchange earnings, concern also mounted about another aspect of the real cost of aid. The GOP's apprehensions about tied aid were reflected in a Planning Commission/EAD study,[3] which provided detailed evidence of instances where tied aid had prevented Pakistan from importing equipment from the most competitive source. The study pointed out that in some cases, prices as high as 50 to 60% of the internationally competitive price had to be paid under tied credits. Quite apart from such extreme cases, the study highlighted frequent cases where imports were financed by relatively expensive tied aid sources.

In brief, aid resources facilitated the growth of agriculture and industry in the 1960s. Physical infrastructure was built, balance of payments support provided, and private sector capacities enhanced. At the same time, donors were strongly associated with the promotion of the 'functional inequality' approach. Donors helped formulate programmes which ignored basic education and health investments. The net result was an unbalanced approach which was effective in stimulating growth but ignored equity imperatives; a neglect which was to haunt Pakistan in later decades and constituted a major difference with East Asian capitalism.

IMPACT OF AID: 1971-7

This period witnessed a sharp reversal of aid donor influence on policy-making. It was also a time of substantial structural and institutional change in the economy. Ironically, aid played an important part in financing projects which exemplified the change in development strategy. However, the composition of aid donors changed. The Soviet Union and Islamic countries replaced consortium members as the major aid donors. The former largely provided financial and technical resources for projects, such as the Steel Mill at Karachi. Islamic countries provided project and balance of payments support, although a few supported policy changes which they considered desirable.

The relationship of the Pakistan People's Party (PPP) government with the World Bank was marred by continuous and unresolved tension. The World Bank was not sympathetic to a general policy shift towards the public sector. It was critical of the Steel Mill. Consortium donors were also sceptical of the government's nationalization and land reform programme. Further, the World Bank expressed strong concern over a macroeconomic strategy which entailed expenditure increases without sufficient attention to domestic resource mobilization. The Bank was not willing to resume lending on a substantial scale unless the government undertook specific measures to tackle the domestic and external resource gaps. On its part, the new government was somewhat dismissive of World Bank policy advice in the sixties, and held it partially responsible for promoting economic policies which contributed to the break-up of the country in 1971.[4] The regime was also far more sensitive to sovereignty issues and viewed policy dialogue with suspicion. Its idea of self-reliance in policy formulation effectively terminated the policy influence enjoyed by the consortium in the sixties (and later revived in the eighties).

Ironically, as mentioned earlier, this general tension prevented progress in areas where there appeared to be a convergence between the World Bank and the PPP. The latter's populist programme was not in disharmony with the World Bank's emphasis on Basic Needs, which had acquired momentum in Washington during the early 1970s. But the World Bank largely argued for public spending on basic social services, within the context of a private sector led development strategy. It was vehemently opposed to PPP's nationalization of industrial and financial assets. The Bank was wary of the motives and anticipated the difficulties these actions would cause to Pakistan's economy.

Thus, the PPP's social sector programme could not attract World Bank funding because of deadlock over the direction of development strategy.[5] This was perhaps a missed opportunity to rectify past neglect of social services. A key area where aid might have helped was population control, at a time when the GOP appeared to be more inclined to tackle this thorny issue. In the mid-seventies, there was considerable donor interest in the population control programme. Subsequently, political tensions resulted in sharp withdrawals, until UNFPA was the only agency with a continuing commitment to the Family Planning Programme.[6]

The USAID programme dwindled into virtual insignificance, reflected in the reduction of US personnel from over 1000 in the mid-sixties, to just 4 in 1977. A similar politically-motivated withdrawal was evident in 1989, when the USAID office was closed.

Aid from consortium sources fell from $400 million in 1968-9 to $52 million in 1971-2. In the events leading up to the creation of Bangladesh, particularly the military crackdown, Pakistan's international prestige was low–a factor which also influenced the aid response.

The main contribution of the World Bank and USAID was restricted to the import of fertilizer, which relieved some of the constraints to agricultural growth during this period. In particular, the growth of wheat production was primarily based on increased fertilizer usage. The World Bank also began to assist in projects concerned with better water management as a much needed follow-up to the gains from the 'Green Revolution'.

The most significant input of aid in this period related to the establishment of the Steel Mill. The Soviet Union provided financial and technical assistance for the project. However, by the long-gestating nature of investments in large public sector capital projects, the return of aid resources was not evident during the seventies. Aid resources assisted in the structural transformation of the economy, but the wisdom of such projects was highly questionable. They were too capital-intensive, contained obsolete technology, and were poorly managed by a public sector prone to extensive patrimonial influences. The result was the worst of all possible worlds— a capital-intensive plant which was overmanned! Substantial surplus labour was hired on political considerations.

Although donors lost much of the policy influence evident in the sixties, ironically the economy's reliance on aid increased during the seventies. Private savings and investment dried up in response to nationalization. Public savings were negligible and there was little progress in domestic resource mobilization through better tax effort. In such a situation, the government's expansion of its public sector development programme was heavily dependent on aid. As Table 13 illustrates, in some years such as 1974, aid contributed a larger share to investment than national savings.

13. THE MAGNITUDE OF THE RESOURCE GAP
(1969-70 to 1977-8)

Years	Savings as percentage of investment	Resource gap (investment-saving) (Rs million)	Resource gap as percentage of GNP
1969-70	56.8	3257	6.8
1970-1	54.5	3568	7.1
1971-2	66.5	2566	4.7
1972-3	83.5	1428	2.1
1973-4	53.2	5431	6.2
1974-5	36.5	11560	10.2
1975-6	58.8	9386	7.0
1976-7	62.0	10408	6.7
1977-8	80.1	5968	3.2

Source: *Pakistan Economic Survey, 1980-1.*

Apart from the Soviet Union, the Islamic countries emerged as major aid donors during the seventies. The purpose of their assistance, however, was largely confined to the external sector. Aid flows from Arab countries and Iran helped to ease adjustment to the OPEC oil price hike of 1973. To the extent that these resources were available to Pakistan, they mitigated the severity of the energy-import-induced squeeze on the balance of payments. Aid from Muslim countries eased Pakistan's balance of payments difficulties and enabled better adjustment to the oil shock. Pakistan also benefited enormously through manpower export to the Middle East which was more beneficial than the direct aid support.

During the seventies, the debt burden began to bite. Pakistan, for the first time, was unable to meet its annual repayments and was granted debt rescheduling. All debt indicators rose fairly sharply during this period, such as the debt-GNP ratio and the debt servicing-foreign exchange ratio. Indeed, the consortium appeared to be concerned almost exclusively with the debt problem and eased Pakistan's resource squeeze through debt rescheduling in 1974. This was granted after protracted negotiations since Pakistan's unilateral announcement of a moratorium on debt repayments in 1971. The problem of mounting debt problems was worsened by the economy's increased reliance on external resources during the course of the decade.

The PPP government was beset by economic difficulties due to a combination of a troubled inheritance, adverse international developments, and insecurities generated by institutional reform. The legacy of the sixties included a civil war which broke up the country, a rising growth rate of population (which had risen from 2.3 to 2.8% during the sixties), and substantial popular concern about rectifying inequities. Soon after coming to power, the government was faced with the first oil price hike and the subsequent world recession. Matters were made much worse, however, by inept economic management and erratic policies. Nationalization and half-baked land reforms intensified ethnic tensions and increased insecurity without any substantive·compensatory gains. The public sector expanded without financial discipline. The result was economic stagnation, a growing debt crisis, and increased dependence on external resources.

In this difficult environment, the government launched a substantial public sector investment programme. The domestic resources to finance this investment were inadequate. An indication of the shortage of resources is provided by Table 13. As the table shows, investment requirements exceeded domestic savings by a wide margin. For example, as noted earlier, domestic savings could finance only 36% of investments in 1974-5.

Another indicator of the inadequacy of domestic resources is provided by Table 14, which demonstrates how most of the domestic resources went into financing non-development expenditure. As a consequence, nearly 65% of development expenditure was financed by foreign capital in some years. The secular rise in aid commitments is illustrated in Table 15. The proportion of aid to GNP rose from 5.9% in 1973 to nearly double—10.5% by 1977. Pakistan's debt service ratio, namely debt service payments as a percentage of foreign exchange earnings, rose to 20% by 1976-7. Pakistan's ratio

was twice that of the average of 10% for low income
countries.

14. GOVERNMENT REVENUE AND EXPENDITURE

		1972-3	1973-4	1974-5	1975-6	1976-7	1977-8
1.	External resources as a percentage of development expenditure	68.97	50.87	69.34	62.43	41.11	38.56
2.	Non-development expenditure as a percentage of domestic resources	92.85	82.31	92.12	86.82	71.22	72.47

Sources: *Pakistan Basic Facts, 1979-80.*
Annual Report 1979-80, State Bank of Pakistan.

15. FOREIGN AID COMMITMENT

	1952	1956	1960	1964	1968	1973	1977
Foreign Aid (Rs million)	5	472	1068	3105	3334	3557	13902
Proportion of GNP (%)	0.02	2.1	3.4	7.5	5.8	5.9	10.5

Sources: *Annual Report 1979-80*, State Bank.
Pakistan Basic Facts, 1979-80.

It is evident from the above that the government of Pakistan
could not have carried out the structural transformation of
the economy without provision of aid investment resources.
Many donors remained unconvinced of the wisdom of plants
such as the Steel Mill. However, it was perhaps both apt and
ironic that the GOP exercised almost exclusive control over
economic policy yet managed to become more dependent on
external finance for its capital goods sector investment
programme. This was partly because economic policies
during this period did little to encourage foreign exchange
earning. Private sector led manufacturing export expansion
was logical, as Pakistan should have moved from import-
substitution to greater outward-orientation. This would have
been very similar to the East Asian experience. But such
prospects in Pakistan were undermined by nationalization
and insecurity.

Pakistan's economic structure paid a heavy price for populism in the 1970s. Half-baked measures prevented any of the structural reforms which a serious commitment to socialism might have brought. Powerful groups within government prevented effective land reforms or implementation of measures such as mandatory primary education. At the same time, capitalist development was thrown off course by random and erratic nationalizations. Neither fish nor fowl, the economy became a confused hybrid of contradictions.

IMPACT OF AID: 1978-88

In 1982, the World Bank-led consortium pledged $1 billion for Pakistan. By 1984, consortium aid commitments more than doubled to $2.2 billion. Consortium aid had resumed after relative insignificance in the seventies. The revival of consortium aid since the early eighties was accompanied by extensive policy dialogue. Perhaps more than ever before, aid resources were closely tied to rectifying perceived deficiencies in macroeconomic and sectoral policy-making. The process of trying to improve the policy environment for growth can be divided into three phases.

The first phase was concerned primarily with macroeconomic issues. The framework for discussion was provided by the World Bank's Structural Adjustment Loan and IMF's Extended Fund Facility. One of the outcomes of this dialogue was the delinking of the rupee from the US dollar in 1982. The subsequent decline in the value of the rupee increased export incentives in a policy regime which was otherwise highly favourable to import substitution. A positive distributional side effect was an increase in the rupee value of remittances.[7]

Other areas of progress included the following: (i) supply side measures aimed at 'getting prices right', improved efficiency in fertilizer and water use, and accelerated growth performance in agriculture; (ii) steps were taken towards foreign trade liberalization, and (iii) there was a substantive improvement in the policy environment for private investment. There was some denationalization, particularly of smaller units.

In general there was a reversion to the private sector led development strategy pursued since independence but abandoned in the 1970s. But the process of reversion was not smooth and encountered numerous difficulties, since many of the state-owned enterprises were bankrupt. Greater success was achieved through policy reforms which promoted new enterprises, rather than denationalization.

The first phase of policy dialogue, however, was to some extent, marred by tension and frustration. The final instalment of the EFF was withheld by the IMF because of non-fulfilment of monetary targets. The GOP felt that the IMF ignored certain' structural constraints and was unwilling to meet IMF targets which would conflict with support of the commodity producing sectors.[8]

Similarly, the GOP surprised the World Bank by indicating reluctance to proceed with the second phase of the SAL.[9] The low ebb in otherwise harmonious relations between donors and GOP was symbolized by the Finance Minister, Ghulam Ishaq Khan's[10] comment on the scale of policy intrusion: 'I will not hand over the management of the Pakistan economy to the World Bank for $250 million.'[11]

For their part, donors were frustrated by the pace of progress towards institutional reform. But the complexity of the process and the diplomatic skills needed for efficacy in this area led to poor results, partly because of fluctuations in US-Pakistan relations. The new recruits of USAID simply did not know the country well enough to be effective in the nitty gritty of institutional reform.[12] A stable, long-term relationship is more conducive to success in this complex area.

The second phase of policy dialogue was marked by a transition from macro to sectoral issues. Macroeconomic issues were not entirely ignored. But the experience of EFF and SAL suggested that sectoral dialogue, supported by aid resources, could be more efficacious in the short term. Donor-encouraged reforms were acknowledged to be more successful at the sectoral rather than macroeconomic level.[13] In the energy sector, for example, World Bank-USAID had a substantive input on pricing and other important supply-related issues. USAID, in particular, was keen to encourage private sector investment in energy and helped to establish an energy sector policy framework which encouraged private investment. In the agricultural sector, better production incentives were accompanied by measures to reduce subsidies as part of increased economy-wide reliance on the market mechanism. Sector dialogue also concentrated on improving recurrent cost policies through extension of user charges. Donors also emphasized the need for institutional reform at the sector level. The ADB agricultural sector loan to ease fertilizer imports, for example, was conditional on the issues mentioned above. The World Bank sector loan also emphasized similar conditionality concerns.

The third and ongoing phase of policy dialogue is perhaps more extensive than either of the previous stages. Current policy concerns emanate from a broad consensus on Pakistan's recent development—that the high growth performance is not sustainable without major structural reform to improve: (i) domestic resource mobilization; (ii) the state of physical and social infrastructure; (iii) the balance of payments position, and (iv) human resource development.

Donor reviews reflected this analytical consensus, with phrases such as 'the Pakistani economy is...living on borrowed time'[14] and 'structural imbalances in the economy and fiscal system of Pakistan constitute serious obstacles to continued economic growth and development.'[15] The need to rectify these structural deficiencies has led to extensive dialogue on macroeconomic and sectoral issues. In 1988, negotiations with the IMF and the World Bank led to the signing of a loan under the Structural Adjustment Facility (SAF).[16] This outlined details of macroeconomic and sectoral policies required for adjustment.[17] The release of SAF resources was subject to IMF scrutiny of performance at regular intervals.[18] A tougher stance on resource mobilization was evident in the World Bank's withholding of a loan in the agricultural sector because of conditions not being met.[19] USAID also got involved with macro-dialogue, through separate annual reviews of GOP policy. The other major donor, the Asian Development Bank, remained a more project oriented institution and left much of the policy dialogue to the Bretton Woods institutions. To the extent that it did occur, ADB's policy dialogue was more project and sector oriented and shied away from macro issues.

The Finance Minister, while acknowledging tough negotiating conditions and the need to swallow bitter resource mobilization pills, termed donor advice as having one central message—that Pakistan should live within its means.[20] GOP officials often expressed a certain ambivalence about the policy dialogue. While there were nationalist concerns about the scale of foreign influence on policy-making, many expressed the view that donor conditionalities play a useful role in constantly stressing the need for fiscal responsibility and structural adjustment on fiscally lavish politicians.

GROWTH, INVESTMENT, AND SAVINGS

Pakistan's high growth performance in the 1980s had a dual input from aid agencies. The provision of investment resources was closely related to the policy dialogue discussed above. This emphasized the revival of the private sector and supply side incentive reforms. Second, aid resources were targeted towards investment in the production sectors—energy, agriculture, and industry.

Aid was involved in meeting investment resource shortages in the 'hard' sectors, including dams.[21] Some aid agencies also indicated willingness to provide resources for industrial estates,[22] which would provide concentrated infrastructure and thus relieve one of the critical constraints to rapid industrial growth.

Aid-financed investment was particularly important in an era where high growth rates were achieved partly by running down past infrastructure. The current aggregate investment ratio is low. The high efficiency of capital implied by an incremental capital-output ratio of 2.8 is not plausible.[23] Future investment needs for infrastructure in energy, transport, and social sectors imply a rise in ICOR, as more capital per unit of output is required.

The relationship between aid and savings is complex. Unlike the sixties, domestic savings have fallen in the last decade. The fall in the domestic savings rate was most severe during the Fifth Plan period.[24] Although there has been a modest revival, the low level of domestic savings continues to plague the economy. There are several reasons for poor savings performance. These include a shift towards a high consumption orientation of society due to the Gulf boom and smuggling, political uncertainties, insecurities in a financial system moving ostensibly towards interest-free banking, poor returns in the financial sectors, and statistical underestimation.

There are three avenues through which aid may have contributed to a deteriorating resource position. First, the high political profile of US aid resumption may have weakened policy dialogue on domestic resource mobilization. USAID commitments were not tied to policy conditionality and the agency recognized that this may have weakened the domestic resource mobilization effort.[25] Second, PL-480 sales provided the GOP with counterpart rupee funds, which were used to finance the budget deficit. This reduced the pressure to raise public savings.

Finally, the foreign assistance packages may have encouraged unproductive expenditures. Development aid was, for example, accompanied by heavy security assistance.[26] The emphasis on defence has tended to put a squeeze on more productive investment. The government's annual development plan fell, as a percentage of national income, from 8.4% in 1981-2 to 7.4% in 1986-7. More than 50% of the annual development plan was financed from external sources. The fiscal squeeze has meant that in some cases, counterpart funds were not available for foreign-assisted projects.

BALANCE OF PAYMENTS

Pakistan's balance of payments performance has been deeply influenced by the robust growth in remittances from the Middle East. By 1984, remittances constituted the largest single source of foreign exchange earnings. They were four times greater than the net aid inflow. At their peak, they were equal to 86% of the trade deficit.[27]

During the course of the eighties, USAID contributed a substantial part of its resources to balance of payments support. Quick disbursing commodity imports accounted for $900 million of the $1.6 billion economic aid package. This formed the major part of the aid programme and was primarily targeted towards the import of energy and agricultural commodities and equipment.

Partly designed to offset the balance of payments effect of the military modernization programme,[28] flexible USAID resources have effectively acted as a source of foreign exchange reserves. Purchases of rupees for local costs of aid projects have directly added to foreign exchange reserves. In addition, USAID resources for the import of agricultural and energy commodities provided balance of payments support. Approximately 33% of these imports were financed by the PL-480 programme. This was used almost exclusively for the import of edible oils. Edible oils account for nearly 7% of all imports. By providing an annual sum of $50 million, PL-480 provided direct balance of payments support. Balance of payments support is not as visible as prestige projects and often goes unnoticed. It has, in the recent past, provided flexible aid resources which have eased commodity shortages and balance of payment strains.

It is, of course, true that the United States has had a surplus of vegetable oil for which commercial interests have a stake in gaining a market.[29] None the less it should be stressed that a USAID financed study and policy dialogue accompanying PL-480 have made strong recommendations for increased domestic production of oil seeds. The supply response so far has been poor but it is to be hoped that, just as with the case of PL-480 wheat assistance in the past, the balance of payments support is used to facilitate greater domestic production through improved producer incentives.

However, the prospects of expanding domestic oil seed production at prices which are competitive with countries such as Malaysia appear slim. Pakistan is one of the major importers of Malaysian oil and it seems unlikely that without a period of protection, a domestic oil seeds industry will develop.

INFLATION

Relatively modest inflation[30] over the 1980s was due largely to a conservative monetary policy, allied to measures which effectively deferred inflationary pressures. In particular, fiscal deficits were largely financed through non-inflationary mechanisms. This was due principally to a financing of the deficits by accumulating domestic debt. Thus, while inflation was kept low temporarily, a huge domestic debt bill was passed on to the economic managers of the 1990s.

Donor influence on inflation-related policies was evident at three levels. First, monetary restraint and credit ceilings are an important component of policy dialogue which involved the IMF. Monetary targets were central to the EFF (1980)[31] and to the SAF negotiations. Second, aid has sometimes provided selective relief from inflationary pressures. For example, aid-financed imports of cotton and wheat at times of periodic shortages have increased supplies and contained immediate inflationary pressures. Third, to the extent that aid resources have contributed to the revival of commodity-producing sectors, they have contributed to releasing inflationary pressures on supply which had built up in the seventies.

However, support for policies which increase user charges, eliminate subsidies, and depreciate the rupee are likely to have contributed to short run inflationary effects.[32]

As evident from the above, policy dialogue has become a key component of the aid relationship in recent years. During the 1990s in particular, World Bank-IMF conditionality has been far tougher, partly due to the failure in the 1980s to undertake necessary reforms. This delay has led to accumulating unresolved problems, which are threatening a default on debt payments. In the 1990s, donors have also been more singular in the pursuit of policy reforms. Far from undermining the policy dialogue through unlinked resource disbursements as occurred in the 1980s, bilateral donors have tended to support IMF-World Bank conditionalities.

Over the last three decades, there has been a sharp reversal of the trend evident in the seventies, whereby donors were almost exclusively confined to project finance or to general balance of payments support. The World Bank has played a leading role in policy dialogue. However, in the early eighties, donor policy co-ordination was relatively weak. As noted earlier, in some areas, the availability of bilateral resources weakened macro-policy conditionality. The success of the dialogue has been uneven. Success with regard to liberalization has been fairly rapid, in areas such as trade reform, deregulation, and privatization. However, domestic resource mobilization and structural balance of payments problems remain intractable.

On account of past failures to effectively tackle these resource gaps, recent World Bank-IMF negotiations entail detailed policy prescriptions. By 1996, the Bretton Woods institutions had linked conditionalities on direct taxation of rural incomes to the release of resources, leading to intense friction with the Benazir Bhutto government, somewhat reminiscent of the deadlock with her father's regime. They were also pushing for restructuring public spending priorities towards basic education and health. Somewhat ironically, these external financial institutions were seen to be pressing for progressive reform measures against reluctant domestic regimes, dominated by rich and powerful interest groups.[33]

During the 1980s, the Asian Development Bank emerged as a major multilateral donor. In some years, it was the single largest donor. Although it acknowledged the need to incorporate macro and sectoral dialogue into lending procedures,[34] its structure is that of a project-based institution. Its involvement in macro-policy dialogue is and likely to remain peripheral.

The increased emphasis on policy dialogue in the 1980s and 1990s has occurred in spite of the steady decline in net aid flows. In 1994-5, they were barely 30% of gross inflow (*see* Table 16). In other words, more than twice as much

16. AID INFLOWS, DEBT SERVICING, AND NET TRANSFERS ($ MILLION)

Year	Gross Disbursement	Debt Servicing	Net Transfers	NT as % of GD
1960-1	342	17	325	95
1988-9	2487	1125	1362	55
1989-90	2202	1232	970	44
1990-1	2045	1316	729	36
1991-2	2366	1513	853	36
1992-3	2436	1648	788	32
1993-4	2561	1731	830	32
1994-5	2584	1810	774	30

Source: Ministry of Finance.

goes into debt servicing than the amount Pakistan actually receives. In 1995, for example, the total amount transferred to Pakistan was $774 million, while the debt servicing for the year amounted to $1810 million. Effectively, most of the $2.5 billion given to the country went into servicing debt. The magnitude of the change is illustrated by comparing the figure for 1960. In that year, only 5% of aid went into debt servicing. This of course reflected the early days of the aid relationship. Grants were prominent and debt was yet to be accumulated. But the comparison is useful to the extent that it provides a reminder of the intense short term pressures faced by present governments. Problems have accumulated and the vicious circles discussed in Chapter 2 have begun to bite.

Over the last decade, the national external debt has gone up, on average, by $1 billion every year. Total outstanding debt was $21 billion by 1995, approximately 40% of the nation's income. Such a situation adds to the intense pressure on the country to grow in the region of 6 to 7% annually. A bad half-decade, as the 1990s have been, create immediate pressures on debt servicing, employment, and living standards.

In view of the declining role of aid in augmenting available resources, the policy influence is disproportionately high. This is largely because globalization and opening up of economies have effectively conferred the status of credit ranking agencies to the Bretton Woods institutions. Foreign private capital looks to adherence with a World Bank-IMF programme as an indicator of stability. The more prosperous countries of Eastern Asia do not need such an endorsement but those with weaker economies, such as Pakistan, wishing to attract FDI and to service their debts need to maintain credibility.

The debt servicing burden is mounting at present and it seems plausible that Pakistan will ask for debt rescheduling in the near future. While the volume is quite substantial, the debt has been acquired at an average interest rate of 4% and the repayment period is generous. These concessional terms are further eased by bilateral adjustments. The 1980s $4.2 billion USAID package was virtually a grant, except for the PL-480 component. In spite of this concessional profile,

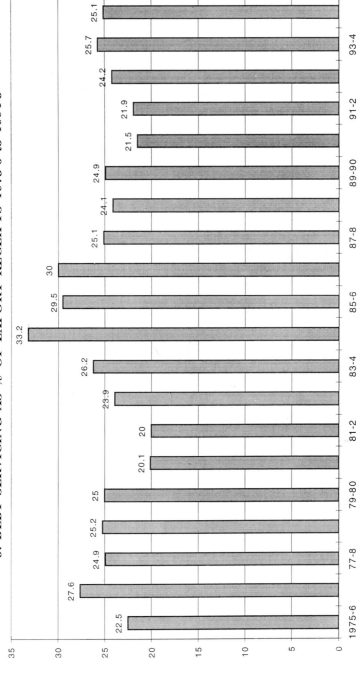

5. DEBT SERVICING AS % OF EXPORT RECEIPTS 1975-6 to 1994-5

6. DEBT SERVICING AS % OF GNP 1975-6 to 1994-5

Year	Value
1975-6	1.8
	2
77-8	1.7
	2.1
79-80	2.3
	2
81-2	1.5
	2
83-4	2.1
	2.5
85-6	2.5
	2.9
87-8	2.9
	2.8
89-90	3.1
	2.9
91-2	3.1
	3.2
93-4	3.4
	3.4

Pakistan's ability to manage its debt position remains precarious. The economy has made slow progress towards undertaking structural reforms which would assure a better capacity to earn foreign exchange through export expansion.

By the mid-1990s, a quarter of export earnings were going into servicing debt (*see* Figure 5). This amounts to 3.4% of national income (*see* Figure 6). In other words, Pakistan is now spending more on servicing debt than on education and health combined. Indeed, while the expenditures on education and health have been cut since the start of the stabilization programme in 1988, debt servicing commitments have risen. These are ominous trends for a country with a literacy rate of 30% and a population growth rate of 3%.

The sharp growth in short-term commercial borrowing to buttress foreign exchange resources and the exponential growth of domestic debt are even more worrying. As noted elsewhere, domestic debt has been acquired at very high interest rates. Domestic public debt is partly crowding out private investment with public consumption. The persisting fragility of the economy forbids any complacency on debt management.

In this regard, one of the measures to consider is linking privatization of state assets to writing off the high interest rate domestic debt. This has been part of the privatization agenda but has not been implemented. Instead of stalling on the privatization programme, the sale of public assets ought to be linked to the retirement of debt.

In sum, in each of the four sub-periods under review, aid has been an important component of the process of structural transformation of the economy. In the 1950s, aid helped lay an infrastructural base and supported a private sector led development strategy. In the 1960s, aid resources and policy input assisted in the acceleration of growth. The 1970s witnessed a shift in government priority towards the development of a capital goods sector. Aid resources played a pivotal role in this transformation. During the 1980s, the revival of the private sector and the maintenance of an impressive growth momentum were assisted by policy dialogue and donor investments. Commodity aid not only provided important balance of payments support but has also periodically assisted in inflation-control policies.

During the 1990s, the aid relationship entered a more confrontational phase. Shrinking global aid budgets and the transfer of resources to the former Soviet Union have been exerting pressure on donors to either withdraw or reduce their activities substantially. At the same time, the cold and the Afghan war-related political imperatives for giving aid to Pakistan are gone.

In addition, Pakistan's economy has performed badly in the 1990s with slow growth, poor employment generation, low domestic savings, high budget deficits, and mounting debt problems. Progress in a number of reform areas has stalled. As a result, donor policy dialogue on direct income tax on agriculture has intensified. Other donors such as the UNDP have raised concerns about the wider problems of governance affecting economic development, particularly Karachi and law and order difficulties. Such donor-financed initiatives have emphasized how the lack of social cohesion is damaging economic prospects.

FUTURE DIRECTIONS

Pakistan's needs remain considerable. In some areas, such as social indicators, South Asia in general and Pakistan in particular is lagging behind parts of Africa. As the largest repository of poverty, South Asia will remain a recipient of aid over the next few years. But the volume of aid to any given country is likely to be disbursed partly as rewards for demonstrated commitment to reforms. In the absence of political imperatives, aid resources will be allocated more through 'competitive bids' based on progress with policy reform. Unless Pakistan undertakes some major reforms, many of which are listed in the last chapter, it is likely to lose out to other South Asian countries as far as aid inflows are concerned.

The move from narrow, project-based lending to a wider, policy-based approach is necessary. While it provides policy substance to the aid dialogue, it is a sad comment that after half a century, Pakistan does not have the domestic institutions to recommend these policy changes. Most of the country's best economists are abroad while others work mainly as consultants for international agencies. The major national institutions, such as the Pakistan Institute of Development Economics (PIDE) and the Applied Economics Research Centre (AERC), are not nearly as effective or important as they should be. In the interests of a more mature aid relationship and greater self respect it is important that these institutions be strengthened. Technical assistance could help fund this institutional restructuring but as important as the resources is the importance given to these institutions by domestic policy-makers.

In view of the relatively small level of inflows and rising debt burdens, Pakistan ought to be developing a framework for a phased elimination of aid. This entails serious measures to raise savings and earn foreign exchange. The move towards more self-reliant growth underscores the need for urgent steps to improve domestic resource mobilization and the strengthening of an export base.

The many contributions and shortcomings of aid in Pakistan's development have been outlined above. In the short-run, aid donors can further assist in policy changes for greater outward-orientation of industry and provision of resources to relieve key physical infrastructure shortages. Donors should also support the introduction of mandatory primary education. But the true test of successful aid is its self-destructive role. The longer term horizon requires a programme for a phased withdrawal. This should be the last decade of aid to Pakistan.

NOTES

1. By the late 1980s, the views of many donors had changed in the face of obvious evidence of the consequences of earlier neglect of social investments. These changes are discussed later.

2. See, for example, Pyatt, G, Noman, O et al.: *Unbalanced Development,* (UNDP, Islamabad, 1988).

3. Planning Commission/EAD: *A Study on High Costs of Aided Projects,* (Islamabad, 1970).

4. The tone of a tense relationship was established in the first meeting between R. McNamara, the World Bank President, and Dr Mubashir Hasan, Finance Minister. Details of the meeting were narrated to the author by the latter in Lahore in 1988.

5. For example, the PPP government approached the World Bank for funding low cost housing as part of the Katchi Abadi scheme. Partly because of government requisitioning of private land, the World Bank expressed unwillingness to get involved.

6. For a discussion of donor involvement and GOP policy on family planning, see Jeffalyn Johnson and Associates: *A Review of United States Assistance to Pakistan, 1952-80* (Washington, 1981).

7. Since most of the remittances are targeted towards poorer segments of society, the rupee depreciation can be expected to have had a positive distributional impact.

8. For further details about the EFF experience, see F. Bilquees: *The IMF Stabilization Package and Pakistan's Stabilization Experience,* (PIDE, 1987).

9. The World Bank was expecting to proceed with a second SAL tranche. See World Bank: *Review of a Relationship,* p.20.

10. Ghulam Ishaq Khan became President in 1988.

11. Comment on Ministry of Finance memo on SAL, quoted by GOP officials, Islamabad.

12. The USAID review of activities takes a candid view of these difficulties. See USAID: *US Economic Assistance to Pakistan,* p.58.

13. Ibid., p.51.

14. World Bank: *Review of a Relationship, 1960-84* (Washington, 1986), p.32.

15. USAID: *US Economic Assistance to Pakistan,* (Washington, 1988), p.34.

16. A structural adjustment facility was backed by sectoral loans in agriculture and energy.

17. World Bank: *Pakistan–Growth through Adjustment,* (Washington, 1988).

18. This point was stressed by the World Bank's Mission Chief in a meeting with the author in Islamabad in October, 1988.

19. Mentioned by the Chief, International Division, Planning Commission during an interview with the author in October, 1988.

20. Dr Mahbubul Haq's meeting with the author, October 1988.

21. Aid agencies have already provided substantial seed money for technical feasibility studies of the Kalabagh dam. The operative constraint is political. Unfortunately the dam has become a symbol of intra-provincial tensions.

22. ADB's willingness is indicated in *Strategies for Economic Growth and Development,* (Manila, 1985), p.39.

23. Indeed, a Planning Commission study suggests that low ICOR is partly due to accounting features such as omission of livestock investment and underestimation of small scale and informal sector investment. In internationally comparable sectors, Pakistan ICOR was not appreciably different. Comments made by Dr Akram Sawati, Chief Macroeconomist, Planning Commission during an interview in October, 1988.

24. Domestic savings rate fell from 7.8% to 5.4%.

25. 'The international donor community now has grave concerns about the size of the chronic deficits which the GOP has been running. With the benefit of hindsight, we now believe the USAID may have contributed to the problem by permitting CIP and PL-480 generated local currencies to pick up a portion of the GOP budget deficit, thereby reducing the pressures for needed policy reform.' USAID: *US Economic Assistance to Pakistan.*

26. 'Economic aid has been the hand maiden of Pakistan's defence requirements...Pakistan's military build-up has placed in jeopardy its ability to meet pressing economic and social investments.' Ibid, p.6.

27. GOP: *Pakistan Economic Survey, 1983/84.*

28. USAID: *Economic Assistance to Pakistan,* p.21 and p.13.

29. It should also be noted that PL-480 edible oil imports fill only part of the demand-supply gap. The rest is made up mainly by private sector imports. PL-480 prices are typically higher than privately imported sources. Terms of PL-480 assistance are generous: 3% in 30 years. Shipping costs are met by the United States government. Data provided by Mr Abid Hussain, PL-480 Desk Officer, Economic Affairs Division.

30. Average annual inflation during the Fifth Plan was 8.8%. During the Sixth Plan it was 6%.

31. Indeed, it was discord regarding overshooting of monetary targets which terminated the EFF in the third year of operation.

32. There is considerable debate on the extent to which these changes provide a 'one-off' inflationary spurt, as opposed to continuing excess monetary expansion, which would have occurred in the absence of these changes. To some extent, these policies are designed to relieve inflationary pressures elsewhere in the economy. But the correction of resource allocation distortions often releases 'suppressed' inflationary pressures, e.g. if removal of fertilizer subsidy raises food prices which have a ripple effect on the rest of the economy.

33. Growing tensions between aid donors and the government of Pakistan have been evident in recent years. These were apparent, for example, in the cancellation of the World Bank President's visit to Pakistan in September 1996 and the withholding of IMF loans. There are many areas where sound macroeconomics and equity are linked. If such reforms continue to be blocked the current political order is likely to collapse under intense pressures.

34. For details see the Asian Development Bank: *A Country Development Strategy for Pakistan,* (Manila, 1995).

CHAPTER 7

IMPRESSIVE GROWTH WITH
LOW HUMAN DEVELOPMENT
The Paradox of Pakistan's Development

If you can look into the seeds of time
And say which grains will grow, and which will not,
Speak then to me...

Shakespeare
Macbeth, 1.3.56-8

You *Tell Us What to Do*

When we launched life
on the river of grief,
how vital were our arms, how ruby our blood.
With a few strokes, it seemed,
we would cross all pain,
we would soon disembark.
That didn't happen.
In the stillness of each wave we found invisible currents.
The boatmen, too, were unskilled,
their oars untested.
Investigate the matter as you will,
blame whomever, as much as you want,
but the river hasn't changed,
the raft is still the same.
Now *you* suggest what's to be done,
you tell us how to come ashore.

When we saw the wounds of our country
appear on our skins,
we believed each word of the healers.
Besides, we remembered so many cures,

it seemed at any moment
all troubles would end, each wound heal completely.
That didn't happen: our ailments
were so many, so deep within us
that all diagnoses proved false, each remedy useless.
Now do whatever, follow each clue,
accuse whomever, as much as you will,
our bodies are still the same,
our wounds still open.
Now tell us what we should do,
you tell us how to heal these wounds.

An extract from *The Rebel's Silhouette,* a collection of Faiz Ahmed Faiz's poetry, translated by Agha Shahid Ali (Gibbs Smith, Utah, 1991)

تم ہی کہو کیا کرنا ہے

جب دُکھ کی ندیا میں ہم نے
جیون کی ناؤ ڈالی تھی
تھا کتنا کس بل بانہوں میں
لہو میں کتنی لالی تھی
یوں لگتا تھا دو ہاتھ لگے
اور ناؤ پورم پار لگے
ایسا نہ ہوا، ہر دھارے میں
کچھ ان دیکھی منجدھاریں تھیں
کچھ مانجھی تھے انجان بہت
کچھ بے پرکھی پتواریں تھیں
اب جو بھی چاہو چھان کرو
اب جتنے چاہو دوش دھرو
ندیا تو وہی ہے ناؤ وہی
اب تم ہی کہو کیا کرنا ہے
اب کیسے پار اترنا ہے

جب اپنی چھاتی میں ہم نے
اس دیس کے گھاؤ دیکھے تھے
تھا دیدوں پر وشواس بہت
اور یاد بہت سے نسخے تھے
یوں لگتا تھا بس کچھ دن میں
ساری بپتا کٹ جائے گی
اور سب گھاؤ بھر جائیں گے
ایسا نہ ہوا کہ روگ اپنے
کچھ اتنے ڈھیر پرانے تھے
ویدوں کی ٹوہ کو پا نہ سکے
اور ٹوٹکے سب بیکار گئے
اب جو بھی چاہو چھان کرو
اب چاہو جتنے دوش دھرو
چھاتی تو وہی ہے گھاؤ وہی
اب تم ہی کہو کیا کرنا ہے
یہ گھاؤ کیسے بھرنا ہے

لندن ۸۸ء

INTRODUCTION

Pakistan[1] has a record of an impressive growth of incomes but its human development is low, leading to severe constraints.[2] Pakistan's GDP growth performance has been the highest in South Asia, while its social indicators have lagged behind. This is reflected in Pakistan's real per capita GDP, $1970 in purchasing power parity terms, which is approximately 41% higher than that of India's.[3] At the same time, the profile of the country's social indicators is one of the worst in the world, and compares favourably only with countries such as Afghanistan and the poorest of the sub-Saharan African nations. Indeed in some areas, such as female literacy, parts of Pakistan have a poorer record than that of almost all of Africa.[4] Further, as documented later in the chapter, Pakistan's income distribution and poverty trends have worsened sharply in recent years. During the 1990s, the economy is suffering from a degree of stagflation, since inflation has nearly doubled while per capita output has stagnated. Therefore, pursuing a more equitable development strategy entails policy and institutional reforms which can revive the growth-generating capacity, while altering major allocative and distributional shortcomings.

This chapter is divided into three sections. The first provides a summary of the strategic challenges confronting the economy. Sustaining rapid growth and improving social indicators require that Pakistan should address strategic imperatives which are discussed below. The emergence of these particular concerns at this juncture of the economy's evolution is a reflection of the pattern of development pursued since independence.[5] The second section attempts an explanation of how Pakistan was able to achieve high growth with low human development and why the strategy followed thus far has run into bottlenecks. Finally, the third section provides a review of the government of Pakistan's (GOP) policy response to these challenges. This analysis examines the achievements and the difficulties encountered in the process of reform.

STRATEGIC IMPERATIVES CONFRONTING PAKISTAN'S ECONOMY

Economic management during the 1990s is confronted with the dilemma of addressing certain critical concerns some of which entail difficult policy choices and conflicts particularly in the short run.

(i) The first policy responsibility of the GOP is to ensure low inflation and stable growth through macroeconomic stability.[6] By the late 1980s, growing fiscal and balance of payments deficits were reflective of unsustainable imbalances. Subsequent efforts to control the macro-imbalances have been mixed. Current attempts at stabilization have entailed a contraction in demand, as well as rising real interest rates. In the short-run, neither contributes to the stimulus required for reviving growth. None the less, providing a stable macroeconomic environment remains a critical objective. This stability has to be accompanied by measures to **increase the pool of investible resources;** national savings and investment rates have to improve appreciably, while foreign capital inflows are also needed to ease the savings and foreign exchange constraints to sustained growth.

(ii) The second key aim, and the test of the efficacy of the liberalization programme, is a substantial **expansion in exports of manufactured goods**. The thrust of the current reform programme is to shift incentives in favour of production for external markets. An adequate supply response in labour-intensive manufacturing exports is a key element in poverty alleviation.

(iii) **Reducing population growth** is the third concern. Pakistan is in the midst of a population explosion and continues to have one of the worst fertility ratios in the world. Pakistan's population growth rate is the highest amongst the ten most populous countries in the world.[7] Both direct measures such as improved access to contraceptive supplies, and indirect measures such as an expansion in girls' primary education need concerted attention.

(iv) The fourth issue is the **quality of Pakistan's human capital**. Pakistan's prospects for diversifying its economy are constrained by the shortage of technical, scientific, and managerial manpower. Improving the capacity to manage and transform a modern economy requires human capital deepening, while the expansion in literacy and cognitive capacity are important facilitators for a more efficient, open economy. While it is widely recognized that Pakistan's development strategy has to undergo a fundamental change as far as attention to human capital development is concerned, it is worth noting that the shares of both public education and health expenditures in GDP have declined since the start of the Structural Adjustment Programme.

These four key outcomes require a careful balance between the instruments of the market and the state. There is little doubt that efficient growth requires increased use of the market, and a general withdrawal of the state from production and trade. However, markets alone cannot ensure equitable development. The state has to take responsibility for effective execution of some key functions; the two tasks discussed below need, in particular, to be performed more effectively than is the case at present.

(v) The **quality of social sector service provision** requires major improvement. The reduced role of the state implies a narrower concentration and a more effective machinery for the delivery of social services. However, the quality of the government's basic service provision is low and deteriorating. In areas such as education, the issue is not exclusively one of resource shortcomings. There are fundamental institutional problems, one of the most serious of which is the lack of quality manpower at the technical and managerial level. Similar systemic problems affect the provision of virtually all economic and social services. Addressing these shortcomings is a necessary precondition for defining future directions in the supply of government services.

(vi) Finally, the state in Pakistan needs urgently to **improve the calibre of governance**.[8] Two issues of governance have a direct impact on economic development—(a) the failure to maintain reasonable control over **law and order** and (b) the exercise of arbitrary power by the institutions of the state due to the absence of a **separation of powers**. At present, the government is unable to perform adequately the responsibility for ensuring law and order. Further, the effectiveness of government operations is handicapped increasingly by the lack of separation of powers between the executive, the legislature, and the judiciary. While the causes for such institutional disturbance are rooted in the country's political evolution, their impact on economic development is increasingly significant. For example, the civil unrest in the principal commercial city and port, Karachi, is likely to have a direct bearing on exports of manufactured goods and foreign direct investment in tradables. No country in the world has become a successful manufacturing exporting nation in which the central commercial city and port are in the shape that Karachi is in.

These six issues of primary strategic concern provide a summary of the key objectives, as well as the instruments required, to shape Pakistan's economy over the next decade. The significance of these issues is highlighted in the subsequent chapters. Chapters 2, 3, and 6 provided an explanation for the economy's evolution and why these particular concerns have acquired such importance.

How fast incomes grow and how widespread the benefits are from this increase in production are outcomes of central concern to economic development. The extent to which policies and institutions can affect these outcomes are the primary consideration for economic management. These issues are universal and much of the recent debate in industrial economies, after the virtual demise of economies with monopoly public ownership, has been on the differing outcomes associated with capitalism. Most of the industrial economies have impressive records on poverty alleviation but the degree of inequality differs considerably. Japan is by far the most egalitarian society in terms of the distribution of income, and is followed by Germany and Sweden. The most unequal of the richer societies is the United States, followed by Australia, New Zealand, and Switzerland.[9] Over the 1980s, inequalities have grown in societies such as Britain and the

United States due largely to excessively market-oriented liberalization policies.

Thus, not only have development strategies in industrial economies differed in their equity outcomes but recent policy shifts have also adversely affected income distribution in many countries. There is convincing evidence that the more egalitarian societies have greater social cohesion, as reflected in the scale of crime. It is also argued that this greater equality has not been at the cost of high growth and poverty reduction. Indeed, labour productivity growth appears to have been faster in the more equal capitalist societies in recent years.[10]

The differing outcomes associated with capitalist economies have led to debates about the effect of the state intervening directly in markets or influencing outcomes through economic and social policies.[11] The same set of issues has emerged in attempts to understand the reasons why East and South East Asian economies have been so successful in achieving highly equitable development.[12] In this section, Pakistan's record on growth, poverty alleviation, and income distribution will be assessed, bearing the East Asian experience in mind. In addition, this analysis will be complemented by examining other sources of divisiveness or cohesion in Pakistan. It is argued that the concern over governance issues relates to the manner in which they have contributed to growing divisions in Pakistani society.

To what extent have the poor benefited from Pakistan's economic development? How equitable has the development strategy been? The answers to these questions are complex. Recent trends suggest that the first half of the 1990s has been a period of considerable stress for large sections of the poor, while income distribution has worsened and social expenditures have been cut. A longer-term perspective suggests that Pakistan has a rather impressive record as far as reducing the worst forms of poverty is concerned. The proportion of population without the minimal calorie intake requirement has been reduced substantially since independence. Income distribution trends tend to be strongly correlated to growth; periods of high growth tend to improve income distribution, whereas low growth has tended to

worsen it.[13] In recent years, income distribution has worsened
sharply and is now worse than it was in the 1950s.

PAKISTAN'S ECONOMIC EVOLUTION

*The section below is a summary of Pakistan's evolution,
which has already been described in Part A of this book.
Readers may wish to go on to the section on poverty and
income distribution. The book is designed so that Parts A
and C are self-contained, hence the repetition.*

The pattern of growth has had a direct bearing on poverty
and income distribution.[14] Once the economy recovered from
the shock of partition, it has been able to sustain growth,
which was particularly high in the 1960s and the 1980s. The
slowdown in growth during the 1990s should be temporary
and a revival of the growth momentum is likely if certain
policy changes are implemented. However, our concern is
not merely with the revival of growth, important as it is for
poverty alleviation. Other actions are required to create a
less divisive and more cohesive society. These measures are
discussed after an explanation is provided for why Pakistan
has been able to sustain such a respectable rate of growth.[15]

In examining the long-term reasons for the country's output
expansion, four deserve particular emphasis. Many of these
points were made earlier in the text, but the review below
consolidates and summarizes the argument. The first was
the early decision to create and harness an entrepreneurial
class for private sector led development. Unlike India, the
state in Pakistan chose not to take over the 'commanding
heights of the economy'. The role of government was viewed
as very strongly supportive of private sector development.
However, it was recognized that leaving markets to produce
the desired result would not be sufficient. Accordingly, the
state intervened extensively in markets. Financial sector
institutions were created to direct credit, industrial output
was protected through tariffs, and fiscal incentives were used
to bolster profits and thus the return to capital. In other
words monetary, fiscal, and trade policy was used to create
and facilitate the private sector. In some instances, the state
went further and actually established industrial enterprises

in areas where the private sector was reluctant to invest, and then handed over these enterprises to private owners. Thus, with respect to extensive state support for the private sector, Pakistan's experience was similar to that of much of East Asia. Virtually all countries in South East and East Asia went through a phase of import substitution,[16] with strong state support for private sector led development. In Pakistan, the decision to create an enabling environment for the private sector, associated closely with Jinnah,[17] provided an entrepreneurial stimulus frequently absent in other South Asian countries. The private sector has played a dynamic role in both industry and agriculture.

The second explanatory feature for Pakistan's growth performance is the generally high quality of macroeconomic management. Inflation has remained low and fairly stable. External sector management has been sound. These achievements are mirrored in relatively low budget and balance of payments deficits.[18] Thus, with respect to sound macroeconomic management too, the experience of Pakistan has resembled that of East Asia.[19]

The third important factor has been the high returns to research and the commercial application of the results. 75% of Pakistan's crop production is under irrigation. This received a major boost through the 'green revolution' seed-water-fertilizer technology of the 1960s, which was so favourably suited to irrigated agriculture. While agricultural growth in the 1960s largely represented returns to international investments in research, the productivity increases in cotton during the 1980s were due principally to the work of domestic research institutes. In both cases, agricultural research provided a strong stimulus to growth. In this respect too, Pakistan's growth momentum benefited in a manner which was similar to that of East Asia although perhaps not on the same scale. Agriculture in the latter has benefited enormously from an efficient and high quality research and extension service.[20]

Finally, variables associated with Pakistan's external linkages have assisted the growth process. Migration to the Middle East in particular provided a strong demand stimulus because of the large volume of remittances.[21] Migration also reduced pressure on the domestic labour market and thereby assisted in real wage rises, both from the demand side in the output markets, as well as the supply side in the labour market. The other aspect of external links which aided growth has been aid inflows. Pakistan has been a major recipient of aid which has helped relieve the investment constraint, particularly on physical infrastructure and the balance of payments constraint on growth (*see* Chapter 6).

These four factors provide an explanation for Pakistan's good growth performance. Most of these determining variables were also evident in much of South East and East Asia. While these similarities are extremely important, they contain a partial explanation since our focus has been exclusively on growth generation. There are other respects in which East Asian development differed fundamentally from Pakistan's.[22] Perhaps the most important divergence has been in the sense of the more inclusive capitalism[23] pursued in the more eastern parts of Asia. This is most evident in education, health, and population welfare indicators.

Explanations for the divergence in development performance need to account for a mix of economic and political factors. During the 1950s and 1960s, the parallels between Pakistan and East Asia were obvious. Both were governed by an ostensibly modernizing elite, pursuing a private sector led development strategy, with a strong supporting role of the state. This framework considered 'right wing' at the time has led, ironically, to highly equitable development in East Asia. A similar result has not been evident in Pakistan. In spite of the analogies there were important differences in policy which account for the wide divergence in outcomes. Both the resemblance and the considerable contrast were analysed in Chapters 1 to 5.

The manner in which Pakistan's development strategy differed from that pursued in Eastern Asia is explored in more detail below.

In order to examine the dissimilarities with Eastern Asia, one has to examine critical differences, particularly with regard to social investments. Some of the major policy decisions which determined the difference can be divided into two time periods: 1950-70 and 1971-95. An explanation of the differences is attempted after the summary of the dissimilarity in policy-orientation.

1950-1970

Perhaps the single most important indicator of the divergence in the development ethos between Eastern Asia and Pakistan is the explicit pursuit of 'functional inequality' in the latter. The concept of functional inequality was articulated in formal policy documents and reflected in the statements of planners.[24] The rationale of the policy was a redistribution of incomes towards profits, which would raise the rate of private savings[25] and thereby accelerate the rate of growth of the economy. Thus, unlike the inclusive capitalism of Eastern Asia, Pakistan's development strategy, while sharing the emphasis on private sector led growth, differed fundamentally in its approach to equity. It is therefore not surprising that a sense of divisiveness has been far more prevalent in Pakistan.

This development ethos also implied targeting government expenditures in support of the higher income groups. Thus, the pattern of government expenditure was disproportionately skewed towards the higher income classes. A logical outcome was the neglect of social investments at the primary level. These were left to the market, with the obvious result that those without effective demand were not provided with basic education, health, or population planning services. The impact of this neglect was clearly not appreciated at the time. The absence of such social investments, particularly when they are accompanied by measures which reduce infant mortality, have typically contributed to enormous demographic .pressures. Such investments in the social sectors played a significant role in reducing supply side pressure on the labour market in Eastern Asia.[26] They assisted in raising per capita incomes and appear to have had a strong influence in altering the role of women in the labour market. Pakistan's neglect of basic social investments in the first two decades, on the other hand, contributed to explosive demographic pressures and reinforced the pattern of low female participation in the labour force.

The third influence on Pakistan's pattern of development were aid donors. The country's participation in US-sponsored regional security pacts[27] provided access to substantial infusions of bilateral aid resources.[28] Along with the aid resources came policy advice. This took many institutional forms,[29] but seems to have provided intellectual support for the doctrine of functional inequality. Thus, donor policy advice reinforced the bias towards a development strategy which proved to be divisive.

The fourth influence relates to the restrictions on public expenditures. A resource allocation decision often put forward for Pakistan's low investments in human capital is said to be defence expenditure. While it is true that Pakistan's fragile security situation implied a relatively heavy emphasis on defence expenditures, the importance of this factor should not be exaggerated. Public expenditure priorities lay elsewhere, even when account is taken of defence commitments. The pattern was established in the first two decades, when Pakistan incurred substantial costs in the construction of a new capital city, Islamabad,[30] partially at the expense of basic social expenditures.[31] This pattern was to be repeated in the early 1990s, when the launching of a major motorway squeezed resources for the social action plan. Further, countries such as Israel who have had an even more serious security problem than Pakistan have not neglected important social investments. Similarly, South Korea, Taiwan, and Indonesia are examples of countries with specific security concerns but who maintained reasonably equitable policies in the social sectors. In brief, high allocations to defence were not incompatible with a more sustained effort in basic education and health.

1971-1995

The first phase of policy-making involved an assortment of decisions, as noted above. These set the mould for a development strategy which paid little attention to equity considerations. While the break-up of the country was due to regional political differences and was perhaps inevitable,[32] economic policy did little to ease the strains. In view of this record, it is somewhat ironic that economic policies after the break-up of the country did not yield different results. This was in spite of the fact that the 1970s witnessed a radical departure in many areas, and constituted a far more explicit recognition of equity imperatives. The three policies which affected growth, poverty, and income distribution in the second phase are summarized below.

The first point to emphasize is that attempts to address the inadequacy of social investments during the 1970s occurred in a very different economic and institutional context. Two changes from the development path chosen since 1947 need particular emphasis. The PPP· government's response to the perceived inequities of the Ayub era was to nationalize industry and engage in widespread civil service reforms.

While both factors were motivated by equity concerns, the anxiety about ethnic redistribution had a strong influence on reforms.[33] The reforms resulted in certain undesirable consequences, which curtailed the implementation of social investments. In particular, the nationalizations which affected the industrial, agricultural, and financial sectors reversed the private sector led development strategy pursued since independence. Private sector investment plummeted and the growth momentum suffered. Unlike any country in Eastern Asia, Pakistan nationalized and through the process squandered the stability that was associated with the consensus on private sector led development in the East. At the same time, civil service reform undermined the efficiency of the executive.

Again, in sharp contrast to Eastern Asian states which protected the efficiency and autonomy of technocratic civil servants, Pakistan's reforms moved in the opposite direction. While in principle they were designed to increase professionalism, in practice they led to a rise in patrimonial influences. Due to the increased induction of political appointees, the public sector started providing an employment subsidy. As the experience of other countries shows, such employment subsidies adversely affect the efficiency of performance.

The result of these reforms was that the government was unable to execute its mandate in the social sectors. Lower growth had deprived government of much needed revenues, while a more insecure bureaucracy was unable to adequately handle its expanded role. Conflict with aid donors over the broader reforms prevented many, such as the World Bank, from supporting the expansion of the social sectors.[34] Thus the opportunity to redress the neglect of social investments was missed in the 1970s due to the wider policy shocks to the economy.

The second important factor, particularly for poverty and income distribution, was the GOP's response to the opportunities provided by the oil shock of 1973-4. Pakistan took advantage of the resultant Middle East boom by adopting a policy of exporting manpower. Since much of the migration was of semi-skilled and unskilled labour, there were extremely positive effects on poverty and income distribution. Conversely, the end of the Gulf boom has contributed to the worsening of income distribution in the 1980s, documented later in the chapter. Thus, during the decade between the mid-1970s and the mid-1980s, Pakistan witnessed more equitable development, not due so much to internal reform but because of labour exports. By the 1990s, this fortuitous source had a much reduced impact, as remittances fell sharply from the peak achieved in 1982-3.[35]

Finally, as in the 1960s, the high growth performance between 1980-8 had beneficial impacts on both poverty reduction and income distribution. Improvements in both aspects of equity were due to a mix of the Middle Eastern boom and the rapid growth in incomes. But there was a general absence of measures to address structural problems. There was virtually no attempt at asset redistribution, expanding direct taxation of wealthier groups, or investing in the human capital of the poor. Indeed, there were periods during the 1980s when public education expenditures fell while the economy was growing rapidly. Even worse was the attitude towards population planning in a country in the midst of a demographic crisis. The government's attitude to population control measures bordered on hostility, which was in sharp contrast to the attitude adopted in all of the Eastern Asian countries.

In sum, the second period of economic policy-making was dominated by conflicts over the relative roles of the public and private sectors. Unlike Eastern Asia, Pakistan underwent a sharp reversal of a private sector led development strategy. The 1980s represented a reassertion of the pre-1970 strategy towards private entrepreneurs and led to the related reversal of nationalizations. The struggle over the relative roles of the private and public sectors disguised the neglect of critical social investments. While the public sector relinquished its role in production and trade, it failed to perform critically important functions required for equitable development. Even in service sectors such as education, the private sector mushroomed while the state was unable to make the necessary adjustments to improve the quality of primary or higher education.

Consequently, this period marked a sharp divergence in the forms of capitalism pursued in Pakistan and Eastern Asia. The latter having retained the supremacy of the private sector in production and trade moved, with extensive state support, from import substitution towards export led growth. Labour-intensive manufacturing exports were critical for poverty alleviation and improvements in income distribution. Further, the state broadened its role in social investments, expanding and improving the primary sectors in education and health. At higher levels, the state concentrated on upgrading technology and management capacity. The policy shifts and uncertainties in Pakistan on the other hand had prevented a concerted drive towards export expansion and diverted the state from playing an important role in regulating markets and intervening in social sectors.

There are several social and political reasons for the inconsistencies and differences between the development strategies pursued by Pakistan and much of Eastern Asia. These deeper causes were explored earlier and are summarized below: (i) Communal and ethnic divisions in South Asia have tended to dominate class polarizations. This led to a mixture of motives in state intervention in the economy. Pakistan's nationalizations of industrial and financial assets were due partly to ethnic elite conflict. But the consequences were important for both export performance and social investments. (ii) The threat of communism was more intense in Eastern Asia. In particular, the Chinese revolution exercised a considerable influence on elite response. This took different forms in particular countries—such as extensive land reforms in Korea and Taiwan and a serious commitment to the expansion of primary education and health in most countries.[36] As a result, none of the Eastern

Asian countries adopted functional inequality as an objective of development policy, leading to a major difference in the form of capitalism which drove the modernization process. (iii) The model of inclusive capitalism pursued in Japan in the aftermath of the Meiji restoration of the late 19th century exerted a strong influence on the region. Thus, countries wanting to avoid a communist take-over were under pressure to pursue a type of equitable capitalism, a practical model for which was provided by the Japanese experience.

In Pakistan the lack of a perceived threat from 'below', and the salience of ethnic/regional cleavages, may have eased the adoption of functional inequality in the first phase, and led to damaging nationalizations in the second. Irrespective of the underlying socio-political causes, it is quite evident that the outcomes associated with the two forms of capitalism were strongly influenced by the pattern of social investments.

TRENDS IN POVERTY AND INCOME DISTRIBUTION IN PAKISTAN

There are different dimensions to indicators of equity. These different aspects are not as well correlated as may be expected. Three different aspects of equity are worth noting. The first is the trend with regard to the extent of poverty. This is usually quantified in terms of the proportion of the population under a basic income or calorie level. Such measurements are particularly useful as indicators of what has been happening to those at the 'bottom of the pile'. Poverty line indicators are typically influenced by the rate of growth of the economy since they are linked to employment, a variable which is strongly associated with the rate of output expansion. This is not to deny that the employment elasticity can be determined by policy decisions in the factor markets, so that the jobs associated with a given expansion of output can differ. But the basic point is that employment generation, which is critical for poverty alleviation, is strongly related to growth. Therefore, it follows that economies with a good growth performance are more likely to show a reduction in poverty than those who are unable to grow. Indeed, as documented below, this is the case for Pakistan whose rapid growth is captured in the data on the poorest groups.

A second aspect of equity is trends in income distribution. In principle, this can improve while everyone is worse off and worsen while all groups are better off. This is so because income distribution is not concerned with the level of aggregate incomes but in the manner in which it is divided. Having noted this caveat, it is none the less desirable that income distribution improve or at least does not worsen in a growing economy. This is particularly important if the initial distribution of income is quite skewed. The distribution of income is usually quantified by a measure known as the Gini Co-efficient. Trends in Pakistan's income distribution suggest a strong correlation between high growth and improved income distribution. The latter has, therefore, tended to fluctuate in different periods. However, the important point to emphasize is that Pakistan's income distribution in the 1990s is worse than it has ever been since records are available.

The third aspect of equity is how widespread has been the acquisition of human capital. This is typically measured in terms of variables such as literacy levels and infant mortality trends. Pakistan's development record in these areas has not been encouraging. Further, public expenditures on education and health have fallen during the first half of the 1990s.

The remaining sections of this chapter document poverty and income distribution trends. It is then suggested that recent adverse trends during the 1990s are compounded by other sources of division in Pakistani society which are leading to increased polarization. These additional factors have more to do with problems of governance and politics, rather than economic policy *per se*.

17. SURVEY OF ESTIMATES OF HEAD-COUNT POVERTY IN PAKISTAN
Per cent of Households

Study	Poverty Line	Year	Rural	Urban
Malik (1988)	Rs per capita	1987-8	24	19
Ahmad and Allison (1990)	Rs per capita	1987-8	20	16
Malik (1991)	Calorie intake	1990-1	16	7

Source: Srinivasan (1993).

The results of recent estimates of the population under the poverty line are summarized in Table 17. Malik's study, using a per capita income level as the base line, estimated that 24% of the rural and 19% of the urban population were below this level. Ahmed and Allison's study suggested smaller proportions under the poverty line (20 and 16% respectively). A more recent study by Malik, using a minimum calorie intake as the cut-off point, showed 16% of the rural and 7% of the urban population below this level. A cross-country comparison of Pakistan's performance with regard to the worst forms of poverty is contained in Table 18.

18. PERCENTAGE OF POPULATION BELOW THE POVERTY LINE

Country	Years	First Year	Last Year
India	1972-83	54	43
Indonesia	1972-82	58	17
Malaysia	1973-87	37	14
Pakistan	1962-84	54	23

Source: *The East Asian Miracle*.

This shows that between 1962 and 1984, the proportion of Pakistan's population below the poverty line fell sharply from 54% to 23%. This compares very favourably with India, where 43% of the population remained below the poverty line. The records of Indonesia and Malaysia are even more impressive than Pakistan's and confirm the point mentioned earlier about high growth and poverty reduction. Minimum poverty trends over three decades in Pakistan are summarized in Table 19. While the various studies on poverty come to somewhat different estimates due to problems of data and differences in methodology, there is no argument about the general trend—the worst forms of poverty have declined considerably since independence. Between 1963 and 1985, the proportion of the rural and urban populations under the poverty line declined from 43 to 20%, and 55 to 16%.[37] Dividing the population between the poor and non-poor in conditions of mass poverty is a somewhat arbitrary and limited exercise. But what such calculations do capture

19. SUMMARY OF POVERTY ESTIMATES FOR PAKISTAN, 1973 to 1991

Study	Measure	Poverty line	63-4	67-70	71-2	78-9	84-5	87-8
Naseem (1973)	1959-60 Rs/capita	Rural 250 300 Urban 300 375	43 61 55 70	26 60 25 59	19 58 25 63			
Allauddin (1975)	1959-60 Rs/capita	Rural 250 300 Urban 300 375	57 67 50 71	36 61 30 60	42 65 42 62			
Naseem (1977)	% of 2100 cals RDA	95 92 90	72 54 45	68 46 36	74 55 43			
Mujahdid (1978)	% of 2100 cals RDA	Rural 250 300 Urban 300 375	27 40 36 52	35 48 29 46				
Irfan & Amjad (1984)	1979-80 Rs/capita	109 95	41 32	55 43	41 29			
Kruijk & Leeuwen (1985)	1978-80 Rs/household	Rural 700 Urban 700		73 50	51 30			
Malik (1988)	1984-5 Rs/capita	Rural 159 172 Urban 185 207	37 43 40 49	44 51 34 43		29 35 24 31	24 29 19 26	
Ahmad & Allison (1990)	1979 Rs/capita	Rural 100 Urban 110				25 20	20 16	
Malik (1991)	2550 cals RDA	Rural Urban					21 11	16 7

Source: Compiled from various studies.

are the trends in extreme forms of poverty, which suggest that Pakistan's aggregate performance in this respect has been fairly respectable.

The data on poverty does not, however, capture the developments during the 1990s. As Chapter 2 emphasized, the doubling of inflation and sluggish growth are likely to have had a substantially adverse impact on the poor, including the poorest groups. More recent data on poverty is not yet available but the indications are not promising.

Trends in income distribution are documented in Table 20. The fluctuations in income distribution reveal an interesting pattern. Periods of high growth are typically accompanied by an improvement in the distribution of income. Thus, the period between 1963 and 1968 witnessed an improvement from 0.386 to 0.336. The lower growth of the 1970s was accompanied by a worsening of income distribution, from 0.33 to 0.373. This was followed by the high growth period of the 1980s, which led to an improvement in income distribution between 1980 and 1988. However, a very sharp deterioration is evident towards the early 1990s. As a result, Pakistan's income distribution is currently worse than at any point since reasonably reliable statistics have been available.

20. HOUSEHOLD INCOME DISTRIBUTION IN PAKISTAN 1963-4 to 1990-1

Year	Gini Co-efficient	Income share lowest 20%	Income share middle 60%	Income share highest 20%	Quintile Ratio
1963-4	0.386	6.4	48.3	45.3	7.1
1966-7	0.355	7.6	49.0	43.4	5.7
1968-9	0.336	8.2	49.8	42.0	5.1
1969-70	0.336	8.0	50.2	41.8	5.2
1970-1	0.330	8.4	50.1	41.5	4.9
1971-2	0.345	7.9	49.1	43.0	5.4
1979	0.373	7.4	47.6	45.0	6.1
1984-5	0.369	7.3	47.7	45.0	6.2
1985-6	0.355	7.6	48.4	44.0	5.8
1986-7	0.346	7.9	48.5	43.6	5.5
1987-8	0.348	8.0	48.3	43.7	5.5
1990-1	0.407	7.3	48.2	44.5	6.1

Source: Federal Bureau of Statistics.

This deterioration is particularly worrying in view of the doubling of inflation in the 1990s. These trends in income distribution are confirmed by another measure of equality—the Theil index.

21. THE THEIL INDEX

Year	Theil Co-efficient
1979	0.27
1984-5	0.26
1985-6	0.23
1986-7	0.22
1987-8	0.23
1990-1	0.30

Source: Federal Bureau of Statistics.

An explanation for the link between rapid growth and improvements in income distribution is through the related impact on the labour market. The derived demand for labour accelerates during rapid growth, with the resultant tightening of the labour market leading to increases in real wages.[38] The very sharp recent decline can partially be explained by the slowdown in growth. But clearly other factors are also at work—such as the decline in overseas migration. This factor may be particularly important since it not only puts additional pressure on the labour market on the supply side but also has led to a decline in income flows for many poor families. Thus, with the aggregate labour supply increasing by over 3% annually, the downward pressure on wages can be severe, particularly during a period of slow growth. Other factors, such as the persistent inability to extend the direct tax base and numerous tax exemptions for new firms, may also have contributed to the worsening of income distribution in recent years.

OTHER SOURCES OF INCREASING DIVISIONS IN SOCIETY

The damaging trends in income distribution and poverty during the first half of the 1990s are bad enough. But they do not provide a comprehensive picture of the sense of division and insecurity[39] prevailing in Pakistan. A disenchantment with elite groups is evident[40] amidst a polity increasingly divided in terms of access to power and authority. These sources of divisiveness are largely related to the political arena, although some are related to social policy. The section below provides a summary of the principal arguments regarding sources of insecurity and division.

(i) A divisive factor not related directly to politics is the education policy pursued since the beginning of the 1980s. The decision to allow the private sector into education was a sensible one. Educational standards had fallen substantially since nationalization. The liberalization of the education sector has led to the emergence of a very robust and thriving private sector. While it remains unregulated and the quality varies enormously, many of the private institutions provide a reasonable level of education. Further, they are improving consistently and show every sign of consolidation and quality enhancement.[41] It is probable that the private sector will provide high quality education for the urban middle class. At the same time, the bulk of the education system under public control continues to disintegrate. A very poor quality public sector,[42] in the presence of a dynamic private sector catering for the relatively privileged classes, is a structure which contributes to social divisions.

(ii) Perhaps the most critical problem of governance relates to the lack of separation of powers. There is no apparent constraint on the actions of the executive. This is most evident in cases of political victimization after a regime changes. The new government is able to unleash tax inspectors, security agencies, and other instruments of the state in support of vendettas. In particular, the absence of an effective legal framework sustains the image of a largely unaccountable, if squabbling, elite. The arbitrary manner in which state institutions are used provide visible evidence for the lack of separation of powers. Thus, there appear to be no effective curbs on the misuse of power. Further, the perception that those in power are above the law creates a wide gulf between those who have access to authority and those who do not.

(iii) The capture and ruin of the public sector controlled financial system appears to have contributed to widespread cynicism against rent-seeking elite groups. Credit was rationed not by price but more through political access. Those who acquired loans through such a distorted process have also tended to default on their loans and use access to power to have loans written-off. The publication of lists of those who have abused resources through access to the state contributed to public awareness of the scale of corruption.[43]

(iv) The extensive magnitude of corruption is widely recognized but little determined effort is undertaken to address the problem. This sustains the impression that those in power are net beneficiaries of corrupt practices and therefore have little interest in controlling it.[44] The problem appears not so much that there is corruption in Pakistan; more damaging is the fact that little is done by the legal system to tackle it. Indeed, there are numerous instances where no action is taken even when the evidence is openly available. Such instances can create hostility and contribute to a sense of alienation from the state.

SUMMARY

The above analysis suggests that Pakistani society is under considerable stress during the 1990s. Not only has income distribution worsened sharply but recent impacts on the poor also appear to be discouraging. In addition, social policy and governance problems appear to be contributing to a sense of division and insecurity. In such circumstances, Pakistan can no longer afford to ignore the imperative for undertaking measures which will lead to more equitable development.

The final chapter of the book returns to these issues and contains some policy recommendations.

NOTES

1. Sections of Part C are based on a report on Pakistan's development written by the author for the UNDP, Islamabad, 1995.

2. These constraints have been noted in a number of recent documents. See, for example, The State Bank: *Annual Report, 1993/94*, (Karachi, 1994); The World Bank: *Pakistan: Progress under the Adjustment Programme*, (Washington, 1993), and the

World Bank: *Pakistan: Growth through Adjustment,* (Washington, 1988).

3. India's real GDP per capita (in PPP $) is $1150. The data is for 1991 and is derived from the United Nations' *Human Development Report 1994.*

4. The 4% female literacy rate of Balochistan province, for example, is worse than that of any African country.

5. Pakistan's development experience has been analysed and reviewed in numerous publications. For details see, *inter alia,* Pyatt et al.: *Balanced Development—Towards a Prescription for Social Action,* (UNDP, Islamabad, 1992); Amjad and Ahmad: *The Management of Pakistan's Economy,* (Oxford University Press, Karachi, 1985); Hussain, A: *Strategic Directions for Pakistan's Economy,* (Progressive Publishers, Lahore, 1988), and Noman, O: *The Economic and Political Development of Pakistan,* (Routledge and Kegan Paul International, London, 1991).

6. The macroeconomic stabilization programme is discussed in more detail in Chapter 2.

7. Pakistan is the ninth most populous country, with an estimated population of 124 million, growing at 3% per annum.

8. The reference is not to any particular regime, but to the generic nature of the problems encountered by the state.

9. For a documentation and analysis of trends in income distribution see The Institute of Fiscal Studies: *Income Inequalities,* (London, 1994).

10. For details on this point see Persson, T and Tabellini, G: 'Growth and Inequality', *American Economic Review,* June, 1994.

11. For details, see The Institute for Public Policy Research: *Paying for Inequality,* (London, 1994).

12. The East and South East Asian experience has been subjected to a number of analyses. See, *inter alia,* Evans, P: *Predatory, Developmental and other Apparatuses—*'A Comparative Political Economy Perspective on the Third World State', *Sociological Forum,* (Vol 4, No.4, Fall, 1989); Deyo, F (ed.): *The Political Economy of the New Asian Industrialism,* (Ithaca, Cornell University Press, 1987); Wade, R: *Governing the Market— Economic Theory and the Role of Government in East Asian Industrialisation,* (Princeton, Princeton University Press, 1990), and the World Bank: *The East Asian Miracle,* (Washington, 1994).

13. The explanation is largely to do with the labour market, with high growth tending to tighten the labour market, and therefore exert upward pressure on real wages. The reverse is the case in periods of low growth.

14. The links between growth, poverty, and income distribution are explored later in the chapter.

15. The causes of Pakistan's high growth are discussed in a number of studies. See, *inter alia*, Burki, S.J: *Pakistan's Economy in the Year 2000: Two Possible Scenarios;* Korson, J (ed.): *Contemporary Problems of Pakistan,* (Westview Press, Boulder, 1994); Ahmed & Amjad: *The Management of Pakistan's Economy,* (Oxford University Press, 1984); Kemal, A.R: *Towards an Efficient and Export Oriented Manufacturing Sector,* (Pakistan Institute of Development Economics, Islamabad, 1994); Hussain, A: *Strategic Issues in Pakistan's Economic Development,* (Progressive Publishers, Lahore, 1990), and articles by Mohsin Khan, Mahmoud Hasan Khan, and Naved Hamid in James and Roy (eds.): *Foundations of Pakistan's Political Economy,* (Sage Publications, London, 1993).

16. The only country not to have gone through an import substitution phase appears to be Hong Kong.

17. Mohammad Ali Jinnah, (1876-1948) the leader of the movement which led to the creation of Pakistan, practised law in the commercial city of Bombay. Historians have documented his early and unwavering commitment to a private sector led growth path for Pakistan, in a period where such views were often considered right wing and contrasted sharply with the socialism of the Congress Party under Nehru and Gandhi. For details, see Jalal, A: *The Sole Spokesman,* (Cambridge University Press, 1983); Wolpert, S: *Jinnah of Pakistan,* (Oxford University Press, 1981), and Bolitho, H: *Jinnah, Creator of Pakistan,* (Macmillan, London, 1954).

18. There are however more troubling indicators of macro-management in the 1980s in Pakistan, with signs of reduced restraint on fiscal and balance of payments deficits which has led to the rapid accumulation of debt. These trends were documented in Chapter 2.

19. The quality of macroeconomic management, and its impact on savings and investment, has been emphasized as among the most important aspects of East Asian economic performance. See earlier references on the East Asian experience for details.

20. A number of country studies have documented the importance of technology adoption and the emphasis on research and extension in Asian growth performance. See, for example, Teh Hoe Yoke & Goh Kim Leng: *Malaysia's Economic Vision,* (Malaysian Economic Association, Pelanduk Publications, Darul Ehsan, 1992).

21. At their peak, remittances amounted to $3.2 billion in 1982. For details of the impact of remittances see Gilani, I: *Impact of Middle East Migration on Pakistan's Economy,* (Pakistan Development Review, 1983) and Noman, O: 'Migration and Economic Development' in Hastings and Donnan: *Economy and Society in Pakistan,* (Macmillan, London, 1992).

22. For details of the comparison see the UNDP's *Human Development Report 1994* (New York, 1994).

23. Socialism, on the other hand, was typically associated with extensive direct public ownership of production and trade. In South Asia, the contrast was symbolized by the Indian approach which was strongly biased against the private sector until the 1990s and Pakistan which apart from the 1970s largely followed a more explicit capitalist development strategy.

24. For a discussion of functional inequality, what it implied in terms of policy, and its social consequences, see Griffin, K and Khan, A (eds.): *Growth and Inequality in Pakistan,* (Macmillan, London, 1972).

25. The domestic savings rate was assumed to rise because of the higher marginal propensity to save amongst the richer groups in society.

26. Virtually all of the successful Eastern Asian societies took population planning issues much more seriously than did South Asia. This was evident not only in the expansion of family planning services but in investments in basic education and health which contributed to the desired outcome.

27. For details of the US-Pakistan relationship, see Taher-Kheli, S: *US-Pakistan Relations,* (Yale University Press, New Haven, 1982); Burke, S.M. and Ziring, L: *Pakistan's Foreign Policy—A Historical Analysis,* (Oxford University Press, 1990).

28. Israel, Egypt, and Pakistan have been the major security-related recipients of US aid.

29. Perhaps the most prominent was the presence of the Harvard

advisory group during the 1950s and 1960s, which had a strong influence on the planning commission and other economic policy-making bodies.

30. The capital was shifted from Karachi to a location which borders the provinces of Punjab and the Frontier. There appears to be little rational justification for the creation of Islamabad, either on cost efficiency or regional grounds. Regionally, it alienated the Bengalis, who wanted a shift to Dhaka. Islamabad thereby became a physical representation of where power lay.

31. The transfer of resources and the expenditure priorities it signified were discussed in Chapter 1.

32. The rushed carve-up of the Indian subcontinent in 1947 created fundamentally unsustainable geographical boundaries. Pakistan came into being as a somewhat unique nation-state, separated into two halves by more than a 1000 miles of politically hostile Indian territory. The possibility of such a country succeeding was remote. For accounts and explanation of the break-up, see Hasan, Z: *The Separation of East Pakistan,* (Oxford University Press, 1994) and Jahan, R: *Pakistan—A Failure in National Integration,* (Oxford University Press, 1974).

33. For discussions of the mix of motives influencing reforms in the 1970s see, *inter alia*, Lodhi, M: 'The Pakistan People's Party', (Unpublished Ph.D. thesis, London School of Economics, 1981) and Kennedy, C: *The Bureaucracy in Pakistan,* (Oxford University Press, 1988).

34. Tension between the GOP and the World Bank led to the refusal of the latter to support the social sectors. This point is acknowledged in The World Bank: *Pakistan and the World Bank: Review of a Relationship,* (Washington, 1988).

35. Remittances peaked in 1983-4 to $3.2 billion and fell steadily towards the $1 billion level by the mid-1990s.

36. Indeed, the UNDP's human development report has emphasized the difference amongst countries with respect to the attainment of education and reduction of poverty, for any given level of national income.

37. As mentioned in the text, the precision of the figures should be treated with caution.

38. Real wage data in Pakistan is not as timely and efficient as that produced in many South Asian countries.

39. Part of the insecurity over law and order is the aftermath of the Afghan war, which has resulted in the proliferation of weapons.

40. Numerous commentators, particularly political scientists and journalists, have written extensively on the disillusionment with elite groups, the lack of law and order, and the virtual denial of access of the poor to judicial institutions.

41. This is reflected in the establishment of private teacher training institutes, frequently with the collaboration of foreign universities. The latter include universities such as Oxford, Bradford, the London School of Economics, and Hull.

42. This is particularly important in a country like Pakistan, where there is a limited expansion of primary education. Restructuring public education expenditures, away from the tertiary to the primary may, however, be counter-productive. This can leave a highly frustrated and discontented group of students in poor quality public institutions at the tertiary level. They can be a powerful and vocal source of social discontent. Rather than restructuring, increase is required in aggregate allocations for public education along with institutional reform.

43. Such lists were published by the interim regime headed by Moeen Qureshi, in 1993.

44. The coping strategy under these circumstances can be to seek patronage from those who wield power. But such patron-client relations can undermine the legitimacy of state institutions.

CHAPTER 8

MACROECONOMIC TRENDS AND THE STRUCTURAL ADJUSTMENT PROGRAMME

Hodja was getting old and was having a hard time making ends meet. One day they asked him, 'Hodja, why did God create men?'

Hodja answered without hesitation, 'So they climb hills and pay debts.'

Nasreddin Hodja
15th century Turkish Humourist

INTRODUCTION

The primary aim of economic policy is to ensure rapid growth and reduce poverty. A complex set of variables affects economic growth and the relative importance of the various components influencing growth has frequently been the subject of intense debate. The importance given to particular instruments is a function of the stage of a country's development and the characteristics of an economy. None the less, there is considerable agreement on many of the economic policies required to stimulate growth. In addition to the objective of reducing poverty, the second aim of economic management is more short-term in nature. This has to do with managing aggregate resource flows in a manner which ensures stability. The key factors for a stable economic environment in the short-run are reasonably low inflation and the ability to maintain the country's external liquidity.

Short-term stability can be threatened by macro-imbalances reflected in unsustainable fiscal and current account deficits. Large and growing macro-imbalances[1] essentially reflect the fact that a society is 'living beyond its means'. The causes of the imbalance between aggregate supply and demand may be domestic or exogenous but macro-stability would require contractionary measures.

It is important to recognize that the measures taken to address the dual objectives of economic policy can temporarily be in conflict, i.e. a growth rate may become unsustainable if it causes macro-imbalances, to correct which a reduction in the pace of economic activity is required.[2] These demand contractionary measures can also adversely affect social sector public spending and lead to falling investment. The extent of the impact on long-term growth prospects would depend on how temporary or deep the cuts were. A brief stabilization period is unlikely to undermine the growth potential, while a protracted period of extended cuts in growth-sensitive areas can clearly have a lasting impact on longer-term development.

In this chapter we examine the causes leading to the adoption of the Structural Adjustment Programme in 1988 and how the demands of short-term stabilization have interacted with the need for structural reform to sustain the momentum for equitable growth.

CONSTRAINTS TO SHORT-TERM GROWTH AND LONG-TERM DEVELOPMENT

The first half of the 1990s in Pakistan has been characterized by relatively low growth and high inflation. While the annual average growth in GDP was 6.4% during 1980-9, it fell sharply to 4.7% during 1990-5.[3] A similar adverse development was that the annual average inflation rate rose to 12% during 1990-5, which was considerably higher than the 1980s average of 7%.[4] The much slower growth in incomes along with higher price increases has been due partially to the economic unsustainability of the growth process of the 1980s. While output growth has been adversely affected by exogenous supply side shocks in some years,[5] unsustainable macro-imbalances accounted for the reversal of the 1980s pattern of higher incomes with low price rises.

By the beginning of the 1990s, Pakistan's development strategy had run into two different types of constraints. On the one hand, **immediate growth prospects** were threatened by macro-imbalances, while **longer-term development** and economic diversification were being constrained by the country's previous neglect of human capital investments.

As far as the sustainability of immediate growth was concerned, two related deficits had acquired serious proportions. Budget deficits in the region of 7 to 8% of GDP were financed largely through the creation of domestic debt. However, the rapid accumulation of this debt burden made it impossible to sustain the high budget deficits without recourse to monetary financing. In other words, during the 1980s, the government of Pakistan (GOP) was financing fiscal deficits through a method which, while it was crowding out private investment, was keeping inflation low. While it was possible to do this for a short period, the strategy effectively meant delaying tough decisions and storing up difficulties for subsequent macro-management.

The fact that the GOP was avoiding the implementation of necessary revenue-raising measures as well as curbing some prices by not allowing public service charges to keep up with inflation, imposed difficult choices for macro-management in the 1990s. This uncomfortable macro legacy was the result of inflation being artificially suppressed by administrative control over certain prices, while domestic debt accumulation was temporarily delaying the need for increased tax mobilization. Thus, higher income earners were not being taxed adequately while the spectre of monetary financing of the deficit began to loom as the limits of debt accumulation were reached.

The return to democratic rule during the late 1980s also implied that the burden for taking these tough macro decisions was being transferred from the military to civilian regimes. The civilian governments were unable to adequately address the immediate pressure to contain the fiscal deficit by radical reform of the direct tax system. On the contrary, some regimes[6] continued to expand expenditure and financed the still high deficit by the only remaining possibility— inflationary monetary expansion. Thus pressures of democratic politics pushed for expenditure increases while avoiding the tough decisions which were required in the inherited fiscal climate.

The other major indicator of macro economic imbalance, apart from the continuing fiscal deficiency was the current account deficit, which had risen to 4.3% of GDP by 1988. Growth in the size of the external imbalance was caused by a mix of reduced remittances from the Middle East[7] and a narrow export base on the side of inflows. At the same time, an increase in the debt servicing ratio and a growing import bill were exerting pressure on outflows.[8] While a depreciating rupee was increasing the cost of imports and the accumulation of past debt imposed increasing servicing requirements, the increase in foreign exchange earnings was not rapid enough to compensate for falling remittances.[9]

While these two macro-imbalances have brought the short-term sustainability of high growth into question, the 1990s is also a period in which Pakistan has had to confront the accumulation of problems generated by its previous neglect of human development. The poor quality of human capital was having a detrimental effect on important sectors of economic activity. Government management quality, technology adoption capacity, and productivity increases were being impeded. This was reflected in factors such as a growing aid pipeline due to poor absorptive capacity in the public sector. The lack of quality human capital was one of the critical determinants of project disbursement delays.[10] Similarly, the absence of professionals with adequate technological capacity was evident in the poor functioning of research and extension services for agriculture[11] and public institutions for technology-development in the industrial sector.[12] Such support services have a key role to play in productivity increases and their poor quality in Pakistan was another cost of human capital neglect.

In addition, the lack of social investment led to a dramatic growth in population. This, in turn, was manifested in negative effects on the balance of payments and fiscal position due to rising food import demand and pressures on government expenditure for the provision of services. A related problem was the rapid growth in the labour force which imposed increasing demands on creating productive employment opportunities.

THE POLICY RESPONSE

In order to address these immediate constraints and longer-term shortcomings, the GOP launched an extensive and complex Structural Adjustment Programme (SAP) in 1988. The SAP was developed in close collaboration with the World Bank and the IMF. In accordance with the nature of the problems outlined above, the SAP contained a mix of stabilization, liberalization, and medium-term structural reform measures.

The SAP involved complex sequencing, the implementation of which has been far from ideal. The stabilization measures were concerned with reducing the level of demand and economic activity, thereby easing the pressure on the fiscal deficit and the balance of payments. At the same time, the liberalization component was aimed at improving the incentives for private sector production, particularly for exports. Finally, the medium-term structural reform measures were aimed at improving some of the social indicators and the quality of human capital. This was largely to be done through a multisectoral social action plan.

The principal policy objectives and targets for each of the three aspects of the SAP are summarized below. First, as far as immediate stabilization is concerned, the SAP envisaged a sharp fall in government expenditure from 26% of GDP in fiscal 1988 to 24.6% by fiscal 1990.[13] This demand contraction was supposed to contribute to a planned reduction in real GDP growth to approximately 5.5% per annum for the first three years of the SAP, down from the high growth rates for the 1980s.[14] Thus, fiscal reform was the key to the proposed stabilization measures. It was intended that the immediate expenditure reduction would restrain import demand and reduce the fiscal deficit. Simultaneously, revenue raising measures were anticipated as having a substantive impact in the third year of the adjustment programme, thus easing the contractionary pressures introduced by the expenditure cuts.

The second set of policy measures related to the incentive reform associated with the liberalization process. These included: (i) trade liberalization provisions, consisting of both export promotion and import liberalization; (ii) continued domestic deregulation of principal agricultural crops;

(iii) removal of remaining controls on industrial investments, and (iv) reform of financial markets, including rationalization of interest rates along with more market-oriented debt financing.

Finally, the longer-term human development bottlenecks were to be addressed partially through a social action plan, concentrating on primary health and nutrition, primary education, population planning, and rural water and sanitation. Associated with the social action plan were institutional reform programmes, which were aimed primarily at addressing the deep-rooted governance issues hampering the functioning of the public sector.

IMPLEMENTATION, ACHIEVEMENTS, AND DIFFICULTIES ASSOCIATED WITH THE STRUCTURAL ADJUSTMENT PROGRAMME

In some respects, Pakistan's Structural Adjustment Programme did not constitute an entirely new policy reform initiative. Aspects of the 1988 programme represented a continuity with the process of liberalization evident since the early 1980s. While such continuity was quite evident in measures to expand the role of the private sector through deregulation and privatization, there were substantive changes associated with the SAP. Perhaps the most significant addition was the much delayed attention accorded to social investments in Pakistan. The other important feature of the SAP was the ostensible coherence of a consolidated package of policy and institutional reform. In principle, the structural adjustment process involved a set of inter-linked measures to control short-term macro-imbalances and longer-term measures to sustain the growth stimulus. Measures with regard to the latter implied that the development path previously pursued by Pakistan—consisting of incentives for import substitution and a general neglect of social investment—had run into serious structural constraints. These limitations were hampering the capacity, *inter alia*, to export manufactured goods, while the low level of human development was imposing multiple pressures.

The Structural Adjustment Programme attempted to define a development strategy to deal with these challenges. It was, however, quite evident that implementing this excessively ambitious agenda of simultaneous reform was going to pose substantial problems. Some of the potential implementation difficulties were anticipated:

> The **sequence** of the measures is as important to the success of the recommended programme as the policy reforms themselves. It is difficult to move ahead with structural reforms without a manageable fiscal deficit...a large fiscal deficit makes import liberalization risky, as excess demand spills over into imports and could negate the benefits of introducing more of a market orientation into the financial sector, as extensive borrowing pushes up interest rates...both trade liberalization and domestic deregulation, by opening up protected areas to competition and by changing relative prices, will involve substantial adjustment for firms and workers.[15]

While the importance of proper sequencing was acknowledged, the logic of the argument was not pursued in practice. Since, as we shall document below, the precondition of a 'manageable fiscal deficit' was not met, the wisdom of proceeding with many of the liberalization measures was questionable. Indeed, the imbalanced adjustment process led to a severe foreign exchange crisis in 1992-3.[16] Further, not enough attention was paid to the issue of how social investments were to be protected, let alone increased, at a time when debt servicing payments were to increase. As it happened, increased debt servicing commitments, along with poor revenue mobilization and public expenditure increases on physical infrastructure, meant cuts in social sector expenditures.[17]

A review of the implementation of policies under the ambit of SAP suggests that there has been considerable progress in measures to promote private sector activity. A number of policy changes have also been directed at improving efficiency and transferring more investment resources towards the private sector. Four private sector promoting activities are worth noting:[18]

(i) An extensive privatization programme was launched, resulting in the sale of seventy industrial units and two of the four nationalized banks. The privatization programme has further reduced the role of the state in production and trade thereby reversing many of the nationalizations of the 1970s.

(ii) Policies for stimulating increased private sector activity have taken the form of numerous measures to deregulate the economy; these include abandoning of investment sanctioning and the opening up of areas for private sector investment which were previously reserved for the public sector.

(iii) Trade policy reforms included the reduction of the maximum tariff from 225% to 80%, reduction of non-tariff barriers, abolition of import licensing, and the incorporation of import surcharges into the tariff schedule. Accompanying these measures was a real, effective exchange rate depreciation of 14% between 1988-9 and 1992-3 to maintain international competitiveness

(iv) There were extensive market-oriented financial sector reforms such as the introduction of an auction system for government securities in 1991. Further, the State Bank of Pakistan was made more autonomous with regard to its responsibilities for monetary management and regulation of the financial sector. Private sector scheduled and investment banks were launched as part of the financial sector reforms aimed at increasing savings mobilization and reducing disintermediation.

While these measures created a more favourable climate for the operation of markets, the domestic private sector found itself in a more hostile economic and political environment. Demand contracted due to spending cuts, and interest rates rose while remittances also fell, further reducing demand. Cuts in development spending occurred at a time when shortages of physical infrastructure and utilities were hampering the competitiveness of business enterprises. In addition to adverse economic developments, political violence in Karachi and instability in the policy regime added to the problems of business.

Political economy bottlenecks stalled crucial policy reforms in the fiscal sphere, culminating in open deadlock with the IMF in 1996. Most noticeable was the lack of progress in broadening the tax base and improving the tax administration system. This was reflected in stagnation of the tax revenue-GDP ratio at 14%. Political impediments to expanding the tax base led to measures which further antagonized the environment for business. In the panic to restore the gap in revenue targets, various indirect taxes were levied; for example, in 1996, a 10% increase in excise tax was levied on gas distribution and petroleum products. Instead of lowering taxes, expanding the tax base, and reducing corruption in tax collection, such panic measures worsened the environment for business. Many of these urban groups were in any case opposed to the government in power in 1996 which led to vociferous protests, further fuelling the downward spiral in business confidence.

At the same time, efforts to rationalize expenditures were not successful. Continuing regional security concerns increased military expenditures and the consequences of past accumulation of debt led to the increase in interest payments. Each of these amounted to approximately 6% of GDP annually and consumed nearly 66% of current expenditures.

The failure to address the fiscal deficit while proceeding with financial and other reforms affected performance under the Structural Adjustment Programme in several ways. As noted earlier, the SAP envisaged the necessity of fiscal reform as complementary and/or prior to many of the other reforms. As the analysis below documents, some of the adverse impacts have been a decline in public investment and an acceleration of inflation. Further, the rate of growth of national income has also been 1.5% less every year since the SAP started, compared to the previous six year period.[19]

All of the three above-mentioned adverse developments during the six years of structural adjustment are likely to have had an unfavourable impact on the poor. A slower rate of growth in GDP created less employment than was the case in the six years prior to SAP, and higher inflation is the heaviest tax on the living standards of the poor. However, such before and after comparisons create difficulties and raise complex questions regarding causality. What is incontestable is that the relative performance of aggregate indicators was worse in the six years of SAP than in the previous six years.

The positive stimulator impact of policy liberalization measures could not outweigh the restraining influence of stabilization measures[20] and inappropriate sequencing, as well as domestic and external shocks.

The aggregate comparative performance is summarized in Table 22 below. The comparison demonstrates that average GDP growth fell from 6.3% per annum in the six years prior to SAP to 4.7% in the six years since the launching of SAP. Average annual manufacturing growth fell from 7.9% to 5.7%. However, the decline in the agricultural sector was marginal. The relatively poor performance in the commodity producing sectors was accompanied by a worrying acceleration in inflation, as the rate at which prices were rising nearly doubled. The average inflation rate increased from 5.3% to 10.0%.

As far as the performance of the macro-imbalance indicators was concerned, the results were also disappointing. The average fiscal deficit declined somewhat, from 7.6 to 7.2%, while the average current account deficit actually rose from 3.2 to 4.4%.[21] Thus, the basic objective of the stabilization programme—sharply reducing macro-imbalances—was not achieved. As noted earlier, a sharp rise in inflation and a foreign exchange reserve crisis were the result.

22. SUMMARY OF COMPARATIVE AGGREGATE PERFORMANCE, BEFORE AND DURING STRUCTURAL ADJUSTMENT
(Average annual Growth Rate over 6 years)

	1982-3 to 1987-8	1988-9 to1993-4
National Income*	6.3%	4.7%
Agriculture	3.7	3.6
Manufacturing	7.9	5.7
Inflation**	5.3	10.0
Fiscal Deficit***	7.6	7.2
Current Account Deficit***	3.2	4.4

Source: Ministry of Finance: *Economic Surveys* and the State Bank of Pakistan: *Annual Reports.*

* As measured by the growth of GDP.
** As measured by the consumer price index.
*** Both fiscal and current account deficits are % of GDP.

In sum, there is little doubt that the aggregate performance of the economy was worse in the six years under the Structural Adjustment Programme than in the previous six years. The worsening trends were due largely to the macroeconomic management problems which had accumulated during the course of the 1980s and the reluctance of the GOP to impose a sharp fiscal contraction on the economy. This was due to a mix of institutional rigidities with regard to tax reform, and political pressures to expand expenditures at a time when there was a return to democratic rule. But the new civilian regimes[22] did not have the macroeconomic space to postpone much needed but politically contentious revenue reform. The inability to do so resulted in an inflationary upsurge. This was accompanied by supply side shocks which collectively contributed to the tough economic landscape of Pakistan in the 1990s.

IMPACT ON THE POOR UNDER STRUCTURAL ADJUSTMENT

If the Structural Adjustment Programme had gone according to the planned sequence, three transitional costs on the poor could have been anticipated. These would have been: (i) a reduction in the rate of growth of employment due to the restraint on output growth from stabilization measures in the first three years; (ii) sub-sectoral employment losses in areas where protection was reduced or withdrawn, as well as job losses due to privatization, and (iii) measures to deregulate major crops, particularly wheat, could imply a reduction in food subsidies to the urban poor and the rural landless.[23]

However, an acceleration in the general rate of inflation was not anticipated in the design. Neither was the cut in social expenditures, as government expenditure cuts bore down heavily on both health and education budgets. Thus, the proportion of national income devoted to both health and education fell during the first six years of structural adjustment,[24] while the social action plan was extremely slow to get off the ground.

The impact on the poor has to be judged not by how the SAP was planned but the manner in which it was implemented. In practice, the first half of the 1990s was characterized by a highly inhospitable economic environment, particularly for the poor. Poverty and income distribution worsened, social expenditures declined from an already low base, inflation nearly doubled, and employment generation was sluggish due to low growth. Further, there has been little evidence of a substantial supply response in manufacturing exports, which is the key test of the success of incentive reform and a critical component of effective poverty alleviation in Pakistan.

Economic trends during the six year period since the SAP was launched are documented below. The macro review is divided into five sections: growth performance; savings and investment trends; fiscal performance; balance of payments, and monetary trends. In each area, the six years of the SAP covering fiscal years 1988-9 to 1993-4[25] are compared with the performance in the previous six years. This provides us with some basis for comparison regarding the impact of policies accompanying the SAP, compared to the period before the SAP.[26]

GROWTH PERFORMANCE

The aggregate annual growth performance since the start of the structural adjustment programme is summarized in Table 23. Except for one year, the growth in GDP has been consistently below 6%, which was the average achieved during the decade of the 1980s. None the less, while growth has been slower, it still has been at a pace sufficient to ensure a rise in average income, since per capita income over the six year period has grown by 5.9% (*see* Table 23).

The fluctuations and the lower level of aggregate growth performance were accounted for by a mix of domestic and external factors. In general, contractionary influences on the demand side, both domestic and external, tended to dominate the potential impact of the supply side reforms introduced through the liberalization process. Thus, while many economic agents were made more efficient, these improvements were accompanied by reduced demand for their products.[27] In

23. ANNUAL GROWTH PERFORMANCE SINCE THE START OF STRUCTURAL ADJUSTMENT

	1988-9	1989-90	1990-1	1991-2	1992-3	1993-4
a) Growth Rates						
GDP	4.8	4.5	5.5	7.7	2.2	3.9
Agriculture	6.8	3.0	4.9	9.5	-5.2	2.6
Manufacturing	3.9	5.7	6.2	8.2	5.3	5.6
Services	3.8	4.4	5.2	6.7	4.5	3.8
b) Value						
GNP*		418,881	439,647	455,462	485,362	496,946	515,959
Per capita GNP**	3913	3984	4003	4137	4112	4146

Source: *Economic Survey, 1993-4.*

* Rupees Million, in constant factor cost of 1980-1.
** Rupees in constant factor cost of 1980-1.

addition, as mentioned earlier, recent growth performance has been affected by supply side shocks. The principal causes for reduced economic activity during the SAP period are summarized below.

DOMESTIC

(i) Part of the slowdown in growth was due to demand contraction accompanying the Structural Adjustment Programme. Curbs on government expenditure, particularly the decline in public investment, contributed to the reduction in economic activity.

(ii) The strong growth momentum in the years 1985-8 when the manufacturing sector grew annually by 8.3% was arrested by a decline in the demand stimuli which had fuelled the expansion. The growth had been evidence of an effective supply response to industrial policy reforms initiated since 1984. Relatively adverse domestic and external demand trends as well as law and order related problems in some years have contributed to a poorer performance. Consequently, the growth of the manufacturing sector as a whole fell to 3.9% in the first year of the adjustment programme (*see* Table 23). Indeed, the rate of growth of large scale manufacturing plummeted to 1.1% from the 10.5% recorded a year earlier.

(iii) Exogenous supply side shocks such as the curl cotton virus and extensive floods severely affected agriculture in selected years such as 1992-3 and 1993-4. Agricultural output plummeted in some years, and had corresponding impact on other sectors.

EXTERNAL

(iv) Adverse external developments have also contributed to a reduction in the demand stimulus. Pakistan's terms of trade have fallen, largely due to lower cotton prices and a rise in oil prices. The TOT, for example, fell by 7% in 1989 and a further 13% in 1990.

(v) Exogenous shocks such as the Gulf War affected remittances adversely and thereby added to the reduction in aggregate demand in some years. While many countries were affected by the Gulf War, the poorer nations with a relatively strong economic exposure to the Middle East through the labour market, such as Pakistan, bore a comparatively higher burden. Another adverse external development was the cut-off in US bilateral aid in 1990, which also contributed to the decline in demand and a degree of tension between the GOP and the donor community.[28]

INVESTMENT AND SAVINGS

Pakistan's recent investment and savings performance has to be viewed in the context of a virtual stagnation, at a relatively low level, over the last 25 years.[29] This plateau, however, was reached after a rapid escalation in the investment ratio during the 1960s. Whereas the first decade of independence was characterized by an extremely low investment ratio of 7% of GDP, there was a dramatic acceleration in the early 1960s as the ratio tripled to 21.1% in 1964-5. The doubling of the domestic savings rate from 6 to 12% of GDP financed part of the growth in investment, but a substantial increase in aid inflows was responsible for meeting the savings-investment gap.[30] The pattern of aid financing of a significant proportion of total investment has been maintained subsequently. This is evident in Table 24, which shows the extent to which foreign savings have financed Pakistan's investment.

The 1980s witnessed a substantial decline in the proportion of investment financed by foreign savings, as this share fell from 32% to 20% (*see* Table 24). This decline was largely due to the growth of remittances from the Middle East and, therefore, the increased significance of national savings as a source of investment finance. However, the first half of the 1990s led to a reversal as aid[31] financed a quarter of total investment. Thus, one of the key challenges for macro-policy during the next decade is not only to increase the investment ratio but also to finance this investment through national savings and foreign direct capital, rather than through aid inflows.[32]

24. FINANCING OF INVESTMENT. PERCENTAGE SHARES OF NATIONAL AND FOREIGN SAVINGS

(Annual Averages)

	1960s	1970s	1980s	1990-4
National Savings	70.8	67.5	79.2	74.7
Foreign Savings	29.2	32.5	20.8	25.3

Source: Calculations based on Ministry of Finance, *Economic Survey*, various issues.

While the level of investment and savings has more or less stagnated since the late 1960s, there have been noticeable changes in the relative roles of the public and private sectors. The state's expanded control over production and trade through extensive nationalizations in the early 1970s led to major changes in the share of government in total investment. The private sector's share fell, for example, from 53% in 1964 to 32% a decade later. The reversal of the state's economic dominance during the 1980s is mirrored in the fact that private investment regained its 53% share by 1994.[33]

Investment and savings trends since the start of the Structural Adjustment Programme have been positive. The investment ratio[34] has incréased from an annual average of 17.1% in the six years prior to the Structural Adjustment Programme, to 19.1% in the subsequent six year period. Private sector investment grew from 7.7% to 9.4% of GDP, and more than substituted for the fall in the ratio of public investment during the adjustment period. The rise in the private sector share of investment was due, *inter alia*, to the removal of many regulations—such as those on investment sanctioning limits—and the liberalization of domestic and foreign exchange controls.

The national savings ratio has shown a marginal improvement, from 13.9 to 14.2% over the same period.[35] However, the minimal progression in the national savings ratio compared to the growth in investment has led to the increased reliance on foreign savings noted earlier. Recent financial sector reforms appear to have helped stimulate domestic savings, which rose from 10.5 to 12.2% of GDP. However, gross national savings stagnated at around 14% in the first three years of the adjustment programme, largely due to increased international debt servicing and reduced remittances.[36] Subsequently, there was a sharp rise in national savings, due to a large inflow of the savings held by Pakistanis abroad. The inflows amounted to nearly 2.5% of GDP in 1991-2 and were largely a response to the liberalization of the capital account, which allowed Pakistani residents to open foreign currency accounts. A decline in national savings during 1992-3, partly due to political insecurity, was reversed in 1993-4, as national savings rose from 13.4 to 15.2% of GNP. As a result, the proportion of total investment financed by national savings increased from 66 to 77%.

Many structural adjustment programmes across the world have led a to decline in investment ratios.[37] While the aggregate investment ratio has improved in Pakistan, its low level continues to be an impediment to sustained high growth. The country's investment ratio of 19% of GDP compares unfavourably with that of countries such as China (36%), Indonesia (35%), and Thailand (39%) (*see* Table 25). Even within South Asia, India and Sri Lanka have somewhat better investment ratios. The latter's domestic savings performance is not much better than Pakistan's. Further, Pakistan's national savings are considerably larger than its domestic savings due to the relatively high importance of factors such as remittances. None the less, Pakistan's investment and savings ratios are below the average for countries which share the classification of low human development (*see* Table 25).

Thus, Pakistan's investment and savings ratio is comparable to that of many African countries and lags some way behind the average achieved by medium human development countries, particularly those in East and South East Asia.

25. INTERNATIONAL COMPARISON OF INVESTMENT AND SAVINGS RATIOS
(% of GDP. Figures are for 1991)

	Gross Domestic Investment	Gross Domestic Savings
East Asia		
China	36	39
Korea	39	37
South East Asia		
Indonesia	35	36
Malaysia	36	30
Thailand	39	32
South Asia		
India	24	23
Pakistan	19	12
Sri Lanka	23	13
Average for low human development countries	21	17
Average for medium human development countries	27	28

Source: UNDP: *Human Development Report, 1994* (New York, 1994).

Sustainable and higher growth requires a substantive increase in Pakistan's investment and savings performance. Relatedly, reduced dependence on aid necessitates major improvements in the external sector's efficiency, a strategic policy concern emphasized in Chapter 6. Much of the current agenda in financial and trade reforms in Pakistan is aimed at increasing the investment and savings ratios. In addition, a strong supply response in manufacturing exports, as well as increased foreign direct investment, are the key instruments in reducing aid dependence and the associated accumulating debt servicing burdens.[38]

PUBLIC FINANCE

Historically, macroeconomic management in Pakistan has been prudent enough to promote growth while avoiding excessively high inflation. One of the contributing factors for relatively low inflation has been a fiscal stance that was characterized by manageable deficits and modest recourse to inflationary financing. The state of public finances, however, began to deteriorate during the course of the 1980s. The largely political reluctance towards an expansion of the direct tax base contributed to growing budget deficits. These were financed mainly through the accumulation of domestic debt. This method of financing had the immediate virtue of avoiding inflationary expansion of the money supply. Delaying much needed fiscal reform through the course of the decade imposed a heavy burden on macroeconomic management in the 1990s. Having exhausted the avenues for domestic debt accumulation, successive regimes from the late 1980s onwards have had to confront the task of fundamental fiscal reform, either through major revenue mobilization and/or sharp expenditure cuts. This task has proved to be extremely difficult and the failure to undertake disciplined, difficult measures has threatened the stabilization programme.

The period since the early 1980s, before the start of the adjustment programme in 1988, was characterized by a rapid rise in domestic debt. Pakistan's domestic debt more than *doubled* from 20% of GDP to 44% during the course of the decade.[39] By 1990, outstanding internal debt exceeded the level of external debt. Total external debt, as a proportion of national income, has risen only marginally from 34.2% to 34.5% of GNP during the course of the adjustment programme.[40] Although it involves payments in foreign exchange, external debt has been contracted at a subsidized average interest rate of 4%. The average interest on domestic debt is thrice as high, as the GOP borrowed heavily from the public at high interest rates. As a consequence, most of the debt servicing involves payments to domestic lenders. For example, total debt servicing amounted to 5.6% of GDP in 1992-3, three quarters of which went into repaying domestic debt.[41] The aggregate domestic and external debt servicing burden became larger than defence expenditure during the

1990s.[42] Further, in some years, debt servicing costs have been three times as large as public expenditure on education.[43]

Thus, injudicious and politically hampered[44] fiscal management in the 1980s not only led to a rapid accumulation of domestic debt servicing commitments but also crowded out savings available for private sector productive investment. In other words, Pakistan's extremely low savings rate was helping, *inter alia*, to finance public consumption, rather than going to critically needed investments.

The gravity of the debt situation contributed substantially to the macroeconomic imbalances that were to be addressed by the SAP. In view of the above, it is perhaps not surprising that the most serious shortcoming of the SAP was in the area of public finance. The failure to address the fiscal deficit has threatened to undermine the balance of the stabilization programme. Difficulties in the fiscal arena have not only disrupted the necessary sequence of reforms but have also contributed to rapidly worsening inflation. Indeed, the experience of structural adjustment programmes across the world has emphasized the importance of getting the sequence of reforms properly co-ordinated. Globally, dereliction in addressing macroeconomic imbalances through a proper sequence has been one of the most frequent causes of unstable adjustment programmes.[45]

A central component of, and the prerequisite for a sustainable stabilization programme was the excessively ambitious target of reducing the fiscal deficit by 3.5% of GDP in three years. This implied a major revenue mobilization effort, since the room for expenditure cuts was extremely limited, with debt servicing and defence jointly exceeding total tax revenues. Successive regimes have found it difficult to adhere to the stringent discipline required.

One of the principal difficulties in fiscal management is the inability to raise the ratio of public revenues to the country's income. Indeed, the proportion of national income collected in tax revenue has actually declined during the course of the adjustment process. The tax-GDP ratio has declined from 13.8 to 13.3 (*see* Table 26). This has largely been compensated for by a rise in non-tax revenues from

3.5% to 4.4% of GDP between 1988 and 1994 (*see* Table 26).
The net result has been a virtual stagnation of the total public
revenue-GDP ratio during the 1990s. As a consequence, tax
revenues continue to finance barely half of public
expenditure.[46]

26. TRENDS IN PUBLIC FINANCE
UNDER STRUCTURAL ADJUSTMENT 1988-94
(Percentage of GDP)

	1987-8	88-9	89-90	90-91	91-2	92-3	93-4
A) Revenue							
Total	17.3	18.0	18.6	16.1	18.4	18.1	17.7
Tax	13.8	14.3	14.0	12.7	13.8	13.4	13.3
Non- tax	3.5	3.7	4.6	3.4	4.6	4.7	4.4
B) Expenditure							
Total	26.7	26.1	25.7	25.6	26.7	26.2	23.7
Current	19.8	19.9	19.2	19.1	19.1	20.6	19.2
Development	6.9	6.3	6.5	6.4	7.6	5.6	4.5
C) Overall Deficit	-8.5	-7.4	-6.6	-8.7	-7.5	-8.0	-5.8

Sources: The State Bank of Pakistan: *Annual Report, 1993-4.*
Ministry of Finance: *Economic Survey, 1993-4.*

The poor resource mobilization performance has implied
that periodic success in reducing the deficit has been largely
due to severe expenditure cuts. This was evident in
1993-4, when a major reduction in the deficit was achieved
despite a fall in the revenue ratio. Slashing public expenditure has provided temporary respite and enabled GOP to
meet IMF targets. Such measures impose severe costs, since
socially and economically important expenditures are cut at
a time when public investment is required in several areas.

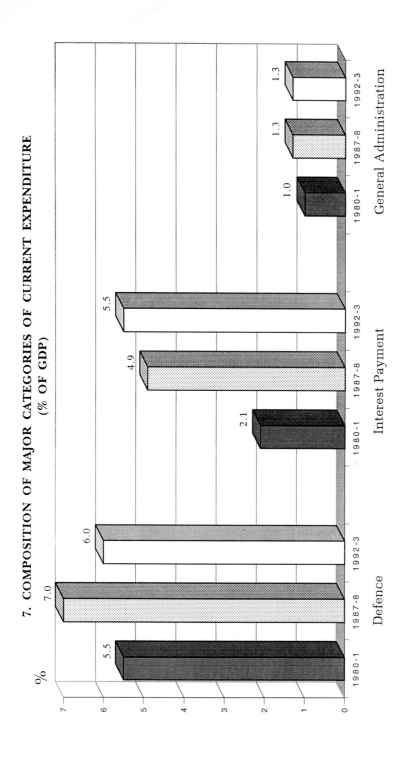

7. COMPOSITION OF MAJOR CATEGORIES OF CURRENT EXPENDITURE
(% OF GDP)

27. TRENDS IN SHARES OF PUBLIC EXPENDITURE
1988-95 (as % of total expenditure)

	1987-8	88-9	89-90	90-91	91-2	92-3	93-4
A)Current Expenditure	74.1	76.1	74.7	75.0	71.6	75.4	80.0
Defence	26.1	25.4	26.5	24.8	23.6	24.9	23.6
Interest	18.4	18.9	21.1	19.2	19.4	21.4	26.3
Subsidies*	4.4	6.6	4.1	4.1	2.5	2.1	2.0
Social services	9.6	9.6	9.1	10.8	14.1	15.7	15.8
Administration	4.7	5.1	5.4	5.2	5.6	5.8	5.9
Other	10.9	10.5	8.9	11.0	6.4	5.5	6.5
B)Development Expenditure	25.9	23.9	25.3	25.0	28.1	24.6	20.0

Source: Ministry of Finance: *Economic Survey, 1993-4.*

* Only current subsidies are included in this category. Development subsidies are included in development expenditure.

An examination of public expenditure trends since the start of SAP reveals a mix of sensible and damaging cuts. The former category consists of admirable efforts to reduce defence expenditure at a time of heightened regional tensions. Thus, in spite of South Asian security concerns particularly over Kashmir, the GOP managed to reduce the share of defence expenditure in total public spending from 26.1% to 23.6% between 1988 and 1994 (*see* Table 27). It should, however, be noted that although the share of defence expenditure has gone down during the course of the adjustment programme, it is still higher than what it was a decade ago. This is illustrated in Figure 7, which shows how the share of defence in GDP rose from 5.5% in 1980-1 to 7% by 1987-8, and has subsequently fallen to 6%.

While recent defence cuts are welcome, and are creditable in view of increasing tensions, the impact of other spending curbs is likely to be damaging. These negative effects assume two forms: they either have a direct adverse impact on the poor and/or they affect the longer-term growth prospects. An important social cost of adjustment has been the manner in which the expenditure has been controlled. Table 27 shows how current subsidies have halved in the first four years of the stabilization programme. As far as the poor are concerned, the most significant feature of subsidy reduction has been the cuts in the wheat and sugar subsidy. This subsidy declined from Rs 7.2 billion in 1988-9, the start of the SAP, to Rs 4.5 billion in 1992-3. Although the decline is exaggerated by the fact that 1988-9 was an exceptional year, in real terms the decline in this consumption subsidy is considerable. Similarly, the edible oils subsidy has been phased out completely. Although there is considerable disagreement on the extent to which these subsidies reach the poor in Pakistan, the reduction of these consumption subsidies are likely to have had a more adverse impact on sections of the poor than the removal of production subsidies, such as those on fertilizer.[47]

Another detrimental aspect of expenditure cuts has been the decline in education and health budgets. These reductions are particularly serious in view of Pakistan's poor record in human development indicators. The decline in social expenditures since the start of SAP, as well as the comparatively low international position of Pakistan, is captured in Table 28. As far as the low relative base is concerned, Table 28 shows how Pakistan's expenditure on education (2.2%) is way below the average for countries in the low human development category, and nearly half of the average spent by countries characterized with medium human development. The case of health is even worse, with Pakistan's expenditures half that of the low human development average, and a third of the medium human development nations. With respect to trends since the start of SAP, health expenditure has fallen sharply from 1% of GNP to 0.7%, while education has fallen from 2.4 to 2.2%. Such declines have occurred at a time when there is a widespread recognition that improvements in education and health are critical if Pakistan is to pursue a more equitable development path.

An indicator of the extent to which social investments have been squeezed by other expenditures is provided by comparing health and education expenditures with debt servicing. During the six years since the start of the adjustment programme, Pakistan's average external debt servicing payments (3% of GNP) have exceeded combined public health and education expenditures.

In recognition of Pakistan's inadequate record on human development and its accumulating negative effects, the GOP launched a Social Action Plan (SOCAP) as part of longer-term development strategy. This is aimed at improving social indicators through more effective delivery of public services in the areas of primary education, primary health, population planning, and rural water and sanitation. Irrespective of the urgent necessity of an extensive social action plan in Pakistan, progress has been extremely limited until 1996. At this point, it is worth noting that the SOCAP was being planned at a time of acute fiscal stringency and related budget cuts in education and health. In an attempt to protect SOCAP expenditures, the GOP allocated specific targeted funds for the programme. The sums involved were modest, with allocations of 0.1 of GDP in 1992-3 followed by 0.2% in 1993-4. However, the latter allocation was not spent and the actual expenditure in 1993-4 amounted to 0.1%.[48] Thus, even if SOCAP expenditure is included, the 1990s witnessed a decline in the share of national income being devoted to public education and health.

Cuts in social expenditures and consumption subsidies have been accompanied by reductions in development spending. As noted in Tables 26 and 27, development expenditure has fallen rapidly in recent years, particularly in 1993-4. Cuts in development expenditure, in a context of an inadequate and deteriorating physical and social infrastructure, are likely to impose further stress on the economy. The GOP is attempting to compensate for these shortfalls through a concerted drive to attract foreign direct investment in infrastructure, particularly energy.[49]

The above sections described how some cuts were sensible while others were potentially damaging. There is another aspect of public expenditure trends which needs to be commented on. This relates to expenditure increases, not cuts. Some of this public spending expansion reflected a distortion of development priorities while increases in interest

28. TRENDS IN EDUCATION AND HEALTH
EXPENDITURES, 1988-94
(% OF GNP)

	87-8	88-9	89-90	90-91	91-2	92-3	93-4
Education	2.4	2.1	2.2	2.1	2.2	2.2	2.2
Health	1.0	0.9	0.8	0.7	0.7	0.7	0.8

International Comparisons

1. Average education expenditure for LHD.*   3.6%
2. Average health expenditure for LHD.   1.6
3. Average education expenditure for MHD.**   4.1
4. Average health expenditure for MHD.   2.3

Sources: Ministry of Finance: *Economic Survey,* various issues.
 UNDP: *Human Development Report, 1994.*

 * LHD denotes Low Human Development.
 ** MHD denotes Medium Human Development.

payments were an obligation bequeathed by the pattern of fiscal management of the 1980s. The rapid expansion in expenditures on large motorways and politically high-profile 'employment schemes' such as the import of taxis were motivated largely by short-term political considerations. It is conceivable that these schemes may have yielded dividends in the electoral arena.[50] But the diversion of resources to these schemes starved much needed social expenditures, particularly at the primary level. Not only did this give wrong signals about development priorities but it also imposed immediate balance of payments and inflationary costs. Without adequate resource mobilization for these populist schemes, the resulting higher inflation is a form of a tax imposed on society, particularly its poorer inhabitants.

The other category of expenditure increases documented in Table 27, shows a rise in the share of current expenditures and a decline in that of development expenditure. The former is not due to greater attention to quality of services and higher operation and maintenance costs. The growth in the relative share of current expenditures was largely due to the rapid growth in debt servicing costs which nearly doubled in a decade, rising from 14.7% of total expenditure in 1984-5 to

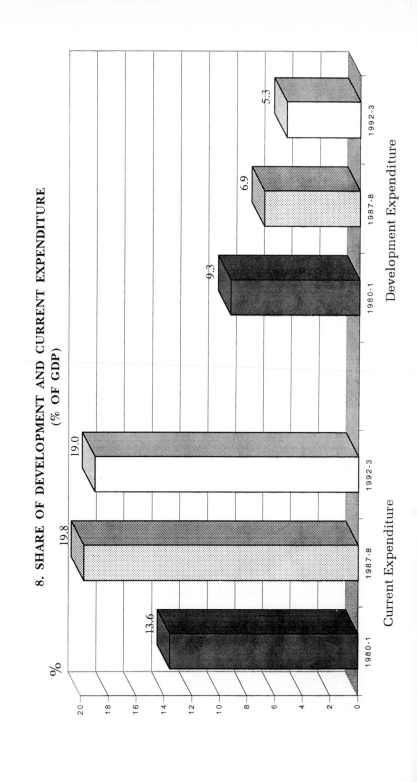

8. SHARE OF DEVELOPMENT AND CURRENT EXPENDITURE
(% OF GDP)

26.3% in 1994-5. The relative decline in development expenditure and the growth of current expenditure is illustrated in Figure 8. The composition of aggregate expenditure has deteriorated in favour of increased debt servicing and reduced development expenditure. This feature is illustrated in Figure 7, which shows how debt servicing has more than doubled in a decade. These expenditure trends threaten a highly destabilizing debt-inflation spiral as the government keeps borrowing or printing money to service the debt.

It is therefore important to retire this debt partly from the sales of privatization, as argued in the final chapter; otherwise future generations will be saddled with an onerous burden.

The true economic costs of the deficit are linked to the trends in the method of financing. Table 29 documents trends in the financing of the deficit. The most worrying feature was the dramatic growth in borrowing from the banking system by the first Nawaz Sharif government shortly after the partial implementation of the financial sector reforms, which raised the cost of credit. A dramatic worsening in inflationary finance of the deficit is noticeable between 1990 and 1993. In 1988, the GOP borrowed a mere 0.1% of GDP from the banking system to finance the budget deficit. The ratio increased to a still low and manageable 0.4% in 1989. The disastrous turning point came in 1990-1, when the borrowing from the banking system amounted to 4% of GDP. Worse was to follow in 1991-2 as the ratio rose to 6.0%. This resulted in an expansion of the money supply (M2) by 20.6%.[51] The inflationary pressure of these two years was sustained in 1992-3.[52]

The dramatic increase in the recourse to the banking system for financing the deficit has contributed substantially to the near doubling of inflation. A sharp fiscal correction was required urgently in order to avoid a further acceleration of inflation and debt. A high interest-high deficit chain needed to be arrested urgently, if macro-imbalances were to be restored without a severe economic slump.

The potential for a serious breakdown in Pakistan's macroeconomic management was averted in 1993-4. As noted earlier, fairly Draconian measures were taken to curb the deficit. Further, there was radical surgery in the method of financing the deficit. Borrowing from the banking system

9. INFLATION: 1980-92
CONSUMER PRICE INDEX

%

13.85 11.1 4.7 7.3 5.7 4.4 3.6 6.3 10.4 6.0 12.7 9.6 9.6

1980 1981 1982 1983 1984 1985 1986 1987 1988 1989 1990 1991 1992

Fiscal Years

was slashed to 0.8% of GDP, thereby avoiding a potentially grave crisis. But these patch-up measures have proved temporary and have not been sustained, as the 1996 crisis illustrated.

29. METHODS OF FINANCING THE BUDGET DEFICIT
1988-94 (Rs Billion)

	1987-8	88-9	89-90	90-91	91-2	92-3	93-4
Fiscal Deficit	-57.5	-56.8	-56.0	-89.1	-89.9	-107.7	-90.7
Financing							
External	12.6	18.1	22.9	22.1	18.0	25.4	22.8
Internal	44.9	38.7	33.1	67.0	71.9	82.3	67.9
Banking System	13.9	0.8	3.5	43.3	72.4	62.6	12.9
Non-bank sources	31.0	37.9	29.6	23.7	-0.5	19.7	55.0
BORROWING FROM THE BANKING SYSTEM AS A % OF GDP							
	2.1	0.1	0.4	4.3	6.0	4.6	0.8

Source: State Bank of Pakistan: *Annual Report,* various issues.

MONEY AND INFLATION

As noted earlier, inflationary pressures have gained momentum during the adjustment programme. Trends in inflation during the 1980s and early 1990s, as measured by the consumer price index, are reflected in Figure 9. The chart confirms the five year period of low inflation during 1982-7, which was also accompanied by rapid growth in national income. Towards the late 1980s, inflation levels reverted to those prevalent in the early part of the decade (*see* Figure 9).

The Consumer Price Index (CPI) is constructed on the basis of retail prices of 357 consumer items prevailing in 12 major cities of Pakistan. The CPI figure is recorded by taking an annual average. The trends in inflation were summarized earlier in Figure 9, which illustrated how a period of relative price stability between fiscal years 1982-7 was disrupted by mounting inflation since the late 1980s. While inflation in Pakistan is not high by many developing country standards, the recent acceleration in inflation has had damaging consequences for the living standards of many poor families.

30. PERCENTAGE CHANGE IN PRICE INDICES AND GDP DEFLATOR

	Consumer Price Index	Wholesale Price Index	Sensitive Price Indicator	GDP Deflator
1981-2	11.10	7.36	15.38	9.37
1982-3	4.67	5.36	2.99	5.28
1983-4	7.28	10.02	7.42	9.66
1984-5	5.67	5.19	8.74	4.54
1985-6	4.35	4.62	3.01	3.29
1986-7	3.60	5.00	2.41	4.52
1987-8	6.29	10.02	7.48	9.61
1988-9	10.39	9.66	13.50	8.59
1989-90	6.04	7.30	6.11	6.45
1990-1	12.66	11.73	12.58	13.07
1991-2	9.62	9.26	9.29	10.07
1992-3 July-March	9.26	7.11	10.28	8.70
1992-3	9.59	6.99	10.78	8.70
1993-4	10.61	12.71	10.05	12.10

Source: Federal Bureau of Statistics.

An indication of the relative impact of accelerating inflation on the poor is provided by a comparison between the Consumer Price Index and the Sensitive Price Indicator (SPI). The latter is an index devised to evaluate the impact of price changes on the cost of living of low income families. The SPI covers the essential consumer items, which have a higher weight in the cost of living of income groups of upto Rs 1000 per month. The trends in both indices are illustrated in Table 30. Since 1988-9, the average annual increase in the CPI has been 10.0%. This compares with an average annual increase in the SPI of 10.4%. In the five years prior to the start of SAP, the annual average increases in CPI and SPI were 5.3 and 5.7% respectively. The price trends during SAP suggest that far from protecting the poor, the general increase in inflation was slightly greater for the commodities of greater significance to poorer income groups.

The recent acceleration in inflation has been caused by four principle factors. The first, discussed above, was the monetary expansion related to the fiscal deficit. The second is the sharp rise in import prices due to a mix of substantial depreciation of the currency and adverse terms of trade movements. The third cause has been agricultural commodity supply shocks, such as the floods in 1992. Finally, the increase in government controlled and administered prices of utilities, fertilizers, petroleum products, and railway fares has also contributed to inflation while the visibility of facilities in the urban areas creates political pressures from the urban poor. Much of the increases in the final category were also related to fiscal strains, since they were motivated by the need to restore financial viability, primarily to government supplied goods and services.

Thus, the near doubling of the inflation rate is not exclusively caused by the policies pursued since the start of the adjustment programme. This would be an erroneous conclusion. To a certain extent, the recent inflationary surge reflects the consequence of earlier policies which had repressed inflation artificially. This suppressed inflation within the system was reflected in growing macroeconomic imbalances. In attempting to rectify these imbalances, the GOP has had to contend with releasing some of the inflationary pressures. Increasing administratively controlled utility prices, for example, was inevitable due to the financial unsustainability of the public corporations which supply these services.

However, the worrying increase in inflation has been due to other factors as well, including improper sequencing in the implementation of the adjustment programme, devaluation, and the lack of revenue mobilization. However, perhaps the most important cause for mounting inflation has been ill-advised expenditure increases without corresponding efforts to mobilize resources. Thus, the consequent recourse to monetary expansion created a seriously unstable macroeconomic environment. During 1993-4, the GOP undertook tough measures to prevent the worsening situation from degenerating into a Latin American style hyperinflation. Such an inflationary crisis might well have been the outcome had the rate of monetary expansion, witnessed during 1991-3, persisted over the next couple of years.

The threat of inflation getting out of control was compounded by another indicator of macroeconomic malaise: Pakistan's foreign exchange reserves plummeted in 1992-3 to a level sufficient to cover barely three weeks of imports. The balance of payments difficulties were also related to policy decisions, taken largely with immediate political gains in mind. Providing targeted credit for the purchase of taxis led to a surge in imports; this rapid expansion in import demand occurred at a time of a textile disaster affecting exports. Ironically, restoring macroeconomic stability became an urgent priority after five years of the Structural Adjustment Programme.[53]

The GOP's response in 1993-4 consisted of co-ordinated monetary and fiscal measures. A number of actions were taken to structurally improve the management of monetary policy in Pakistan.[54] In terms of immediate macro objectives, domestic credit expansion to the private sector was curtailed, particularly through the withdrawal of special schemes with a heavy import content.[55] Raising interest rates and tightening lending in concessionary finance schemes also contributed to greater control over the money supply. However, the most important measure with regard to tighter control over monetary aggregates was the major change in the manner that the reduced fiscal deficit was financed. Government borrowing from the banking system was slashed.

In sum the above analysis suggests that poor employment generation in an environment of high inflation contributed to social dislocation and tensions in the trying 1990s.

THE EXTERNAL SECTOR AND THE BALANCE OF PAYMENTS

In a period of a rapid rise in inflation, such as the one encountered in Pakistan during the 1990s, the exchange rate adjustments can be slow to follow. This can have a detrimental effect on export performance. In the case of Pakistan, the poor export performance was not, however, caused by an over-valued exchange. A continuous depreciation has ensured that price competitiveness has generally been maintained. The export-oriented management of the rupee's exchange rate has been part of a policy agenda aimed at increasing the external orientation of Pakistan's economy. The trade policy reforms have been aimed at improving the structural position of the balance of payments while trying to ensure that transitional problems are managed without causing severe economic dislocation.

Apart from the fiscal deficit, the external current account deficit was the second important macroeconomic imbalance that was the target of the SAP. The basic target was to reduce the current account deficit from 4.6% of GDP in 1988 to 2.5% in an unrealistically short period of three years. In addition, the aim was to double the reserve import cover from three weeks to six weeks. The reform programme contained an extensive package of exchange rate, tariff, and regulatory reforms.

As far as trade reforms are concerned, liberalization measures included the elimination of many non-tariff barriers, abolition of import licenses, and reduction in maximum tariff rates. More competitive exchange rate policies have been pursued through a managed float system since 1982. The cumulative decline in the value of the rupee in the subsequent decade has been approximately 67%. Numerous controls and regulations were relaxed in reforms of the exchange and payments system in 1991.

The capital account has been liberalized gradually, while the rupee was made fully convertible on current account transactions in July 1994.[56]

The direction of external sector reform is aimed firmly at creating a more open and competitive economy. The success of this strategy would, above all, require a more diversified manufacturing export base. In addition, increased inflows of foreign direct investment would provide another indicator of achievement.

External sector trends since the start of the adjustment programme reveal a mixed picture. Export performance has tended to fluctuate around the state of the textile sector with little evidence of any substantial diversification of the export base. Except for the occasional year, import growth has not grown excessively after tariff reductions. There has been some success in attracting foreign exchange inflows, which have partially compensated for the continuing decline in remittances.

As far as comparative results are concerned, Table 31 shows how the average current account deficit in the six years since the start of the SAP was considerably worse than during the equivalent period before adjustment. The average annual current account deficit rose from 3.2% of GDP to 4.4%. However, on average, the country was exporting a considerably larger proportion of national income, up from 8.3 to 12.4%, which was accompanied by a much smaller increase in the propensity to import. As a result, the average trade deficit declined during the first five years of SAP from 8.5 to 5.5%. It follows that the worsening of current account deficits was due to adverse movements in the services account, such as declining remittance inflows and increased debt servicing payments.

31. EXTERNAL SECTOR TRENDS BEFORE AND SINCE THE START OF THE STRUCTURAL ADJUSTMENT PROGRAMME
(% of GNP. 6-Year Annual Averages)

	1982-1988	1989-1994
Current Account Deficit	3.2	4.4
Imports	17.3	17.9
Exports	8.3	12.4
Trade Deficit	8.5	5.5
External Debt Servicing	2.4	3.0

Source: Ministry of Finance: *Economic Survey,* various issues.

In the early years of the adjustment programme, the robust trade performance was largely due to the exceptional growth in exports in the late 1980s. However, as mentioned earlier, this was concentrated largely in the textile sector. The share of cotton manufactures in total exports rose from 42% in 1988 to 52% in 1992. Perhaps more encouraging was the growth in leather and non-traditional manufacturing goods. The growth in exports was large enough to absorb the surge in imports, leading to an improvement in the trade balance.[57] On the other hand, there was a depreciation in the services account, largely due to a substantial decline in remittances. Workers' remittances have halved over the last eight years, declining from $2.2 billion in 1987 to $1.1 billion in 1993. In the span of a decade, remittances have come down from 10% of GDP to approximately 3%. In addition to declining remittances, the current account has been hit by increased external debt servicing burdens, which have increased from 2.4% of GNP to 3%.[58] Nevertheless, the liberalization of foreign currency deposits compensated somewhat for this decline as substantial capital flowed into the foreign currency accounts. The pattern of inflows suggested that some of the remittances were deflected into foreign currency deposits.[59]

Workers' remittances have been a major source of foreign exchange earning for Pakistan. The value of remittances was only $136 million in 1972-3 but increased steadily to $2887 million in 1982-3, reflecting an annual growth rate of 35.7%. However, a 40% decline in remittances during 1985-92 is documented in Table 32 below. This trend underlines the need to undertake major reforms in the incentive structure for exports in order to adjust to a structural worsening of the services account.

32. WORKERS' REMITTANCES ($US MILLION)

	1985-6	1986-7	1987-8	1988-9	1989-90	1990-1	1991-2
M.E.	2021	1673	1418	1356	1322	1234	985
Total	2591	2278	2021	1896	1942	1848	1467

The structure of the balance of payments remains vulnerable to changes affecting a narrow band of goods and services. Rising prices of relatively inelastic imports, the potential for increased import demand due to tariff liberalization, a narrow export base, poor human capital levels for an internationally competitive economy, and increased reliance on short-term capital flows are factors which suggest that the balance of payments may remain under pressure. While the direction of reforms to address these external sector difficulties appears to be sound, Pakistan may find the challenge of responding to reduced remittances and increased debt servicing quite demanding. Efforts in this direction are unlikely to be assisted by factors in the political economy of Pakistan. In particular, the prolonged crisis and deterioration in Karachi create an unfavourable climate for, *inter alia*, attracting foreign direct capital for manufacturing exports.

The litmus test of the liberalization programme remains a major supply response in manufacturing export performance.

Recent reforms have improved the price incentives for exporters and considerably reduced regulations. None the less, the GOP's desire to emulate East Asian achievements would require concerted efforts to improve the physical infrastructure and the quality of human capital, as well as bring about a more stable situation in the main port city of Karachi.

SUMMARY

The aggregate performance of the Pakistan economy during the first half of the 1990s is in sharp contrast to the previous decade. Much of the 1980s were characterized by high growth with low inflation. However, this growth path proved unsustainable due to a mix of domestic and external factors. The failure to address urgent resource mobilization imperatives led to a rapid accumulation of debt. Growing macroeconomic imbalances required a contractionary stabilization programme to bring spending in line with national resources. The growth momentum was also disturbed by exogenous factors such as a sharp decline in remittances, an international recession, and supply side shocks to agricultural output.

The GOP has responded to the difficulties through a wide-ranging policy reform process. These have been co-ordinated under the umbrella of the Structural Adjustment Programme which was launched in 1988-9. The stabilization component of SAP has been plagued by the failure to reduce the fiscal deficit, which undermined the envisaged sequencing of reforms. The liberalization component has been more successful, with reduced regulations and incentive reforms improving the climate for private sector activity. Human development initiatives have been slow to get off the ground. Education and health expenditures have been cut, while policy and institutional shortcomings have hampered progress in the social action plan.

This chapter dealt with the macroeconomic framework, the stabilization difficulties encountered in the 1990s, and the broad direction of reforms. The next two chapters examine sectoral issues which need to complement these changes.

NOTES

1. For a period of time, these macro-imbalances can be financed by the accumulation of domestic and foreign debt, as was the case in Pakistan during the 1980s. Excessive debt accumulation is, of course, unsustainable and the structural causes of the macro-imbalances require attention.

2. This point has caused considerable controversy globally in the context of Structural Adjustment Programmes (SAP). Critics of SAP emphasize how longer-term growth prospects are undermined by cuts, while defenders of SAP point to the necessity of taking difficult short-term measures to ensure a stable long-term growth path.

3. These averages have been calculated from the State Bank of Pakistan: *Annual Report, 1993-4* and the Ministry of Finance: *Economic Survey, 1993-4.*

4. This refers to the rate of inflation, as measured by the growth in the Consumer Price Index.

5. These shocks have included floods in 1992 and a virus which affected cotton production in 1993 and 1994.

6. Between 1988, which was the start of the SAP, and 1994 there was a rapid turnover of civilian governments. Some of these regimes, particularly that of Benazir Bhutto's administration in 1988 which reduced the budget deficit, were more fiscally prudent than others. This point is dealt with in more detail later.

7. By the mid-1980s, remittances had peaked to $3.2 billion, which was almost 300% greater than the net aid inflow.

8. The debt servicing ratio rose from 20% of exports of goods and services in 1980 to nearly 30% by 1988, with the result that more exports were required not only to service the debt but also to sustain the growing demand for imports.

9. Pakistan's manufacturing export growth was dominated by yarn, as the country doubled its world share in the yarn trade during the 1980s. However, the country's export performance was generally disappointing.

10. The aid pipeline refers to the difference between aid commitments and disbursements. The pipeline grew substantially during the 1980s. While variables, such as a lack of matching rupee resources affected certain projects, one of the key factors was the absence of qualified personnel. This impact

of human capital scarcity is documented in Cassen, Duncan, Noman et al.: *Impact of Aid on Pakistan* (UNDP, Islamabad, 1989).

11. For details of the poor research and extension capacity and its consequences for agricultural productivity, see the World Bank: *Pakistan—A Strategy for Sustainable Agricultural Growth,* (South Asia Region, Washington, 1994).

12. The poor functioning of public sector technology support institutions has limited diversification and the quality of industries such as surgical goods. For an analysis of the poor functioning of such institutes see the Economic Policy Research Unit: *The Role of the Metal Industries Development Corporation,* (Lahore, 1990).

13. For details, see the World Bank: *Pakistan—Growth through Adjustment,* (Washington, 1988), p.118.

14. Ibid., pages 110-20 have details of the planned reduction in GDP growth.

15. Ibid., p.xiv.

16. Foreign exchange reserves plummeted to a level which barely covered 3 weeks of imports during the 1992-3 fiscal year. This was largely due to increased government expenditures with important balance of payments implications, such as the import of transport vehicles.

17. Of particular importance in the area of infrastructure investment increases was the launching of a national motorway scheme in 1991, which came in for heavy criticism on grounds of fiscal irresponsibility and the diversion of resources from other priorities, such as the social sectors.

18. For details of policies implemented since the start of the SAP, see *Progress Under Adjustment,* op. cit., parts 1 and 2.

19. There is no implication that the persistent fiscal deficit was responsible for directly slowing the rate of growth. On the contrary, a more severe expenditure cut would have exerted a further contractionary force than was already the case due to declining public investment.

20. Such as reduction in public investment demand.

21. These comparative figures have to be interpreted with caution. What they clearly establish is the poor comparative performance in virtually every sphere of the economy. However, such a comparison disguises some of the macro-policy management

achievements, such as the reduction in the current account deficit during the SAP process.

22. While all regimes, in a period of rapid turn-over, adhered to the development strategy outlined under the Structural Adjustment Programme, commitment to the whole package was weak due to both a lack of active involvement in its formulation and policy differences with regard to specific areas. The Structural Adjustment Programme was most closely associated domestically with Dr Mahbubul Haq who was the outgoing Finance Minister in 1988. Dr Haq signed the SAP but was not part of the subsequent elected governments which were in power during 1988-95.

23. Measures to deregulate the major agricultural crops were recommended in each of the first five years of the SAP. See policy matrix in ibid., p. 115-6.

24. The extent of the fall in the social expenditure ratios is documented later. Most areas of government expenditure, including defence, have been affected. The share of interest payments has, however, continued to rise.

25. The cut-off point for the data used in this study is the fiscal year 1992-3. This covers five years of the adjustment programme. Little difference is made to the analysis if we examine the monthly data for the fiscal year 1993-4. In any case, time and data constraints do not allow for examination of monthly statistics for the current fiscal year (1994).

26. Three problems regarding this method need to be noted, although there are no easy remedies for them. The first is that the reform process did not begin with the Structural Adjustment Programme. Many liberalization and deregulation measures had been undertaken in the five year period before the SAP. Thus, one is examining the performance of the economy before and during the SAP, but the period before the SAP was not without reform. The second problem is the familiar one of the counter factual. One can argue that performance may have been even worse without the SAP, since the previous period of more rapid growth was unsustainable. Empirically, this counter factual is not observable and we shall confine our comparative analysis to the observed impacts on the economy. Finally, there is a need to distinguish between different aspects of the reform process. Clearly, stabilization measures are intended to have a different impact on the economy than liberalization policies which seek to increase efficiency of resource allocation. Because

these policies were introduced at the same time as the stabilization programme, it is difficult disentangle their relative impacts. The contractionary features of the stabilization programme should not be confused with the policy measures taken for liberalization. But a fundamental conceptual and empirical difficulty is encountered when an attempt is made to distinguish between the two types of policies and their impact on the poor. If the net impact of the simultaneous implementation of these policies is to reduce the rate of growth, the magnitude of employment generated, and cut government expenditures of benefit to the poor, then the transitional phase is one in which many groups of the poor suffer. These negative impacts are not frequently due to the sector adjustment loan policies but to the stabilization programme. This was the case in Pakistan and care has to be exercised not to ascribe poorer relative performance in the post-adjustment period to the policies associated with the liberalization programme.

27. This was particularly true for the manufacturing sector, an issue addressed in the discussion of the industrial sector in Chapter 9.

28. The cut-off of US bilateral aid was caused by the invocation of the Pressler Amendment of the US Congress, which requires that the President verify that Pakistan is not acquiring nuclear weapons capability. The Pressler Amendment is viewed by many as a discriminatory and arbitrary legislation, since it does not apply to other South Asian countries such as India which, like Pakistan, is not a signatory to the Nuclear Non-Proliferation Treaty. A view commonly held within Pakistan is that the Pressler Amendment was used in response to the Pakistan chief of army staff's statement during the Gulf War recommending a 'strategic defiance'.

29. For details see Ahmed and Amjad: *The Management of Pakistan's Economy, 1947-82,* (Oxford University Press, 1984).

30. At this stage of Pakistan's economic evolution, the difference between national and domestic savings was negligible. The disparity between the two grew considerably in the 1980s due to substantial migration to the Middle East and the resulting remittances.

31. It should be noted that foreign savings contain flows other than aid, but these other categories are relatively insignificant in the case of Pakistan.

32. Accumulation debt servicing burdens, documented later in the book, make it necessary for Pakistan to shift to more sustainable forms for financing investment.

33. The share of the private sector in total investment was 54% in 1992-3 and 53% in 1993-4.

34. Ratio of total investment to GNP.

35. The national savings ratio figures also represent annual averages over six years before and after the Structural Adjustment Programme.

36. Remittances have declined from a peak of $2.8 billion in 1982-3 to $1.3 billion in 1992-3.

37. For details see the World Bank: *Structural and Sectoral Adjustment Loans—The Second Review,* (Operations and Evaluation Department, Washington, 1992).

38. By early 1995, there has been little evidence of a supply response in manufacturing exports. Commitments for foreign direct investment, however, have increased substantially particularly in infrastructure projects. The energy sector has received special attention from foreign private capital due to GOP guarantees, which ensure a high and safe return to capital.

39. Government of Pakistan: *Statistical Supplement to the Economic Survey, 1992-3,* p.121.

40. Ibid., p.104.

41. Ibid., p.120.

42. It should be emphasized that these debt figures only refer to civilian debt. Figures on military debt are not available. Since the breakdown in defence expenditure is also not available, it is difficult to estimate the magnitude of debt servicing within this aggregate.

43. It should, however, be noted that Pakistan is still a recipient of positive net transfers through aid. In 1992-3, for example, while 68% of the aid disbursed was equal to external debt servicing, there was a net transfer of 32% of total aid disbursement. These external debt servicing figures do not include interest on short-term borrowing and IMF charges.

44. The political influence refers to the fact that through much of the 1980s, the regime appeared to be more concerned with granting fiscal favours and concessions to generate political loyalty, at the expense of executing its responsibility for

increasing direct tax revenues, as part of prudent macroeconomic management.

45. For details of cross-country experience on this issue, see World Bank: *Structural and Sectoral Adjustment Operations—the Second Overview*, (Washington, 1992).

46. During 1992-3 for example, tax revenues financed 51% of total expenditure. This share rose to 56% in 1993-4, not because of increased tax mobilization but due to expenditure cuts.

47. This is also the conclusion reached in the analysis contained in *Just Adjustment*, op. cit.

48. State Bank of Pakistan: *Annual Report, 1993-4,* p.101. The budgeted allocation for 1994-5 amounts to 0.3% of GDP.

49. During 1993-4 in particular, Benazir Bhutto's government launched an extensive programme to attract FDI in the energy sector. The generally positive response by foreign investors was facilitated by the finalization of a large private sector financed energy project, HUBCO.

50. Prime Minister Nawaz Sharif may have consolidated his urban support-base through such schemes, particularly the liberal import of taxis for the unemployed.

51. This monetary expansion was in spite of a sharp decline in net foreign assets.

52. Budgetary support from the banking system amounted to 4.6% of GDP in 1992-3.

53. It amounted to a mere Rs 13 billion, down substantially from the Rs 70 and Rs 64 billion borrowed in the previous two years.

54. These included greater autonomy for the central bank through an amendment of the State Bank Act, which gave it greater authority in managing monetary policy. Improved co-ordination of fiscal and monetary management was also attempted through the creation of a monetary and fiscal policies co-ordination board. Such measures were part of the wider financial sector reforms, which have the aim of reducing the direct participation of the public sector while improving its regulatory capacity.

55. Credit facilities for importing taxis were withdrawn in 1993-4. These were linked, in any case, with a regime which was no longer in power and the new government had no political attachment to the scheme.

56. Only 18 other countries have assumed the obligations of Article VIDI of the IMF's articles of agreement which cover the exchange and payments systems operated by member countries.

57. This improved from 6.6% to 4.6% between 1988 and 1992.

58. This implied that, on average, Pakistan had to devote 14.5% of its foreign exchange earnings to debt servicing during 1988-94 as compared to 12.8% during 1983-8.

59. In the fiscal year 1992 alone, $1.2 billion came into these foreign currency accounts. This constituted nearly 2.5% of GDP.

CHAPTER 9

THE PROSPECTS FOR INDUSTRIAL AND AGRICULTURAL DEVELOPMENT

> *Previously in some places people suffered a great deal because they did not take the long view and neglected economy in manpower and material resources and the expansion of production. The lesson is there and attention must be called to it.*
>
> Chairman Mao's Red Book

INTRODUCTION

The key challenge for poverty alleviation is to implement the policy changes required to stimulate and sustain higher growth in industry and agriculture. The rationale and direction for these reforms is discussed in this chapter, in the context of historical trends since independence.

Along with measures to increase aggregate incomes, policy attention has to be paid to the impact on the poor and the improvement in equity. The purchasing power of the poor is determined largely by employment.[1] These primary incomes are a function of labour market demand conditions which are strongly influenced by the level of activity in the markets for goods and services. Since most people derive their livelihoods from industry or agriculture, the performance of these sectors is, therefore, of critical importance for poverty alleviation.

As far as services are concerned, their main **direct** role in generating primary incomes has been through the export of manpower. Another possible source of services income, tourism, is unlikely to play a significant role in Pakistan. Services such as the financial sector play a **facilitative** role in supporting the growth of industry and agriculture. Financial sector reforms, including the possibility of expanding postal savings institutions, are needed in Pakistan to raise the level of savings and investment. Finally, the returns to investment in services such as education and health have been stressed in earlier chapters. In the long run, these productive service investments can determine the pace and pattern of growth. In the immediate future, however, policies and investments which influence the growth of agriculture and industry are critical for the further alleviation of Pakistan's poverty. This growth should be used to finance social investments which can in turn accelerate per capita growth and assist in diversification.

As noted earlier, Pakistan's growth performance since independence has been a respectable one. This was illustrated in Chapter 1, which demonstrated how the economy has grown over four decades. There have been fluctuations, with the 1960s and 1980s being marked with particularly high growth, but an average annual GNP growth of 6% has been sustained over nearly half a century.[2] The first decade was consumed largely by the need to adjust to the traumas of partition.[3] The high growth of the 1960s was followed by the slowdown of the 1970s, due not only to exogenous international shocks but also to a serious reversal of the development strategy pursued since independence. Again, the **alternating** pattern across the decades was repeated by the good performance of the 1980s and the relative stagnation in the first half of the 1990s.

The broad reasons for this output performance were discussed earlier and can be summarized as follows: The early decision to go for private sector led growth was combined with effective state intervention in support of commodity production. This implied a set of inter-related policies which sustained growth. These included financial sector policies such as directed credit and the creation of private financial institutions. Trade policy protected industry, thus enabling high returns to the capital employed in the initial phase of import substitution. A part of the agricultural surplus was transferred to industry through pricing policies, while agricultural growth was aided by technological innovations in both the 1960s and 1980s. External influences have, by and large, been positive. While Pakistan's export performance has not been as good as may have been

33. CMI VALUE OF PRODUCTION AND VALUE ADDED
(Rs MILLION)

Major Industry	Value of Production				Value Added			
	1984-5	85-6	86-7	87-8	1984-5	85-6	86-7	87-8
Food	31.183	33.146	36.682	43.791	9.236	9.760	9.375	11.854
Beverages	1.986	2.292	1.930	2.379	1.176	1.221	1.026	1.333
Tobacco	7.498	7.117	11.465	9.074	5.920	5.612	9.776	7.488
Textiles	26.157	28.342	35.538	40.361	8.202	8.596	10.887	12.895
Apparel	1.553	2.123	2.830	4.152	283	625	616	1.167
Leather and Products	3.216	3.927	6.192	7.552	602	1.062	727	991
Ginning, Pressing and Bailing	9.732	10.120	9.436	12.095	747	1.147	632	1.091
Wood and Products	354	445	469	662	144	156	137	254
Furniture and Fixtures	238	120	261	305	89	44	80	89
Paper and Products	1.659	1.820	1.777	2.952	526	622	592	828
Printing and Publishing	1.416	1.570	1.834	1.947	573	622	758	707
Drugs and Pharmaceutical Products	4.944	5.270	5.907	7.532	2.055	2.369	2.343	2.802
Industrial Chemicals	8.888	9.584	11.328	11.484	4.469	4.596	5.388	5.185
Other Chemical Products	3.923	4.243	6.038	5.875	1.611	1.942	2.103	2.598
Petroleum and Coal Products	1.138	1.088	1.305	1.420	268	227	338	550
Petroleum Refining	19.169	20.605	17.545	19.852	719	3.194	5.539	4.379
Rubber Products	2.024	2.171	1.874	2.040	648	861	709	695
Plastic Products	995	981	1.302	1.340	327	318	398	344
Non-Metallic Mineral Products	6.657	7.793	10.015	11.723	3.559	4.079	5.760	6.480
Iron and Steel Basic Industries	10.814	9.601	13.662	16.112	5.441	2.194	5.051	4.827
Fabricated Metal Products	1.318	1.219	1.729	2.109	523	468	564	770
Non-electrical Goods	5.343	4.966	5.540	5.562	1.269	1.340	1.263	1.319
Electrical Machinery	4.668	5.196	7.055	8.668	1.558	1.857	1.702	2.428
Transport Equipment	5.505	6.341	7.627	10.195	1.324	1.384	1.596	2.706
Measuring, Photographic, Optical Goods	443	395	493	706	121	80	90	202
Sports and Athletic Goods	252	302	375	518	57	69	104	141
Others	315	347	346	480	124	133	117	187
Total:	161.388	171.124	200.555	230.886	51.571	55.298	67.671	74.310

Source: Federal Bureau of Statistics.

expected,[4] the country has benefited considerably from manpower export and periodically from concessional aid inflows.

There are, however, major impediments to raising the growth rate in both industry and agriculture. A discussion of the policy direction required to remove these shortcomings follows the analysis of the evolution of each sector respectively.

(A) THE INDUSTRIAL SECTOR

Evolution, performance trends, and basic characteristics

Pakistan's industrialization drive, from a virtually non-existent base at independence[5], has tended to build naturally on its agricultural foundations. Indigenous raw materials such as cotton provided the inputs for the merchant capital, which was converted into an industrial bourgeoisie during the first two decades.[6] The early industrial development was concentrated in Punjab and Sindh, particularly Karachi, which turned rapidly from a small fishing town into the country's major financial and trade centre.

While the share of industry in GDP has grown from 8% in 1950 to 28% in 1995, the product composition of Pakistan's industry remains narrowly based on agro-industrial units. More than two-thirds of manufacturing value added in the early 1980s was generated from domestic raw material, principally in food and beverage processing, cotton textiles, leather tanning and products, garments, and cement. The dominance of domestic raw material based agro-industries in the large manufacturing sector is reflected in Table 33.

The growth performance of the manufacturing sector during the 1980s was impressive. The sector grew at an annual average of 8.2%, following the relative stagnation of the previous decade. The manufacturing growth performance was fuelled by a combination of yarn and garment exports, growing domestic demand aided by large remittance inflows, and fairly robust agricultural growth through the decade. The manufacturing growth performance between 1990-4, however, shows a lower rate of growth, with an annual average of

5.9%: the relative slowdown appears to be due largely to demand contraction over the period as a whole and supply side shocks in agriculture in some years.

Recent trends in investment in the manufacturing sector reveal an interesting picture. In general, Pakistan has a low investment ratio, which tends to hover around 18%. Within this aggregate figure, the share of manufacturing has tended to be quite low. During the 1980s, the annual average investment in the manufacturing sector has been 3.2% of GDP. This is illustrated in Table 34, which documents investment trends between 1980-94. While the aggregate investment ratio did not alter in the 1980s, there was an underlying shift in the public-private sector shares. Public investment declined from 1.7% to 0.3% of GDP, while private investment more than doubled during the course of the decade (from 1.6 to 3.3%). As a result, investment in manufacturing was almost exclusively undertaken by the

34. INVESTMENT IN MANUFACTURING INDUSTRIES DURING THE 1980s AND 1990s

Year	Investment in Manufacturing as Percentage of GDP			Share of Private Investment in Total Investment in Manufacturing
	Private	Public	Total	
1980-1	1.6	1.7	3.4	48.5
1981-2	1.7	1.4	3.1	53.9
1982-3	1.9	1.4	3.3	57.0
1983-4	2.0	1.4	3.4	60.0
1984-5	2.1	0.8	2.9	72.1
1985-6	2.4	0.9	3.3	72.6
1986-7	2.4	0.6	2.9	81.0
1987-8	2.4	0.5	2.9	84.4
1988-9	3.0	0.4	3.4	86.7
1989-90	3.3	0.3	3.5	88.9
1990-1	3.3	0.3	3.6	92.5
1991-2	4.5	0.3	4.5	94.5
1992-3	4.4	0.3	4.7	94.6
1993-4	4.4	0.2	4.6	95.2

Source: Based on data obtained from *Economic Survey, 1990-1*.

private sector by the mid-1990s, reflecting the withdrawal of the state from production. By 1994, for example, the share of the private sector in manufacturing investment was over 95% (*see* Table 34).

The other aspect of recent investment trends worth noting is the rise in the manufacturing investment ratio during the early part of the 1990s. The share of manufacturing investment in GDP has risen to an average of 4.4%, which is substantially higher than the 1980s average of 3.2%. Policy measures such as liberalization of investment sanctioning procedures and trade reform which have made imports easier, along with the textile export boom in the early 1990s, appear to have contributed to the increased investment ratio.

As far as export performance is concerned, the 1980s have witnessed an increase in the export-orientation of Pakistan's economy. Export earnings as a proportion of GDP have increased from 10% in 1979 to 15% in 1994. During this period, the average annual rate of growth in manufacturing exports has been nearly 13%. This impressive export performance has been led mainly by cotton yarn and garments. However, the export base generally remains narrow and too dependent on low value added items.

While Pakistan's ratio of manufactured exports to GDP is higher than the average for low income countries, it is far below the achievements evident in Eastern Asia. Malaysia's ratio, for example, is a very high 45%. Pakistan's share in world trade has improved marginally in recent years, going up from 0.16% to 0.18% between 1987 and 1992. There has been a noticeable increase in Pakistan's share of the cotton yarn trade, but this has been offset by declining shares in the trade of leather products and carpets.

It is useful to examine the recent export performance of specific manufacturing sub-sectors since it provides indicators of the areas which are likely to lead a labour-intensive manufacturing export drive. For this summary review, the principal sub-sectors can be divided into three categories— textiles, leather, and miscellaneous products. The latter include items such as sports goods, surgical instruments, and carpets.

35. STRUCTURE OF EXPORTS OF MANUFACTURED GOODS

	1980-1		1989-90		1991-2		Growth Rate		
	$US (Million)	Percentage Share in Exports of Manufactured Goods	$US (Million)	Percentage Share in Exports of Manufactured Goods	$US (Million)	Percentage Share in Exports of Manufactured Goods	1980-1 to 1991-2	1980-1 to 1989-90	1989-90 to 1991-2
Fish preparations	7	0.4	17	0.4	16	0.3	7.1	9.3	-3.0
Cotton yarn	217	13.1	838	21.2	1178	21.1	15.1	14.5	18.6
Cotton cloth	241	14.5	560	14.2	820	14.7	10.7	8.8	21.0
Made-ups	182	11.0	430	10.9	602	9.2	11.5	10.0	18.3
Garments and hosiery	75	4.5	669	16.9	1039	18.6	24.5	24.5	24.8
Synthetic textiles	129	7.8	212	5.4	419	7.5	10.3	5.1	40.8
Carpets and rugs	227	13.6	230	5.8	230	4.1	0.1	0.1	0.1
Leather	90	5.4	280	7.1	241	4.3	8.6	12.0	-7.2
Footwear	10	0.6	24	0.6	23	0.4	7.1	9.1	-2.0
Petroleum products	126	7.8	44	1.1	40	1.6	-2.8	-10.0	43.0
Chemicals and drugs	23	1.5	22	0.6	23	0.4	n.a.	-0.4	2.1
Sports goods	32	1.9	108	2.7	141	2.5	13.3	10.7	14.0
Surgical instruments	27	1.6	70	1.8	91	1.6	10.7	10.0	14.0
Engineering goods	51	3.1	34	0.9	38	0.7	-2.5	-4.0	5.0
Other exports	225	13.5	418	10.6	744	13.3	10.5	6.4	33.0
Total exports of manufactured goods	1662	100	3956	100	5672	100	10.6	9.1	18.0

Source: Kemal, op. cit.

Pakistan's export earnings are dominated by textiles, which typically accounts for 65 to 75% of manufacturing exports. This is illustrated in Table 35, which not only shows the shares in manufacturing exports but also illustrates the significance of cotton yarn in the 1980s export boom. In $ terms, cotton yarn exports increased by nearly 550% during the decade. The importance of the other major category, garments, is shown by the fact that garment and hosiery exports went up from a mere $75 million to over $1 billion (*see* Table 35). The success of the spinning sector, while welcome in terms of export dynamism, raises wider questions about textile policy. Part of the reason for the spinning boom was the rapid growth in cotton production due to technological breakthroughs, price controls, and an export tax on raw cotton.

Some studies suggest that spinning is not an activity in which Pakistan has a comparative advantage, i.e. the value added is negative when inputs and outputs are measured at world prices. Other studies suggest that this is actually not the case and that the value added on spinning is positive when measured at world prices. Irrespective of the question of whether spinning is an efficient industry in Pakistan, there is a wider issue of whether the country should be relying excessively on such low value added exports. Higher quality yarn and other textile products need to be promoted. The production of higher count yarns was being aborted by trade policy, which imposed high tariffs on inputs such as caustic soda, bleaching power, and dyestuffs. The reduction of tariffs on these inputs, announced in the 1993-4 budget, was expected to promote exports of higher count yarn. This is also likely to accelerate the recent growth in higher quality fabric exports. The other major component of textile exports during the 1980s was garments which, as in Bangladesh, emerged as a significant export sector. Even in garments, the concentration has been on a relatively low quality output; quotas for slightly better garments remain unutilized. Shortcomings in such areas represent a form of a human capital constraint to economic development. The absence of design, marketing, and quality control skills constrain the development of better quality output. In the absence of good quality manpower, it is easier to concentrate on simpler, lower value added products. This is an area in which sector-specific training support can play an important role in overcoming such constraints. These need to be allied to price reforms which provide the incentives to export higher value added items.

Along with garments and yarn, the relatively rapid expansion in manufacturing exports during the 1980s was led by the leather sub-sector. Leather exports grew at an annual rate of just over 13% in $US terms. The pattern of leather exports is somewhat similar to that of the textile sector—leather garment exports have risen sharply but the concentration of the leather sector remains on relatively low value added products. Skill, design, and marketing constraints, along with trade policy anomalies, appear to have hampered higher value added exports. None the less, the potential in the leather sector suggests that this could be an important component of a labour-intensive export drive.

36. EXPORTS OF SPORTS GOODS

Year	$ Million
1980-1	32
1981-2	30
1982-3	35
1983-4	49
1984-5	44
1985-6	49
1986-7	58
1987-8	65
1988-9	71
1989-90	108
1990-1	138
1991-2	141

Other sub-sectors which have been performing reasonably well in export markets are: (i) engineering goods, or more specifically, surgical instruments. However, most of these tend also to be at the lower quality end. Given the considerable history of surgical goods production in Pakistan, there appears to be a promising potential for upgradation and expansion.[7] The rapid increase of surgical goods exports[8] disguises the general decline in the export of other engineering goods. Many of these industries are estimated to be activities in which Pakistan has a comparative advantage and therefore appear, in principle, to be a promising area for policy and infrastructural investment support for an export drive. (ii) Football exports have been the driving force in sports goods exports, which grew at an annual rate of 14% during the 1980s. The export earnings are given in Table 36. Pakistan produced the footballs for the 1994 soccer World Cup in the United States, a success which could be built upon.[9] Again, in view of Pakistan's experience in sports goods production, this is an area where labour-intensive exports could increase substantially if technological and marketing innovations were made. (iii) Other areas where Pakistan appears to have an export potential in the short-run are carpets and food processing. In carpets, Pakistan has suffered a decline in world export share, while in food processing exports, the country has not competed effectively in large nearby markets, such as the Middle East. Again these subsectors appear to be promising but would require concerted government policy support.

It follows that a more coherent and aggressive industrial policy is needed to shift towards higher value manufacturing exports. This would place new demands on the state. As it withdraws from production and trade, it needs to support a concerted export drive through a mix of price reforms, technology transmission institutions, training support, and physical infrastructure investments. This role is required of the state in order to improve the quality and the technological capacity to export more sophisticated and demanding products.[10] More details of the policy direction necessary for labour-intensive exports are discussed after a review of recent policy influences and constraints to future growth.

Policy influences on recent outcomes and constraints to future growth

The performance and structure of the industrial sector has been deeply influenced by the policy environment. Industrial sector policies have had five types of impact: (i) incentives which have promoted growth in general and exports in specific manufacturing sub-sectors; (ii) policy distortions which have discriminated against manufacturing exports; (iii) policy and institutional shortcomings which have led to excessive capital intensity and low employment elasticity; (iv) policy biases which have affected the level and efficiency of investment, and (v) shortages of public investment in energy and physical infrastructure. This set of policy influences on the recent development of the industrial sector is examined below in the context of the policy reforms initiated in the 1980s.

The first category of recent policy influences—growth and export-generating incentives—were initiated through major structural reforms during 1981-3. The GOP's reform programme was supported by several adjustment loans from international agencies.[11] The general thrust of the reforms was towards creating the appropriate price incentives for the private sector. Accordingly, some of the key reforms included the delinking of the Pakistani rupee from the United States dollar in 1982, followed by an extensive deregulation of prices which were previously controlled administratively.

These international and domestic price reforms were accompanied by asset ownership changes in the form of a far-reaching privatization of state-owned enterprises.[12] Further, in addition to the exchange rate reform, a set of trade and fiscal measures was introduced to promote exports.[13] Imports of intermediate goods were liberalized, while specific incentives were extended, such as duty draw back schemes[14] and tax allowances. Collectively, these measures fuelled the export drive and contributed substantially to the revival of the private sector.[15]

The second feature of the policy framework have been disincentives towards production for exports. Anomalies remain and several aspects of industrial policy adversely affect export expansion, in spite of the promotion measures referred to earlier. Fiscal incentives to promote specific industries or particular regions have not only created major revenue losses but have also involved arbitrary protective measures, such as tariff protection. Tax holidays and regional development schemes led to enormous revenue losses in the

1980s. It is estimated that over 50% of investment in manufacturing enjoyed a tax holiday.[16] These tax breaks have frequently been combined with tariff protection for locating industries in backward regions. Since equipment is effectively subsidized and output protected from competition, these measures have reinforced the bias in favour of capital-intensive production for the domestic market. Pakistan's trade policy continued to shield many sectors during the 1980s through tariff protection. While tariffs were reduced, they were substituted with other import taxes[17] which frequently left the level of protection unchanged.

Protection of some sectors, while there is a simultaneous promotion of manufacturing exports, can and does coexist.[18] Regional and tax policies in Pakistan, however, have tended to sustain the bias in favour of import substitution. Invest-ment in export industries has had to deal with unnecessary and undesirable policy inconsistencies, such as the arbitrary announcement of distortionary regional schemes.

The relative neglect of a focused export-oriented industrialization is reflected in the fact that the 1989 industrial policy did not even mention export promotion as one of the four major goals.[19] In particular, manufacturing exports have been discouraged by the excessive focus of fiscal, monetary, and trade policies on import substituting industries.[20] During the 1980s, some progress, was made in favour of export promotion. Exchange rate reforms have already been mentioned. In addition, the relative bias against what were classified as non-traditional exports was removed by tax reforms which created a level playing field on export incentives, irrespective of whether they were traditional or not.[21] The removal of such disincentives for diversifying exports was welcome but was not sufficient. More extensive reforms to remove the anti-export bias were required in the 1990s. The agenda is similar to the kind of industrial policy reforms undertaken in East Asia to initially promote labour-intensive manufacturing exports.[22] Estimates of the importance of such industrial reforms for poverty alleviation in Pakistan suggest that the GOP should play particular attention to a more concerted drive towards manufacturing export growth.[23]

The third set of policy influences have been those which have affected factor markets. Of particular importance are distortions which have artificially promoted mechanization by subsidizing capital. A corollary of the above is the related discrimination in the employment of labour. The low employment elasticity of Pakistan's industrial sector has been unfortunate not only for its adverse distributional consequences but also because the neglect of social policy investments has meant intense pressure on the supply side of the labour market. In other words, while population and the labour force have been growing rapidly, the country's industrial policy has discriminated against employment. The large scale manufacturing sector, for example, barely employs 2% of the total work force, while it accounts for approximately 16% of national income. The demand for labour has·been subdued by policy distortions which have made machinery cheap. The price of capital has been lowered by a number of measures. Subsidized interest and tax holiday schemes have reduced capital costs by nearly 50%.[24] Similarly, import tax exemptions for investments in large scale manufacturing (LSM) have encouraged capital intensity. Other fiscal instruments, such as generous depreciation allowances, have also effectively lowered the price of capital.

In addition to these policy biases against employment, institutional failures have also contributed to excessive capital intensity. Financial sector rent-seeking, for example, which may lead to loans for the purchase of capital equipment being 'written off', effectively lowers the price of capital. Similarly, the practice of under-invoicing the purchase price of capital goods, so that the import duty paid is lower than would have been the case at the market price, also encourages more capital intensity. Such institutional disturbances accentuate the policy biases mentioned earlier, which affect factor markets.

Fourth, it is somewhat ironic that the above-mentioned distortions favouring capital intensity have simultaneously reduced the volume of resources available for investment. Repression of interest rates, and related financial disintermediation, have discouraged savings. Thus, while the demand for investment has been high due to policy influences, the same inducements have had an adverse impact on the supply of investible resources. A low savings rate, and a poorly functioning financial system, have acted as a constraint to increasing the level of investment. Further, the efficiency of investment has been hampered by the political control of the financial system, whereby resource allocation decisions were partially determined by patronage. Such institutional factors have often meant that investment has gone into less profitable projects.[25] Inefficiency of capital use has also been encouraged by policy distortions which favour investment in new firms, rather in expansion of existing plants or for modernization of installed capacity. As a result, over 75% of manufacturing investment in the 1980s, for example, was in new firms.[26]

The pattern of public expenditure on physical and social infrastructure was far from optimal, as far as the industrial sector was concerned. Acute shortages of energy and a deteriorating transport network provided immediate constraints to industrial activity, while lack of social investments created both direct and indirect effects. For example, a burgeoning labour force created employment pressures, while a poor skill base restricted the potential for diversification. However, due to lack of effective revenue mobilization efforts, there were chronic shortages of public investment in both physical and social infrastructure.

The set of five types of policy influences discussed above had tended to promote a highly capital-intensive and protected industrial structure. Much of the recent reform agenda in the financial, trade, and fiscal policies has related to the need for shifting incentives away from such an inward-looking, and rent-seeking-oriented industrial structure. Needless to add, such reforms have been resisted by groups who have benefited from the existing pattern of incentives and patronage.

During the adjustment process of the 1980s and 1990s, Pakistan accumulated substantial additional debt, at a time when the previous volume of domestic and foreign debt servicing was leading to an alarming situation.[27] For reasons of debt servicing, as well as the more substantive one of employment creation, a supply response from the industrial sector is critical for the success of the structural reform programme. Further, it is quite important for the export orientation of the industrial sector to deepen and improve on the performance achieved during the 1980s. The relatively poor actual performance of the industrial sector during the 1990s is, therefore, a cause of substantial concern. Part of the reason had nothing to do with the policy reforms *per se*, since the slowdown was due to domestic supply side shocks and some adverse exogenous external developments. However, some of the more intractable political and institutional reasons for disturbance in the industrial sector—such as the spiralling violence in Karachi—are particularly worrying for Pakistan's emergence as a major manufacturing exporter. These wider political economy considerations are discussed after an analysis of the policy direction required for labour-intensive manufacturing export growth.

Policy direction for labour-intensive industrial growth

The first pricing and institutional reforms, initiated in 1981-3, were partial. A set of macroeconomic and sectoral constraints remained and the continuing policy response to the industrial sector's development took the form of a comprehensive agenda of reforms, which were initiated in the late 1980s. A four year structural adjustment loan, covering 1988-9 to 1991-2,[28] was signed between the World Bank, IMF,[29] and the GOP, with strong support from other donors such as the ADB, UNDP,[30] and various bilateral agencies.[31] An extensive series of trade, financial, and fiscal reforms ensued, which have a strong bearing on the future evolution of the industrial structure. These included: (i) liberalization of the capital account and the convertibility of the rupee; (ii) reduction in maximum tariffs from 220% to 80% and a virtual elimination of items on the negative list of banned imports; (iii) deregulation of investment sanctioning procedures so that domestic as well as foreign investors no longer require a license; (iv) no controls on foreign ownership of enterprises or on the repatriation of profits earned therein; (v) financial sector reforms such as the privatization of commercial banks, entry of private investment and commercial banks, and stronger regulatory measures for the supervision of banks; (vi) fiscal reforms, such as the introduction of a general sales tax to compensate partially for the loss of indirect taxes due to tariff reduction and the imposition of taxes on agricultural income and wealth.

This extensive array of reforms is to be built on by another three year Structural Adjustment Programme, which was signed by the GOP in early 1994. In addition to general balance of payments support,[32] the accompanying loans are aimed at addressing the shortages in human capital[33] and physical infrastructure.[34]

One of the central objectives of the wide-ranging policy reform agenda is to create a more efficient, dynamic, and outward-oriented industrial sector. Accordingly, the reforms have been addressing perceived inconsistencies and shortcomings in the existing policy framework. The future evolution of the industrial sector from a largely import-substituting to a more export-oriented one requires that the momentum be sustainined for the policy reforms currently under way. Needless to add, policy distortions such as the dreaded 'regional development schemes' need to be shunned. Apart from pursuing a sound and consistent policy framework, the state needs to support the industrial sector through physical and social infrastructure investments. Investments in physical infrastructure, such as energy, are being expedited through the mobilizatron of both international and domestic private capital for such projects, although progress has been slow.[35] Such investments have partially relieved the public sector resource constraint for infrastructure development.

The human capital constraint for the corporate sector is largely being reduced by the private sector as well. A number of private management and technical training institutions have been opened. Management and technology centres have been established some of which service the needs of specific sectors such as textiles. These need to be supported by more effective public sector education, training, and technology transfer institutions. As mentioned earlier, concentration on these functions is part of the transformation of the role of the state, as it withdraws from production and trade and engages in interventions which support private sector led industrial development.

Accompanying human capital investments played a critical role in the industrial development of East Asia. They not only reduced employment pressures on the industrial labour market by reducing population growth, but also initially aided productivity growth because of the primary education received by the workers.[36] Subsequent diversification and maturing of the industrial sector required a more sophisticated human capital base, the creation of which involved extensive state support.[37]

The GOP needs to play an important role in the diversification of the industrial structure. It has a role in both altering incentives and creating capacities. Fiscal, trade, and financial policy reforms are required to remove the bias towards capital and against labour. Similarly, policy reforms can reduce the incentives towards domestic production and create a more even 'playing field' for exports. The public sector can also help by assisting with marketing information and   technology transmission. The latter can be assisted through joint ventures as well as improving the efficiency of existing technology support institutions.

In brief, policy and institutional reform along with human capital investments can play a critical role in accelerating the transformation towards a more labour-intensive export-oriented manufacturing sector.

Political economy constraints in the development of the industrial sector, particularly export industries

The industrial policy direction noted above is necessary for expanding labour-intensive exports. There are, however, influences on manufacturing development which go beyond those confined to the typical mandate of industrial policy. The impact of these influences has been analysed earlier in the text. The arguments are summarized below, with a view to examining how these obstacles could be avoided in the future.

The evolution of the industrial sector has been shaped by wider political economy considerations, which have had an important bearing on policy. Two features related to the regional/ethnic aspect of who gained from industrialization shaped much of the debate on distributional issues. The most significant feature, initially, was the sense of regional deprivation felt by East Pakistan. East Pakistan's lack of participation in the industrialization process fuelled the wider grievances regarding the distribution of political power. The transfer of the agricultural surplus to industry had an unfortunate regional correlation. Pricing, particularly exchange rate policy, assisted in the transfer of jute incomes generated in East Pakistan to the industrial development of Western Pakistan.[38]

The other ethnic aspect remained subdued under the East-West Pakistan conflict till the creation of Bangladesh. Many of the merchant groups were refugees from India, as was much of the senior bureaucracy. The ethnic background of the entrepreneurs[39] was important since this had a significant bearing on subsequent policy shocks in the 1970s, such as the nationalization of the industrial and financial sectors. During the 1950s and 1960s, however, the Muhajir and Punjabi-dominated industrial class[40] received extensive state support. The emerging industrial class did not exclusively consist of Muhajirs and Punjabis. There was a strong presence of a few Pathan families, who benefited from close linkages with the military rulers, particularly during the 1960s.[41] The ethnic groups which were largely left out were the Bengalis, the Balochis, and the Sindhis. The marginalization of the latter was particularly serious since, in the post-Bangladesh Pakistan,[42] Sindhi resentment at Muhajir-dominated industrialization in their province tilted the balance of power in favour of nationalization. It reinforced the reaction against the emerging bourgeoisie in the Punjab, which led to a movement against private capital in the province. A similar reaction was evident in the NWFP.[43]

In many ways, the industrial business groups became the focus of an attack against the pursuit of functional inequality. They were the beneficiaries in an environment where the equity expectations inherent in the Pakistan movement were not being met. The process of urbanization was unleashing rapid change. The response of the GOP was perceived to be uncaring and unresponsive to the needs of labour. In other words, the obvious neglect of the requirements of social cohesion during industrialization created a political backlash, which led to nationalization.

These political economy factors regarding distributional gains have had an enormous impact on the sector's evolution. The cost of the nationalizations of the 1970s has been immense. The relative decline *vis-à-vis* East Asia began during this period. None of the East Asian countries nationalized. Indeed, as mentioned in Chapter 2, they consolidated their industrial sectors and moved from an import substitution phase towards export expansion. Thus, protection was used to create 'infant' industries, which were then subjected to the efficiency discipline of external markets. The resultant labour-intensive manufacturing exports played a critical role in poverty alleviation.

Pakistan's nationalizations, on the other hand, led to direct bureaucratic control over production units.[44] The uncertainty and instability created by the shock over ownership adversely affected investment in the industrial sector and prevented a major expansion into manufacturing exports. Those who came to dominate the public sector enterprises had little experience of business, leading to gross inefficiencies. Further, the nationalized financial sector became a source of political patronage leading to highly inefficient and arbitrary investment decisions. Much of industrial investment in the 1970s was absorbed by an ill-advised shift towards a heavy basic goods sector. By the 1980s, much of the formal financial sector was bankrupt, largely because of political patronage, which wrote-off loans to major business groups. This plunder of the financial sector has had an extremely adverse effect on the levels of savings and investment.

The result was a deepening of an import substitution strategy. The principle difference was that the output composition shifted towards capital and intermediate goods, while the ownership transferred to those with little ability in business management. Further, these public sector enterprises were frequently run on non-commercial considerations. The inevitable consequence of pricing distortions, ostensibly for social reasons, was the commercial non-viability of the firms, leading to demands on tax resources to sustain them. A steel mill was built in the 1970s, with the assistance of the Soviet Union, at Karachi.[45] This not only absorbed the bulk of investment resources which had high opportunity costs, but also led to excessive overmanning due to political patronage. Thus, a large inefficient plant was created which severely distorted the development of the industrial sector. Moreover, the Steel Mill reinforced the bias towards capital intensity, sustaining the low employment elasticity of Pakistan's manufacturing sector.[46]

The 1980s witnessed a reversal to a private sector led industrial structure. As far as privatization of public sector enterprises was concerned, it was slow in the initial phase, partly because of complex negotiations regarding the transfer of liabilities to the private owners. Much of the emphasis was on reviving the momentum of private sector industrial activity. The policy debate was dominated by the question of the relative roles of the public and private sectors as well as the regional/ethnic spread of ownership.[47]

In sum, the result of this pattern of the industrial sector's evolution is that Pakistan, until the mid-1990s, has had largely inward-looking, capital-intensive manufacturing enterprises. Although there have been notable successes in exports during the 1980s,[48] the policy regime tended to favour manufacturing for the domestic market. Further, rent-seeking gains distorted investment patterns and led to the protection of inefficiencies, particularly since loans were often 'written off' due to political influence.[49] A set of industrial, trade, and financial sector policy reforms is currently under way. Progress has been relatively slow but the general direction of reforms appears to be sound. The financial sector is being taken out of direct political control, while incentive reforms are shifting gradually towards more labour-intensive manufacturing exports. There is an urgent need to expedite the pace of implementation of these reforms while attending to the key political bottlenecks to major ·improvements in export performance.[50]

No country in the world has become a major exporter with its principal commercial city and port in the turmoil that Karachi is in. The causes lie deep in the political system of Pakistan. While problems of drugs, smuggling, and sectarian violence compound the difficulties of the city, the fundamental issue is the failure of ethnic integration. The critical province of Sindh has been devastated by a rural-urban ethnic division. The polarization, which is reflected in the support base of the major political parties, has had a debilitating impact on society and the economy. Recent efforts at resolving the problems of Karachi have failed.[51] What appears to be self-evident is that Pakistan is unlikely to become a major player in manufacturing exports if its port city remains in this perilous state. It is also extremely unlikely that Pakistan can attract major foreign direct investments for manufactured exports with Karachi reduced to its current plight.

The key indicator of the success of Pakistan's wide-ranging structural reforms in the industrial sector is the supply response of labour-intensive manufacturing exports. A substantive political impediment to progress in this area is the ineffective ethnic integration in Sindh province. There are many desirable social and political reasons for a political settlement in Sindh. The imperatives of the economy suggest that the issue is not simply a provincial one. The impact on stable national economic development is obvious. Amongst a myriad of difficulties, this is perhaps the single most important political problem facing the country. Certainly, as far as economic repercussions of structural adjustment are concerned, concerted attention towards reversing the disintegration of Karachi is required urgently.

Finally, the scale of rent-seeking corruption has had a very damaging effect on the pattern of industrial development. The 1980s began, as mentioned earlier, with a reversal of the policy shocks which created considerable uncertainty over property rights.[52] However, the revival of a private sector led industrial strategy consisted of two elements: incentive reforms which promoted private investment and growth, and extensive political manipulation of the financial system. The latter occurred because the financial sector remained mostly under state ownership during the course of the 1980s. This combination of incentive reform and institutional control led to extensive corruption and abuse, and distorted the incentives for exports. The latter occurred indirectly, since rent-seeking yielded high returns to protected domestic-orientated activity through access of industrialists to the political process. There are equity and efficiency consequences of such patronage mechanisms. Entrepreneurs invest too much time in seeking favours and earning related rents.

These distortions take the form, for example, of numerous Special Regulatory Orders (SROs) which periodically provide tax exemptions and special privileges to particular industries. These SROs tend not to be transparent and frequently reflect patronage-related privileges. Further, entrepreneurs without such political access are obviously discriminated against. Such inequities fuel the popular discomfort at the lack of accountability over corrupt practices, thereby contributing to the sense of disillusion with the political process noted earlier.

The measures required to deal with such corrupting distortions include judicial independence, denationalization of the financial sector, and greater regulatory autonomy for the central bank. There is evidence of progress in some of these areas. The 1994 State Bank Act has increased the independence of the central bank, while the financial sector has been deregulated and partially denationalized. The pace of privatization and liberalization of financial institutions needs to be accelerated in order to restore the health of the financial system, which is a necessary precondition to the much needed increase in the savings rate. Reforms which strengthen independent regulatory capacity and loosen direct state trading activities in the financial sector are welcome. These need to be supported by efforts to create a more effective and efficient judicial system.

SUMMARY

Rapid economic growth is necessary[53] for poverty alleviation. Relatedly, the performance of the industrial sector in Pakistan is critical for the pace of employment generation. Pakistan has had a chequered history of industrialization. Major achievements in the 1950s and 1960s were followed by policy shocks over ownership in the form of nationalization. The reversion to private sector led industrial development in the 1980s was accompanied by a much improved export performance.

Pakistan's industrial sector has suffered from policy inconsistencies which are in the process of being ironed out. Recent policy reforms have set in motion a process towards transition from an inward-looking, capital-intensive industrial structure to one which is more open and likely to create more jobs. Apart from sustaining this policy direction, the momentum of reform needs to be supported by public investments in physical and social infrastructure.

(B) THE DEVELOPMENT OF AGRICULTURE

Sectoral trends

Pakistan inherited a good base for agricultural development. While human capital and technological levels were low, the region of Punjab had witnessed major investments in irrigation in the early 20th century. The canals built around the five rivers of Punjab provided a sound base for the development of irrigated agriculture. The first decade after independence was a period of rehabilitation and adjustments to the shocks of partition. General economic growth, including that of agriculture, was subdued. Through the course of the 1950s, agricultural output remained stagnant in per capita terms.

It was during the 1960s that Pakistan became one of the 'green revolution' countries.[54] The high yields embodied in imported technology led to major increases in the output of the leading crops. The chemical seed and fertilizer package linked to increased water supplies led to a rapid supply response. The marketing of high yielding inputs was accompanied by policy incentives for the expansion of water supplies through subsidies for private tubewells. Both food and cash crop production benefited from the green revolution, and agriculture grew at an annual rate of nearly 2% per capita.

The rate of growth was not sustained in the 1970s due to a mix of land tenure insecurities affecting investment, changes in marketing arrangements, and the nationalization of small agro-industrial units. These policy shocks were compounded by natural calamities such as floods and a cotton virus. As a result, the sectoral growth rate was negative in per capita terms for the decade as a whole (*see* Table 37).

The 1980s witnessed a revival of positive per capita growth. This was due to a mix of a strong performance by cash crops such as cotton, and a boom in the livestock sub-sector. Livestock contributes more than a third of agricultural value added and has been a dynamic sub-sector since the mid-1970s. Initially, the growth was concentrated in poultry production, which had been growing at an annual rate of 12% during the 1970s and 1980s. Since then the success of livestock production has spread to cattle and milk production.[55]

37. PER CAPITA GROWTH IN AGRICULTURE, 1950-95

Decade	Annual Average Growth
1950-9	-0.6%
1960-9	2.7%
1970-9	-0.6%
1980-9	2.5%
1990-5	0.2%

Source: Calculations based on *Economic Survey,* various issues, Government of Pakistan.

During the early 1980s one of the milestones of agricultural production was achieved as the country approached self-sufficiency in basic food grains. This is reflected in Table 38, which shows how the extent of wheat imports became relatively negligible, and were used primarily to build reserves and iron out price fluctuations. Further, a surplus of rice was evident in the growth of exports (*see* Table 38). This process was aided by good weather.

These food supply achievements, however, suffered reversals after the gains of the early 1980s. Imports, as a percentage of wheat production, again began to accelerate. The proportion rose to 5.6% during 1985-9 and increased sharply to 10.1% during the 1990s, which partly reflected the impact of natural calamities affecting the variability of wheat production (*see* Table 38).

The proportion of rice which is exported has risen from around 20% in the early 1970s to a level where nearly a third of domestic production is exported. There have been fluctuations in sub-periods, but the proportion appears to have stabilized at around 28% (*see* Table 38).

38. FOOD GRAIN PRODUCTION AND TRADE
(5-year Averages)

Period	Wheat **imports** as a % of total domestic production	Rice **exports** as a % of total domestic production
1974-9	14.1	21.2
1980-4	2.6	32.6
1985-9	5.6	27.8
1990-4	10.1	27.0

Source: Calculations based on *Economic Survey,* various issues, Government of Pakistan.

A major and growing source of pressure on the balance of payments is edible oil imports. These have grown substantially and amounted to nearly $US 600 million in 1994-5 alone, constituting the single largest import item from the agricultural sector. As such, they are the fourth largest commodity import item after machinery, chemicals, and petroleum products.

Aggregate increases in output have to be assessed in relation to the use of inputs in order to get an idea of efficiency. A number of recent studies tend to show that output growth has been due principally to increased input supplies, not to more efficient use of these inputs. Except for a brief period in the 1960s, total factor productivity growth has been static or even declining.[56]

Yields per unit of land suggest that while Pakistan has shown reasonable progress in some crops, the performance remains substantially below potential and low in relation to other countries. Yield performance in cash crops such as cotton has tended to do better than food crops in recent years. Cotton yields, for example, more than doubled between 1982 and 1992, rising from 360 to 750 kg per hectare. This yield performance was the principal source of encouragement in crops during the 1980s; otherwise much of the dynamism came from livestock growth. Rice yields, on the other hand, have declined during the same period, falling from 1750 to

1550 kg per hectare. Wheat yields have shown moderate improvement, rising from 1700 to 2000 kg per hectare between 1982 and 1992. Rice and wheat yields had grown quite substantially in the 1960s in the immediate aftermath of the green revolution.

Land ownership and operation patterns have undergone substantial change since independence. In 1947, there were essentially two categories of farming arrangements. The first involved landlords who either engaged in share-cropping agreements with tenants, or retained tenants-at-will who had no legal or customary rights to the land they cultivated. Large landlords were economically and politically dominant in both Sindh and Punjab. The second category of farming consisted mainly of small peasant proprietors, principally in the NWFP and in parts of Punjab.

Subsequent commercial developments have led to a wider variety of market-based relations, specially in the wake of the green revolution. More commercial, large land owners have emerged who have resumed land from tenants, not only because of increased returns from land but also due to fear of resumption due to land tenure reform. Wage labour has increased in many areas, as have the sources of off-farm rural income. This greater differentiation and complexity of tenure relations is not in contradiction to the continuing, and disproportionate political influence of the larger landlords. It is estimated that the large landlords, i.e. those owning over 20 hectares, own 38% of the land in Sindh, 25% of the land in Punjab, and 14% in the NWFP.[57] This group continues to exercise an exceptional influence on the political system, whether in alliance with military regimes or as part of political parties. Land reforms have done little to change the rural power base.

The picture of a feudal Pakistan is not a static one. There are a number of dynamic changes which are affecting the shape of rural society and its relative importance. There are several changes, such as the pressure on land through sub-division of holdings, within the context of rapid population growth. However, perhaps the most important dynamic is to do with the reduction in the relative share of rural areas in the total population. Approximately 40% of the country now lives in urban areas. The ongoing rapid pace of urbanization implies that Pakistan will be a majority urban country within the next two decades.

The rural areas have not been static as far as social structure is concerned. Links with urban society have been intensified by migration. In a number of regions, agro-industrial development and related urbanization has led to the growth of numerous small towns and cities in previously rural areas. Within the rural areas, different forms of tenurial and land holding patterns have emerged. In some areas, there has been an increased concentration of operated land holdings as owners have resumed land from tenants; in less productive areas the pattern of resumption has not been so rapid.

In 1996, Pakistan had the largest proportion of landlords in cabinet in all of Asia. Most families have strong ties with the military. As a result, the exercise of power is still influenced to a great extent by the large, landed rural families. The growth of urban forces is, however, leading to a clash between rural and urban interests.[58]

The rural-urban divide is already having an impact on the capacity to formulate economic policy. The political opposition of the urban private sector to a government dominated by rural interests has brought a certain paralysis to economic direction in the 1990s. Industrialization has been hampered by the political conflict and urban disturbances. Thus, rural power and urban tensions are juxtaposed in a manner which prevents a clear economic direction to be implemented.

In brief, sectoral trends suggest that taken as a whole, Pakistan's aggregate growth performance in agriculture is respectable, averaging 3% per annum since independence. This pace of expansion has generally enabled the country to feed a rapidly growing population. There have been periods of high growth of food grains as well as the principal cash crop, cotton. The latter has provided the base for the industrialization process. Recent years have also witnessed an acceleration in the growth of livestock production. Further, current yield levels and poor organization of sub-sectors such as livestock suggest that there is considerable room for future expansion. None the less, while the aggregate growth rate over the past has been reasonable, the per capita performance is not as impressive. This is partly on account of the failure to implement an effective social policy. A population growth rate of 3% has imposed strenuous burdens on the agricultural sector's capacity to provide food and assist in the production of clothing. In addition to the difficulties of growing fast enough to provide such basic needs as food and clothing, the high population growth rate has exerted pressures on the labour market, leading to rapid rural-urban migration.

Policy influences on sectoral performance

The influences on sectoral performance have tended to vary. The 1960's green revolution was to some extent exogenous, determined by technological developments outside the country. The application of favourable results of international research was facilitated by public investments in irrigation infrastructure, and incentives to private producers in the form of subsidies for irrigation investment. Output price policies did not tax agriculture on a scale which would be a disincentive to private production. Farmers received a good return on their investment, as evidenced by the supply response in the 1960s. The sector did transfer a surplus to industry but within reasonable limits.

For the industrial sector, as long as agricultural inputs are provided at below the border price, it is a recipient of a policy-induced subsidy. For major agro-industrial sectors such as textiles, the pricing policies have always ensured a favourable transfer, although the scale of the transfer has tended to vary from period to period.

During the 1970s, the policy regime sustained a transfer out of agriculture in the region of 15% of agricultural gross product.[59] The scale of transfers out of agriculture has reduced substantially in recent years, and is estimated to have fallen from 15% to 6% of agricultural product in 1992.[60] Once subsidies and capital investments are taken into account, the net transfer out of agriculture is negligible.[61]

During the 1980s, the results of domestic applied agricultural research, price policy reform, and improved crop management techniques fuelled growth. As noted earlier, there was a particularly sharp rise in cotton and the livestock sub-sector.

The general incentive regime for farmers has been strongly influenced by price and marketing policies. By and large, farming has remained a private business in Pakistan, and the state has refrained from any major involvement in production.[62] The involvement in output pricing, input subsidies, and marketing regulations has, however, played an important role in shaping private returns.

Like governments elsewhere, the GOP has justified extensive intervention in pricing and marketing on the basis of the need to meet multiple objectives; these have included balancing the need to ensure an 'adequate return' to farmers with the stimulus to be provided to agro-industry, protecting the domestic market from fluctuations in international markets, and ensuring the availability of basic food at reasonable prices.

In the 1950s, the GOP maintained a highly regulated marketing regime. Farmers had to sell grain at below market prices to government distribution channels. Farmers also operated under periodic profit controls, price ceiling regulations, and the enforcement of zoning restrictions which controlled the movement of grain from one area to another. A partial liberalization of this marketing and pricing regime occurred in 1959 and provided a more favourable incentive regime for the green revolution.

Support prices and price regulations for all the major crops as well as livestock produce determined the incentive structure for production decisions. Export of crops such as rice has been controlled through government marketing boards In the 1980s, the system of procurement price supports was formalized through the creation of the Agricultural Prices Commission. The APC consults farming groups and other stake-holders in determining the level of prices.

Price and marketing interventions affect all crops. Wheat is procured through provincial agencies at the support price announced. Farmers do not have to sell to those marketing organizations, hence they do not enjoy a monopoly in trade. Export taxes are imposed on cotton trade in order to assure a supply to the domestic textile industry at lower than border prices. The sugar industry receives considerable protection through tariffs and purchases of sugar-cane at support prices.

The country's comparative advantage in growing sugar-cane is, however, open to question.

The net effect of the policy regime on various crops can be summarized as disprotection of wheat, with some estimates suggesting that the degree of disprotection for wheat is one of the largest in the world. These estimates are based on a comparison of import parity prices with the domestic price of wheat after the regulatory interventions. However, a recent study[63] has questioned this basis of comparison, and undertaken a dynamic analysis of the impact of liberalizing the wheat market. The prevailing import parity price is viewed as appropriate for a static comparison, but it is argued that the effect of liberalization would be to lower the market price below the currently prevailing import parity. The implication of such an analysis is that the magnitude of the policy discrimination against wheat is exaggerated, if dynamic price reducing effects of liberalization are taken into account.

Whatever measure is used, there is little doubt that there is a policy discrimination against wheat and cotton, while rice and sugar-cane receive protection through the policy regime. The rationale for the tax on wheat is that it creates more stable and lower prices while the tax on cotton is a transfer to industry. It is questionable whether sugar-cane deserves such policy support in view of its doubtful comparative advantage.

The 'tax' or transfer out of agriculture through policy interventions is not unusual. With the possible exception of Korea, this has been the experience of all the countries of East and South East Asia. Countries such as Taiwan, Malaysia, and Thailand have all had periods when policy has deliberately transferred resources out of agriculture, but within limits which were prudent enough to ensure that the agricultural sector maintained a respectable rate of growth, and diversified into higher productivity activities. What matters is the scale of the transfer and whether the policy regime provides sufficient incentives for efficient and equitable growth.

During the 1980s, Pakistan's agricultural policy underwent a number of reforms. Subsidies to pesticides and most fertilizers were withdrawn, support prices adjusted upwards accordingly, and state intervention in marketing reduced. It was argued that further liberalization could reduce public sector marketing inefficiencies and thereby consumer prices.[64] Policy tried to maintain a difficult balance between the needs of industry, reasonable consumer prices for basic food, and incentives for farmers.

A number of policy reforms under way in Pakistan since the 1980s suggest that the constraint to further agricultural development has less to do with poor incentives and more with the need to improve productivity, water and input management, skills, and extension. Future efficiency gains are related to the ability to use inputs more intensively. The current irrigation system is not efficient in the use of increasingly scarce water. To address this issue, a number of on-farm water management projects have been launched. Similarly, there is the perennial problem of land lost to water logging and salinity, which needs to be reclaimed by measures such as gypsum application. These efficiency considerations require reforms and investments in the following areas: .

- The direction of recent price reform should be sustained. Prices of inputs such as seeds, fertilizers, and pesticides are close to or equal to market prices. These have been accompanied by output price liberalization. Some inputs are still subsidized, such as irrigation water. Credit is also subsidized for those farmers who get access to either targeted credit schemes or use their political influence to get loans written-off. Such subsidies are of course highly inequitable, and require privatization of the financial sector and regulatory discipline. Irrigation price does not at present even cover O & M costs. Defining the long-run marginal cost of this water has been fraught with difficulties and current price policy attempts are to raise the price to cover at least the O & M cost, while treating the capital cost as a physical infrastructure support. Related to the input price reforms are changes in output prices in a manner which would reduce the transfer out of agriculture. Macroeconomic reforms have also been in the right direction. There are no apparent exchange rate or monetary policy distortions impeding agricultural development.

There is no over-valued exchange rate or an interest policy which distorts capital use.[65]

- Price reform such as the above should be matched with reforms of direct taxation. The imposition of direct income taxes and increased wealth taxes is justified not only on grounds of equity but also in the interest of required sectoral investments. A simple mechanism for doing so is to revive the Finance Act of 1977, which eliminated the outdated land tax system and replaced it with direct taxes on income. This Act was repealed by the incoming government in 1977. A number of other options are available[66] but it is time for Pakistan to address this issue head-on, rather than continue to postpone one of the symbols of inequity which tax exemption of income from agriculture constitutes. There is no direct taxation of incomes derived from agriculture. The apologists for this exemption point to the taxation suffered by the sector as a whole, through the price and regulatory regime. This misses the point. After all these interventions are taken into account, it should still be the case that if a person's income is in the taxable range, it is subjected to tax. Some of the wealthiest families in the country do not legally pay any tax. This inequitable exemption also sets a bad precedent for direct taxation in industry, where the higher income tax payers view such an exemption as arbitrary. The argument about sectoral transfers is a subterfuge for the self-interest of those who escape the direct tax net. The scale of the transfer has reduced in recent years; moreover, the question of sectoral transfers should not be confused with individual tax liability. A person in industry is not taxed on the basis of whether his sector is doing well or not. Your tax cannot be assessed on what you may have earned under different policy circumstances. The argument that a person could have earned more is a poor one for seeking tax exemption. The only relevant issue is gross earnings from the assets and/or labour employed in agriculture.

- Increased savings and tax revenues are required to finance a range of supporting investments needed for agricultural development. The first set of investments consists of direct support to physical infrastructure and support services. Efficiency of resource use has been improved recently through programmes for on-farm water management and irrigation system maintenance. Public expenditure is required to sustain and extend these programmes, and to reform the poorly functioning extension service.[67] Public expenditure patterns for social investment also have an important effect, particularly on the medium-term diversification prospects, the health of the rural population, and in reducing pressures on the rural labour market by controlling fertility. In this regard, the importance of the rural-focused Social Action Plan (SAP) should not be underestimated. The SAP is aimed at primary education, primary health, and rural water and sanitation. Its effective implementation requires not only public spending but also, as in other areas, institutional reform to improve the public sector's delivery capacity.

The failure of previous land reforms has sustained the political power and disproportionate command over resources of the large landowners. The rationale which lay behind the previous land reforms remains as, if not more, valid than ever before. Patrimonial practices, the lack of accountability of power, and the arbitrary manner in which authority is exercised, are obstacles to political modernization and equity. Agri-business and capitalist farming need to be encouraged as should mechanisms for involving the landed families in industry. This modernization of rural institutions is critically important. However, while the rationale for land reform can be reiterated and the policy options for different forms of land reform articulated, there is the basic problem of the agency of change. Another land reform under current conditions could be a recipe for disaster. Perhaps the most significant progress that could be made should be through the imposition of an income tax and the holding of an honest census.

In sum, Pakistan's potential in agriculture and industry suggests possibilities for rapid growth. The dynamism the country has shown and the existence of substantial private sector capacities provide the base for reasonable growth prospects. In principle, the country should grow in the region of 7 to 8% per annum. Some of the policy measures outlined for increasing the productivity of agriculture and international competitiveness of industry, require an important role for the state in facilitating the achievement of these growth rates. Measures such as direct income tax and financial sector reform should also facilitate the rise in savings required to achieve higher growth and improve equity. In spite of the current difficulties and the problems of implementation of policy reforms, the prospects for rapid agro-industrial growth suggest that the Pakistan economy could perform even better than it has done in the first half-century.

NOTES

1. The purchasing power of poor households can be affected by measures which influence the prices of the goods that they consume. Thus, subsidies on basic food items can, for example, help determine the living standards of poor families. However, the determinant of primary incomes is the wage level in employment.

2. In per capita terms, the annual average growth in incomes has been 3%.

3. This involved major relief efforts to settle refugees, and created the physical base for the new government.

4. This is particularly true when one compares Pakistan's export performance in the 1960s with that of the successful East Asian economies. In that decade, the difference between the two was marginal. Indeed Pakistan's manufacturing exports were greater than those of Indonesia and Thailand. However, the gap really grew in the next two decades, partly because of nationalization and political turmoil.

5. In 1947, the areas that constituted Pakistan were almost entirely agricultural. East Pakistan produced jute and rice, while West Pakistan's main crops were cotton and wheat. Most of the industrial units remained in the territory of the truncated India. There were a few small agro-processing units in Pakistan. Similarly, a modern financial sector did not exist.

6. For an analysis of the process of Pakistan's early industrialization see Papanek, G: *Social Goals and Private Incentives,* (Oxford University Press, 1966). Professor Papanek was part of the

Harvard Advisory Group which was extremely influential in the early stages of development strategy formulation.

7. For an analysis of the surgical goods industry see Noman, O: *The Metal Industries Development Centre, Sialkot,* (Economic Policy Research Unit, Lahore, 1990).

8. Pakistan's surgical goods exports have tended to concentrate on the US market for basic and disposable hospital kits. Even in this low quality area, there has been periodic lack of attention to quality control issues. The official certification system has not always worked efficiently, leading to trade disputes about the required chromium content of instruments. For details, see Noman, op. cit.

9. There were newspaper reports that the 'Made in Pakistan' label was not allowed to be written on the balls made for the World Cup, which is an indicator of Pakistan's poor reputation in export markets. But many other countries have discovered that it is not difficult to change this perception if you take quality control and marketing seriously.

10. These processes can be accelerated through joint ventures with foreign firms, creation of technology, and marketing-oriented producers' associations and so on.

11. A three-year adjustment programme during 1980-3 was supported by the World Bank and the IMF. This supporting finance included an IMF's Extended Fund Facility (EFF) of SDR 1.2 billion and a 1982 World Bank $250 million structural adjustment loan, directly linked to the IMF programme. Additional sectoral adjustment loans included the Asian Development Bank's programme loans for agriculture and industry and the World Bank's loans for energy and export development.

12. Initially, the privatization programme was slow to get off the ground. By 1988, however, it gained momentum and most of the public enterprises were sold by 1993.

13. Policy reforms for the promotion of exports were expedited through a World Bank sectoral adjustment loan for export development in 1986.

14. Duty drawback schemes are intended to promote exporters. Firms which import inputs can claim a return of the tax imposed if they can show that the inputs were part of exported output. Such schemes raise post-tax profits.

15. For details of the measures taken, see McLeary, W.A: 'Pakistan:

Structural Adjustment and Economic Growth' in Thomas, V (ed.): *Restructuring Economies in Distress*, (Oxford University Press, New York, 1991).

16. For details, see Naved Hamid, op. cit.

17. These included an education tax levied on imports, import license fees, and surcharges.

18. On this point see Noman, A: op. cit.

19. The four goals of the 1989 industrial policy were: (i) dispersal of industries; (ii) maximization of employment; (iii) promotion of key industries, and (iv) promotion of small scale industries.

20. For a detailed analysis of the policy distortions which have acted as a bias against exports, see Hamid and Kemal: op. cit.

21. Before the reforms, goods classified as traditional exports were favoured through subsidies. These typically took the form of compensatory tax rebates. The distinction between traditional and non-traditional exports was subsequently eliminated as far as qualification of promotional subsidies was concerned.

22. For a recent discussion of these reforms and their implication for Pakistan see Little, I: 'Trade and Industrialisation Revisited', (Iqbal memorial lecture, PIDE annual conference, Islamabad, 1994).

23. Studies have estimated high employment generation returns to manufacturing exports. See, for example, Khan, A.H: *Employment Creation Effects of Pakistan's Exports*, (Pakistan Institute of Development Economics, Islamabad, 1991).

24. Studies have estimated that 8-year tax holidays and concessionary finance schemes have reduced the price of capital by 23% and 24% respectively. See Kemal, A and Hamid, N: *Pakistan Industrial Sector Review Study* (Asian Development Bank, Manila, 1991).

25. This point has been made in a number of analyses of Pakistan's financial sector. See, *inter alia*, Fatma Shah: *The Regulatory Environment for Pakistan's Financial Sector*, (Economic Policy Research Unit, Lahore, 1990) and the USAID: *Review of the Financial Sector*, (Islamabad, 1989).

26. For an analysis of these issues see Hamid and Kemal: op. cit.

27. The growth of debt servicing commitments was analysed in Chapter 2.

28. Initially, the programme was for three years and was later

extended by one year due to exogenous shocks such as the floods and the Gulf War, which had a severe impact on the fiscal as well as the balance of payments position.

29. The IMF provided general balance of payments support through a structural adjustment facility of SDR 382 million and a standby loan of SDR 273 million. Agriculture sector loans, of $200 million each, were provided by the ADB and the World Bank. Other policy-based lending included World Bank loans to the financial sector ($150 million) and a second energy sector loan ($250 million), as well as an ADB industrial sector loan of $200 million.

30. The UNDP focused on the institutional change component of the reform process and, therefore, was involved in one of the most difficult and contentious areas of structural reform.

31. For example, donors such as the British ODA and the Netherlands government concentrated on supporting the Social Action Plan.

32. The IMF has agreed to provide an enhanced structural adjustment and extended fund facility of SDR 1 billion.

33. The World Bank is providing a $200 million loan for the Social Action Plan and a $250 million loan for the public sector adjustment loan.

34. Considerable emphasis has been placed on policy reforms which allow an extended role for the private sector, both domestic and foreign, in the provision of physical infrastructure. The main emphasis of the energy policy, for example, has been to reduce the resource constraint by attracting private investment for projects which would alleviate the infrastructural constraints to industrial development.

35. During 1994-5 considerable progress appears to have been made in attracting private investment for such infrastructural development. This has included foreign capital.

36. For an analysis of human capital factors see, *inter alia*, Yoo, Jung-ho: *The Industrial Policy of the 1970s and the Evolution of the Manufacturing Sector in Korea*, (Korean Development Institute, Seoul, 1990); Westphal, Yung Whee Rhee and Pursell: 'Korean Industrial Competence: Where it Came From', (World Bank Staff Working Papers, 469, 1981); Pack and Westphal: 'Industrial strategy and technological change', *Journal of Development Economics*, (Volume 22, No 1, June 1986).

37. For cross country reviews, see Lee, E: *Export-led Industrialization and Development,* (ILO, Geneva, 1981).

38. For an analysis of regional distributional issues, see Griffin and Khan (ed.): *Growth and Inequality in Pakistan,* (Macmillan, London, 1971).

39. For details of the regional and ethnic background of Pakistan's early industrialists, see Papanek, H: *The Social Background of Pakistan's Entrepreneurs,* (Harvard University Press, 1969).

40. For details, see Altaf, Z: *Pakistani Entrepreneurs,* (Progressive Publishers, Lahore, 1988).

41. The family of President Ayub Khan was directly involved in the industrialization process, particularly through his son, Gohar Ayub, who subsequently became leader of the Senate in the 1980s. Other families, such as the Habibullahs, also emerged as major industrial families.

42. Pakistan split into two nation-states in 1971. What was then East Pakistan became Bangladesh, while the territory which was West Pakistan now constitutes the state of Pakistan.

43. Zulfikar Ali Bhutto was the political figure who marshalled these forces into an organized political movement. His party, the PPP, contained a mix of the urban left and the rural landed elite, both of whom had grievances against the pattern of industrialization.

44. These political economy factors were examined in more detail in Part 1 of the book.

45. For details see Sarmad, K: *Pakistan's Economy in the 1970s,* (PIDE, Islamabad, 1982).

46. This was in spite of the political patronage which bloated employment in the Steel Mill. Much of this manpower was not needed by the technology and was effectively an employment subsidy provided by tax resources.

47. Particularly favoured during the 1980s were entrepreneurial groups in the Punjab, some of whom, such as Nawaz Sharif, entered the political arena directly. For details see Weiss, A: *The Rise of an Industrial Bourgeoisie in the Punjab,* (Vanguard books, Lahore, 1992).

48. An analysis of Pakistan's manufacturing export performance is contained in Asad Syed: 'Industrialisation in Pakistan', (Ongoing Ph.D. thesis, Cambridge University).

49. The interim government of Moeen Qureshi published a list of the worst offenders in 1993. Most of the prominent businessmen were on it.

50. As stressed earlier, the law and order situation, particularly in Karachi, not only hampers a major export push but also prevents a substantial infusion of foreign direct investment.

51. These included an ill-thought out army operation which, if anything, exacerbated the political problems.

52. The nationalizations of the financial and industrial sectors, in particular, created a major investment slump and considerable uncertainty over the future evolution of the industrial structure.

53. Growth is necessary but not sufficient for the impact on poverty. For an analysis of necessary and sufficient conditions, see Rolph van der Hoeven: *Structural Adjustment, Poverty and Macroeconomic Policy: Experiences and Reflections in the Light of Recent Theory,* (International Labour Office, Geneva, 1995).

54. For detailed analyses of different aspects of the green revolution, see, *inter alia,* Choudhry, Ghaffar: 'Green Revolution and Redistribution of Rural Incomes—Pakistan's Experience', *Pakistan Development Review,* Autumn, 1982; Mahmood, M: 'The Pattern of Adoption of Green Revolution Technology and its Effects on Land Holdings in the Punjab', *Pakistan Economic and Social Review*, Islamabad, Volume 15, 1, 1977; and Hussain, Akmal: 'Regional Inequalities and Capitalist Development', *Pakistan Development Review*, Autumn, 1974.

55. Pakistan's agricultural output consists principally of crop and livestock production; the contribution of fishing and forestry is negligible.

56. For details of trends in total factor productivity, see Qureshi, S.K: *Agricultural Pricing and Taxation in Pakistan,* (Pakistan Institute of Development Economics, PIDE, Islamabad, 1987); Byerlee, D: *Agricultural Productivity in Pakistan—Problems and Potential,* (World Bank, Islamabad, 1995); Qureshi, et al: *Taxes and Subsidies in Agriculture as Elements of Intersectoral Transfer of Resources,* (PIDE, Islamabad, 1989); and Khan, M,H: *Underdevelopment and Agrarian Structure in Pakistan,* (Boulder, Colorado, Westview Press, 1981).

57. For a more detailed analysis, see Khan, M.H: op. cit. and Hussain, A: 'Distribution of Landholdings in Punjab', (Unpublished Ph.D. thesis, University of Sussex, 1979).

58. This is reflected in political alliances, where groups such as those led by Nawaz Sharif primarily have urban support, particularly in the Punjab, while parties such as the MQM dominate urban Sindh, and the PPP is increasingly associated with rural groups.

59. For details of the impact of the policy regime on the sector, see Hamid, N, Ijaz, N, and Nasim, A: *Trade, Exchange Rate and Agricultural Pricing Policies in Pakistan,* (World Bank, Washington, 1990); and Nadeem-ul-Haq: *Agricultural Pricing Policy in Pakistan,* (International Food Policy Research Institute, Washington, 1993).

60. For a review of the estimates, see The World Bank: *Pakistan—A Strategy for Sustainable Agricultural Growth,* (Washington, 1995).

61. Ibid.

62. There are a few military farms but these are insignificant in relation to domestic production. They are frequently linked to procurement of output by military bases.

63. Byerlee, op. cit.

64. See Ghaffar Choudry and the World Bank, op. cit.

65. Although there are tractor subsidies.

66. For a detailed discussion of the reform issues and their implications, see Khan, M.H: *The Structural Adjustment Process and Agricultural Change in Pakistan in the 1980s and 1990s,* (PIDE, Islamabad, 1994), and the World Bank: op. cit.

67. The extension services require institutional reform, which go beyond the need for resources only. A number of proposals have been made to improve their effectiveness, including ones about linking extension services to the research centres.

CHAPTER 10

SOCIAL SECTOR REFORMS
The Health Sector

Health is the supreme wealth...wisdom is better than wealth.
Buddha

INTRODUCTION

Pakistan's economy has the dynamism and resilience to attain annual rates of growth in the 8% region. Such increases in income, along with equity-enhancing reforms, are central to future prosperity and social cohesion. Measures to stimulate growth were discussed in Chapter 9 and are summarized in Chapter 11. This chapter examines some of the issues which are critical for improved distribution and equity.

The need for an improvement in the quality of social services, particularly education, was stressed in Chapter 3. Some of the issues raised with regard to the education sector are referred to below. However, this chapter illustrates the problems of reform in social service delivery by examining the case of the health sector in more detail.

The previous emphasis placed on higher education is evident in the high quality of professionals produced by Pakistan. A substantial body of bankers, lawyers, economists, and civil servants has been produced, many of whom have excelled internationally. Private spending on education is substantial, and is more than double public expenditures. Annually, a large body of Pakistani students leaves for universities abroad. A number of European and American universities have also established campuses in the country.

In addition, a domestic private sector has mushroomed. During the 1980s, there was dynamic growth of private school chains across urban Pakistan.[1] Most of these schools are mixed in terms of gender, and many perform creditably in a difficult environment. Private schools have created their own teacher training institutions and have begun to send some of their staff for training in international centres. Private universities have also been established, and some provide excellent education in areas such as business administration.

Welcome as this buoyancy of private education may be, it only reaches the urban middle classes and the upper income groups. The gulf between the 'English medium' groups and the rest of society is enormous. The education system reinforces the divisions between these two nations rather than acting as a mechanism for social integration.

The public education system is beset by a number of serious shortcomings. The neglect of primary education has been referred to earlier and analysed in detail elsewhere.[2] In addition to this fundamental flaw in sectoral allocation priorities, a number of other germane problems confront the education sector. Sophisticated and rich languages such as Urdu are denigrated and treated as inferior, as are the regional languages. While English should retain a central role in the education system, the demands of social cohesion and cultural self-respect necessitate recognition of Urdu and the respective regional languages, and their inclusion in a common core curriculum which should be taught across the nation. The reaction to a damaging past should not be to abolish English; on the contrary, its standard has to be raised. What needs to be broken is the assumed link of national languages with conservative and reactionary forces in society. This change needs to be reflected in the development of a liberal multi-lingual curriculum, particularly at the school level.

Mandatory primary education and a more liberal multi-lingual curriculum are key elements of developing an education system which helps build social cohesion while creating a literate society. A strong maths, technology, and science orientation is vital for Pakistan's economic development. Such a technical orientation was vital in East Asian success.

Many of the issues of organization, management, decentralization, and regulatory capacity are endemic to all the social sectors in Pakistan. This chapter examines the institutional problems of the health sector as an illustration. Many issues of sectoral financial reallocation and management reforms in health are virtually identical to the problems confronted in education.[3]

THE HEALTH SECTOR
Past sectoral record and current situation

The frequently expressed concerns regarding the health status of Pakistan's population tend to overlook the progress made since independence. The control over certain diseases, rampant in pre-partition days, has been a substantive achievement. Programmes of immunization have contributed to reduced mortality in infants and children. Maternal mortality has also been reduced. One of the indicators of human development, average life expectancy, has increased by 40%. However, impressive as these figures may appear, their contextual relevance is underscored by a comparative analysis. Most post-colonial developing countries have more impressive health records than Pakistan's; the fact that the country's GDP growth record has been better than average reinforces the image of unbalanced development. The poor relative health performance of Pakistan is reflected in the table below.

39. CHANGES IN LIFE EXPECTANCY AND CHILD MORTALITY
Select Asian Countries 1960-88

Country	Life Expectancy			Under-5 Mortality	
	1960	1975	1987	1960	1988
Bangladesh	40	46	52	262	188
India	44	52	59	282	149
Indonesia	41	49	57	235	119
Kampuchea, Dem.	42	36	49	218	199
Laos, PDR	40	42	49	232	159
Malaysia	54	54	70	106	32
Myanmar	44	54	61	229	95
Pakistan	43	50	58	277	166
Thailand	52	60	66	149	49
Sri Lanka	62	66	71	113	43

Source: UNDP: *Human Development Report, 1994.*

Pakistan's record on some human development indicators such as life expectancy, is somewhat similar to that of India, as pointed out in Chapter 1. However, in other areas, the South Asian record in general and Pakistan's in particular, lags well behind the rest of Asia. This is evident in the trends in under-5 mortality, where only war-torn Kampuchea and Bangladesh fare worse than Pakistan. India's record is seven times worse than Malaysia's and three times poorer than Thailand's (*see* Table 39).

As mentioned elsewhere, the primary reasons for this imbalance were the insecurities associated with a new nation state. Unsure of whether the new country would last, the allocations of public resources were disproportionately biased towards defence. Such distortions were inherent in the geo-politics of partition and the brunt of the security dilemmas was borne by Pakistan, as the country whose existence was in question. A part of the explanation for Pakistan's poor human development record is related to the security strains on public expenditure. However, as the examples of Korea and Taiwan show, high defence spending is not incompatible with major gains in human development indicators (*see* Chapter 4).

As far as the record of past health sector programmes is concerned, the more significant achievements have been in the increased control over several communicable diseases. None the less, the majority of deaths remain attributable to diseases that are preventable. This is illustrated in the Pakistan Demographic Survey of 1988, which noted that 58% of all deaths were due to three causes: (i) infectious and parasitic diseases; (ii) diarrhoea and enteritis, (iii) pneumonia and bronchitis. Similarly, the National Health Survey of 1982-3 found that infectious and parasitic diseases accounted for 52% of total morbidity prevalence, whereas diseases of the respiratory system accounted for 18%. Another critical area of health concern is the high levels of infant and maternal mortality, which are related to high fertility rates in an environment where the support infrastructure of primary health care is negligible.[4]

ORGANIZATION AND MANAGEMENT[5]

The organizational structure of the health service in Pakistan can be described at two levels. The first is the network of over-stretched public sector facilities, whereas the second refers to the mainly urban-oriented, private provision of health services. As far as the public sector is concerned, the 1973 constitution, including its various subsequently amended forms, gives primary responsibility to provincial governments for the administration and provision of the health care delivery system. However, the fact that the federal government is responsible for several important components of health delivery leads to a much more diffuse system of public sector provision.

The federal government undertakes a wide variety of functions, which combine regulatory duties, special programmes, and training responsibilities. Specific functions include national planning and co-ordination, regulation of pharmaceutical supplies, containment of communicable disease, provision of health services for federal government employees, establishment of postgraduate medical centres and colleges, and other responsibilities not borne by the provinces. There are also various special-purpose, vertical programmes: an expanded programme of immunization, and the control of diarrhoeal disease, acute respiratory infections, malaria, and tuberculosis. The vertical programmes are planned and funded primarily at the federal level.

The functions of the provincial health departments include the provision of health services to the entire population—directly in the case of teaching hospitals and special institutions—and through a general health hierarchy headed by the provincial Director General of Health Services, District Health Officers, District Headquarters Hospitals (DHQ) under a medical superintendent, Tehsil Headquarter Hospitals (THQ), Rural Health Centres (RHC), Basic Health Units (BHU), dispensaries, and Maternal-Child Health Centres (MCHC).

The impact of a poorly functioning and inefficient state machinery is felt most keenly in the low priority ministries, such as health. The high profile departments, such as the Ministry of Finance, attract the relatively better staff. The federal government, in general, tends to acquire more qualified employees. Those departments considered low priority, such as provincial health and education, are frequently at the bottom rung of a degenerating public sector. The weaknesses of health sector management have to be seen in this context.

The deficiencies of health sector management can be divided into three categories: fragmentation, centralization, and inadequate procedures. Currently, operational management is rather fragmented. A district health officer does not supervise district hospital staff; a medical officer in charge of a basic health unit does not have power over vertical programmes staff. Reporting lines of authority are ill-defined. For instance, some old BHUs report to RHCs while new ones are directly accountable to DHOs. At the rural level in particular, the organization of health services is not conducive to efficient management. Key rural health staff are in vertical programmes or other departments, and therefore are not under the direct authority of the medical officer in charge of the RHC or BHU. The District Health Officer's management ability is further hampered by excessive workloads resulting from outdated management routines, as well as the constant need to refer upwards for almost all decisions.

As far as centralization is concerned, there is a general absence of delegation of authority for operational decision-making at the district or divisional level. Decision-making for matters such as programme budgeting and finance are restricted to the top level of the provincial and federal hierarchy. This kind of system obviously prevents local authorities from taking any initiative to improve health service delivery. For example, at the district level, the District Health Officers have only limited authority to manage budgets, appoint or fire staff, or plan and co-ordinate activities within their district.

Partly as a result of the above, a pervasive sense of passiveness and weakness dominates overall management and organizational structures. The systemic bias against local initiative, poor quality of health information, virtually non-existent logistical support, and the lack of merit as a criteria for staff appointment and promotion have collectively undermined morale in the health services. Similar problems abound in the education sector.

HEALTH MANPOWER

The quality and quantity of medical manpower are important determinants of the efficiency of the health services. As far as quality is concerned, impressionistic evidence suggests a general decline in recent decades. Apart from exceptional centres of training, medical staff receive their education in indifferent medical institutions. These centres of learning have grown rapidly without adequate care regarding the quality of trainers or the resources available for a proper medical education. The pattern of medical manpower expansion in Pakistan is a reflection of middle class demand pressures being accommodated by heavily subsidized public sector supply. Many parents perceive the rate of return to medical education to be high. During the 1950s, the 1960s, and the 1970s, becoming a doctor was an avenue for high domestic earnings, social status and/or migration abroad. The low salaries and status associated with other categories of medical manpower such as nursing have led to low demand and a consequent imbalance in the health manpower profile.

The gap between private return and social costs widened as a large number of doctors went abroad after receiving a subsidized education. The public sector supply response to the unrelenting private demand pressures led to a rapid acceleration of educational facilities, particularly in the 1970s. Subsequently, the opportunities for migration dried up and the real wages of domestically-employed doctors have declined. The downward pressure on wages is related to the excess supply in urban areas, the preferred location for graduate doctors.

The pattern of past expansion in medical manpower documented in Table 40 is consistent with the above analysis of high demand for doctors and subsidized public supply, accompanied by a neglect of other manpower. Between 1971 and 1981, the number of physicians nearly doubled, and between 1981 and 1990, the number of physicians increased four-fold, reducing the doctor-population ratio by 78 per cent. Over the same period, 1971 to 1981, the number of nurses

40. TRENDS IN HEALTH SECTOR INPUTS BY PROVINCE

Province and Resource	Year			Growth Rate: 1971=100		
	1971	1981	1990	1971-81	1981-90	1971-90
SINDH						
Doctors	2620	3805	21854	145	574	834
Doctor/Pop. Ratio	5240	5022	1136	96	23	22
Nurses	1102	1886	4021	171	213	365
Nurse/Bed Ratio	5.7	5.1	6	89	117	105
Hospital Beds	9749	15097	23954	155	159	246
Bed/Pop. Ratio	1408	1266	1430	90	113	102
PHC facilities	689	1633	2366	·237	145	343
PHC/Pop. Ratio	19927	11701	10493	59	90	53
PUNJAB						
Doctors	3727	7200	23171	193	322	622
Doctor/Pop. Ratio	9788	6593	2663	67	40	27
Nurses	1730	2534	5343	146	211	309
Nurse/Bed Ratio	6	6	6	100	103	103
Hospital Beds	16530	23729	32962	144	139	199
Bed/Pop. Ratio	2207	2000	1872	91	94	85
PHC facilities	2026	3174	4605	157	145	227
PHC/Pop. Ratio	18006	14956	13399	83	90	74
NWFP						
Doctors	371	1287	6803	347	529	1834
Doctor/Pop. Ratio	21930	8521	2121	39	25	10
Nurses	148	328	1059	222	323	716
Nurse/Bed Ratio	27/8	16.4	11	59	67	40
Hospital Beds	6431	8427	11510	131	137	179
Bed/Pop. Ratio	1265	1301	1254	103	96	99
PHC facilities	717	1298	1737	181	134	242
PHC/Pop. Ratio	11347	8449	8308	74	98	73
BALOCHISTAN						
Doctors	227	600	1623	264	271	715
Doctor/Pop. Ratio	10374	7228	3354	70	46	32
Nurses	97	190	345	196	182	356
Nurse/Bed Ratio	12.7	801	10	64	123	79
Hospital Beds	1928	2416	3464	125	143	180
Bed/Pop. Ratio	1221	1795	1571	147	88	129
PHC facilities	253	609	843	241	138	33
PHC/Pop. Ratio	9308	7121.	6457	77	91	69
NATIONAL						
Doctors	7000	13322	53451	190	401	764
Doctor/Pop. Ratio	8982	6336	1991	71	31	22
Nurses	3105	5004	10768	161	215	347
Nurse/Bed Ratio	7/4	606	7	89	106	95
Hospital Beds	36-33	51552	71890	143	139	200
Bed/Pop. Ratio	1745	1637	1480	94	90	85
PHC facilities	3972	7281	9551	183	131	240
PHC/Pop. Ratio	15830	11593	11141	73	96	70

Source: *Annual Report,* Director General of Health; ratios are computed.
UNDP: *Human Development Report for Pakistan,* (Islamabad, 1992).

increased by approximately 60%, and by a little more than 100% between 1981 and 1991. As a consequence, the number of nurses per doctor decreased from 0.44 in 1977 to 0.2 in 1990. By international standards, there should be four nurses per doctor, and thus the data indicate a relative surplus of physicians and a shortage of nurses. Another indicator of imbalance is the fact that while physicians increased seven-fold over 20 years, the number of PHC facilities increased by only 140 per cent. While the pace of expansion of facilities has not matched the rate of growth of physicians, there is evidence to suggest that these facilities are seriously under-utilized.[6]

In addition to the obvious imbalance in rates of growth among various health resources, there are regional disparities. The ratio of nurses per hospital bed is substantially lower in Sindh and Punjab than in the NWFP and Balochistan. The ratio of hospital beds to population has changed little in the NWFP and Sindh and has increased substantially in Balochistan. On the other hand, the PHC facilities-population ratio in Punjab (13 399) is over twice the ratio in Balochistan (6457)[7] (see Table 40).

Another serious imbalance is the concentration of medical facilities and resources in urban areas. While around 65% of the population is resident in rural areas, reports suggest that 83% of employed physicians are in urban areas. In addition, 85% of all hospital beds, 82% of all hospitals, 97% of all TB centers and 58% of all MCH centers were concentrated in urban areas in 1990.

There is no formal structure to provide health services below the BHU unit designed to serve a population of 5 to 10 000, and thus it is estimated that 36% of the population, approximately 39 million rural residents, have no reasonable access to basic health care. As a consequence, there is a strong correlation between distribution of resources and urban-rural mortality rates.

In an effort to meet medical needs, early attention was devoted to training doctors. Development of medical schools increased, however, far beyond the needs of the nation. Currently, there are 17 medical schools producing approximately 4000 doctors annually. During periods of heavy recruitment of professional personnel by the capital-rich, population-poor Gulf States, a substantial number of medical graduates could expect to find employment outside the country. Such opportunities have declined substantially as a consequence of the fall in oil prices during the 1980s. Consequently, it is estimated that there are approximately 8000 doctors currently unemployed or underemployed in the country.

The oversupply of doctors and the limited capacity of the government sector to absorb more and more graduates means an increase in the number of doctors in the private sector. Per force, most of the growth of private sector medical care has been in the most inefficient form of health care provision: the single practitioner working out of a single office.

While there is much to be said for encouraging an open health market, there are also significant problems. First, there is no quality control. There is no annual or regular accreditation system, no license renewal requirement, and thus no follow-up or regular inspection. Nor has any self-regulating professional association developed. Second, the increasing dependence on the private sector means growing pressure for some government subsidies in one form or another. These subsidies result in further centralization of medical capital investments in urban areas. The financial pressure on the government, however, arises not simply from pressures to provide subsidies in various forms, including low cost equipment loans, but also because basic medical education is essentially cost-free to the consumer. Thus, the government is funding the generation of surplus medical personnel in one particular category, and this group in turn places further financial pressures on the state by limiting its practice to the one sector of the population better served by existing resources: the urban population.

In contrast to the surplus of doctors, there is an apparent shortage of personnel in almost every other professional category. The output of medical specialists is estimated to be about 135 per year while the demand is approximately 600 to 700 specialists a year.

While there are 47 nursing schools in Pakistan, the number of applications is low. Nursing remains primarily a female occupation, and the problem of expanding the nursing staff is linked to the undersupply of female health workers at all levels and in all categories. The problem is particularly severe in the rural areas. Efforts at recruiting and retaining female staff in rural areas are complicated by low rural female literacy, the low status of nursing and paramedical professions, regulatory rigidities which discourage re-entry to service, the absence of incentives for working in rural facilities, and general cultural constraints on the employment of women. The cumulative result of these various factors is that there are many vacant posts for nurses and other female health workers.

In summary, the pressures on policy-makers have distorted the supply of health manpower. There is an overproduction and under-utilization of doctors; shortages exist in all other categories. Medical personnel are concentrated in urban areas. The concentration of surplus physicians in urban areas provides the opportunity for private sector expansion, but there are no structures to provide quality control. Moreover, the unbalanced distribution (by category and geographic area) is inefficient. The government is providing essentially no-cost medical education for an increasing surplus of doctors, many of whom will be unemployed and/or underemployed, pressuring the government for employment or capital resources.

FINANCING HEALTH CARE

Many, though by no means all, of the organizational and manpower difficulties discussed above are related to problems of financing. Inadequate resources not only make recruitment of quality personnel difficult, but also provide a fertile ground for excessive distortion of manpower priorities as powerful interest groups capture a small pool of resources. In this section, we shall concentrate on the third aspect of the health sector—finance.

The government's investment in the health sector is minimal. The health sector share of GNP is only 0.90 per cent for FY 1995-6, a figure which is low by any international standards. However, a variety of surveys indicate that private sector involvement, primarily in urban areas, increases the total financing of the health sector to about 3.5 per cent of the GNP, and this level of financing does not compare unfavourably with countries at the same level of development as is Pakistan. Thus, non-governmental investments in health care are approximately 2.5 times that of the federal government.

However, one needs to treat the combined public and private sector expenditure figure with great care. Low government funding accompanied by high private expenditure may reflect the fact that the latter is primarily going into curative measures, disproportionately biased towards the richer urban groups. Such an allocation would be consistent with inadequate health indicators for the population as a whole, which is the case in Pakistan. Public resources directed at preventive measures tend to affect these indicators more strongly than curative facilities.

The Health Care Financing Study[8] of 1986-7 indicated that 53% of total health expenditures were from private households,[9] 34% from **all** levels of government, 7.6% from employers, and 4.4% from foreign aid. The high proportion of private household expenditures on health is reflected in the fact that 57.1% of total expenditures and 69.5% of all recurrent expenditures on health were made in the private sector (doctors, hospitals, prescribed drugs, and traditional medicines). Government services generated 32.8% of total expenditures, 24.5% of recurrent expenditures, but 88.7% of all capital expenditures on health. As noted earlier, one has to be cautious about the link between private expenditure and health indicators. The fact that people get sick more often may explain high private expenditures. More preventive health investments require public resources.

It has already been noted that the amount of federal government investment in health is low by international standards and there is evidence that the funding is allocated in such a way as to be less effective than it could be.

The current picture of health services is one of underfunding, demoralization, and degenerating quality in the public sector, accompanied by a private sector which is expanding rapidly but remains unregulated, uneven, urban, and almost exclusively curative. Inevitably, there are a few excellent prestige hospitals. To restructure the sector requires more than a simple infusion of resources. More funding is necessary but it would have to be part of a package of reform measures.

Outlining desirable changes is not intended to abstract from the considerable difficulties of implementation. The changes suggested below are likely to face problems similar to those which impede the delivery of other social services.

RESOURCE MOBILIZATION AND PROVISION

Having acknowledged that the health sector requires systemic reform, not just a simple infusion of resources, it is worth emphasizing that many of the changes will not be sustainable if they are not supported by additional resources. At the aggregate level, therefore, it may be desirable to set a target for an increase in health sector allocations from 0.9% of GDP to the average for LDC, 1.5%. At present, the trend is in the opposite direction. Education and health expenditures have been cut since the start of the Structural Adjustment Programme in 1988. Reaching and sustaining the higher health expenditure target requires revenue mobilization and, ideally, an increase in economic growth. A sequential expansion should take place which raises public commitment to above the LDC average in order to compensate for past neglect. The low tax-GDP ratio in Pakistan suggests considerable capacity for resource mobilization, an issue examined in more detail elsewhere in the text.

The expansion of primary health spending should be, and should be seen to be, directly linked to the taxation of agricultural incomes. These redistributional equity-enhancing reforms are critical for greater social cohesion.

Public sector expenditure on health and education will require priority claims on expanded tax resources. Without such resource commitments, it is difficult to envisage serious progress in human capital development. Thus, the suggested framework is one where the private sector acts as the engine of growth in production and trading activities, supported by a public sector which raises more tax resources to concentrate on human development activities and provide infrastructure. The focus of the public sector should be to spend these increased resources on primary health care, mainly through decentralized units under the control of local and provincial authorities. This direction of reform should be supported by efforts to incorporate and encourage NGOs. The Punjab Health Foundation (PHF), established in 1991, provided an example of a framework for promoting health NGOs. One-third of resources were to be provided by an NGO, supported by a grant and a loan of one-third of total capital requirements from the public sector.

A second course of additional funding is wider introduction of user charges. In practice, *de facto* user charges have already been introduced in a number of ways. Typically, they have arisen out of the need to fill the shortage created by inadequate recurrent funding. Thus, 'free' treatment in government hospitals is anything but free. Patients have to buy medicine in the private market; the government continues to subsidize treatment by providing beds and doctors, but selective user charges have been introduced by measures such as requiring private purchase of medicine. For political reasons, governments find it difficult to announce withdrawal of ostensibly free services. However, most provincial governments have proposed the introduction of a wide range of user charges, as part of the preparation for the Social Action Plan.

In particular, the SAP submission from Punjab contained very detailed suggestions for user charges in health and education. This is an area where conditions set for aid by donors also exert pressure on the public sector to withdraw from commitments it cannot afford and which impose an unsustainable burden on recurrent budgets.

Indeed, the systemic problem regarding recurrent cost funding is symbolic of the chronic under-funding of social sector programmes. The poor recurrent cost availability to maintain services is an effect of unsustainable promises on the public delivery of services. Put quite simply, the government cannot afford to provide the services that it has taken upon itself to deliver. At the same time, there is continuous pressure to extend the coverage of free or subsidized government services to larger and larger groups of the poor. The demands of political support-building imply that governments find it hard not to succumb to such pressures. This leads to disproportionately high capital commitments.

Thus, the structure and dynamics of public sector health services are such that a small pool of resources are disproportionately allocated to capital costs; the resulting inadequacies in recurrent cost funding imply that the quality of existing services tends to decline at the same time as new services are introduced. The expansion of new services creates more pressure on recurrent costs and the downward spiral of deteriorating quality is accentuated. To rectify this situation, a larger infusion of tax resources has to be accompanied by formalizing user charges and adoption of planning procedures, whereby the recurrent cost implications of capital cost commitments act as effective constraints on politically-determined, random capital expansion.

ORGANIZATION AND MANAGEMENT

As stressed earlier, health sector reform involves more than additional resources. The second set of changes relates to organization and management. A critical issue to be considered is regulation. This concern emanates from a broad redefinition of the role of the government in the health sector. The incapacity to financially sustain the current pattern of public provision of health services has led to a movement regarding the need for a much larger involvement of the private sector and NGOs with the government. However, as the public sector withdraws in service provision relative to the private sector, its responsibilities need to be **reinforced** rather than curtailed.

Particularly important is the regulatory capacity to monitor the private sector. An unregulated private sector can literally be lethal, particularly for the poorer segments of society. Because of the high quality of medical practitioners, along with the relatively substantive resource inputs, the private provision of services for the well-to-do has an element of quality control built into it. The most severe distributional impact of unregulated health services is felt by the poor. Diluted medicine, unqualified staff, and dangerous hygienic conditions form the disturbing milieu for the provision of health services for the poor. One of the preconditions for a more effective curative component of the health sector is to establish an effective regulatory body. This should contain private sector health practitioners as well as public sector representatives. Under the present proliferation of urban private sector health facilities, the most effective role for the public sector may well be to encourage and monitor self-regulation by the providers and consumers of the services. NGO personnel could, in certain circumstances, act as knowledgeable representatives of consumers, specially in areas where they are involved in the delivery of health services to the poor.

The recommendations for the health sector contain a combination of additional resources and management reform. The discussion above was cursory and merely illustrative of the difficulties involved in reform. The key issue is to increase allocations for primary health spending, to be accompanied by the required management and regulatory changes. Similar problems plague the public sector delivery mechanisms for primary education and population welfare. Collective reform of these services is central to the role to be played by the state for a more equitable society. Apart from the direct welfare benefits of primary health investments, a key development objective is the reduction of an exponential population growth rate. Reforms of health, population welfare, and primary education are necessary to address this critical problem facing Pakistan.

NOTES

1. Education chains such as the Beaconhouse School System, City, and Grammar Schools emerged across the urban landscape.

2. For details see Weiner, M and Noman, O: *The Child and the State in India and Pakistan,* (Oxford University Press, 1995).

3. Ibid.

4. There are specific implications arising from poor health, mortality, and morbidity patterns described above. First, both infant and maternal mortality are influenced by fertility patterns; early age at marriage, early first birth, short birth intervals, and childbearing late in the reproductive years of life are related to increased risks of infant and maternal mortality. See J.G. Cleland

and Zeba A. Sathar: 'The Effect of Birth Spacing on Child Mortality in Pakistan', *Population Studies* 38, 1984. Second, high levels of infant mortality reduce birth intervals and may encourage females to persist in childbearing to ensure ending their reproductive experience with a desirable number of surviving children, particularly sons. See A.A. Razzaque Rakanuddin: 'Infant-Child Mortality and Son Preference as Factors Influencing Fertility in Pakistan', *Pakistan Development Review*, XXI:4, Winter, 1982.

5. The issues involved in public sector reform have been the subject of several public administration reports. The most recent, and one which summarizes many of the issues previously raised, is Robert La Porte Jnr, et al.: *The Management Development Report on Pakistan*, (UNDP, Islamabad, 1992).

6. For details, see Dr M. Mohsin Mubarak: *Health Coverage in Pakistan*, (Rawalpindi, The Army Press, no date). Mubarak writes: 'An average BHU (Basic Health Unit) generally attends to 2000 to 6000 patients a year which is less than 10% of the expected number in the target population,' (p.14). For details of the health sector analysis, see the *Human Development Report for Pakistan*, (Graham Pyatt et al. UNDP Islamabad, 1992).

7. This summary is based on the UN's Human Development Report for Pakistan. Dr Beecher was the principal consultant for the health sector. The author was a member of the team which produced the report.

8. GOP, Ministry of Planning and Development: *Health Sector in Pakistan: A Financing and Expenditure Study*, (Islamabad, 1988).

9. Nearly two-thirds of household expenditures were on pharmaceuticals (63% of total household health expenditures), about one-fifth on consultation (21%), and 7% on traditional medicine.

PART C
THE FUTURE IN THE BALANCE[1]

CHAPTER 11

IMPLOSION OR EQUITY?
Scenarios for the future

Reformers have the idea that change can be achieved by brute sanity.

George Bernard Shaw

WHAT LIES AHEAD?

Pakistan's economy has the dynamism and resilience to attain annual growth in the region of 8%. Such buoyancy in income growth, along with measures to improve equity, is central to the country's future prosperity and social cohesion. The policy changes required to achieve these objectives are given below, in the light of the experience of the past five decades.

The turbulence of an anxious half-century masks many achievements. The economy has performed far better than the collapse predicted at partition. Further, as a country, Pakistan is here to stay. Questions about its future viability are no more valid than those confronting other multi-ethnic nation states. Yet it is fashionable to question the future existence of Pakistan whenever there is a serious crisis. This is largely due to the break-up of the country in 1971. However, the creation of Bangladesh was virtually inevitable because of the shambolic manner in which Britain had partitioned India. No one could seriously have expected the deeply flawed physical separation to be sustainable. While the manner in which the country was managed politically did not help[2] it is difficult to see how the security threat to a physically bifurcated Pakistan could have been prevented. Militarily, it was always vulnerable to external intervention.

While Pakistan's existence as a nation-state seems assured, it none the less faces the threat of an internal implosion.

After 50 years of independence, deep pessimism about the country's direction has resurfaced and is evident in public forums.[3] But the decline into the abyss is by no means inevitable. This chapter considers some of the possible interventions which could arrest this decline. In many ways, it is an exciting historical juncture, in which different groups are engaged in a battle over the 'big issues': the place of religion and ethnicity, the clash between landed and industrial interests, and the type of economic structure to be established.

The dynamics of change in Pakistan are rapid. Commentators continue to describe the society as 'feudal'. While Pakistan's landlords still exercise considerable influence, the picture is by no means static. This is evident in the fact that the first and third largest political parties in the 1990 and 1997 elections were both primarily urban.[4] Pakistan will be a majority urban nation by 2010. Indeed, the principal reason for the delay in conducting a census arises from facing up to the reality and consequences of urbanization. The most significant implication is the further shift towards urban centres as the driving force in the political system.

In Europe, North and South America, and Asia, such conflicts have historically been resolved after civil wars. Inevitably, there will be conflicts ahead but the engrossing issue is who will 'win' in Pakistan. Later in this chapter we argue the case for a set of measures required to create a liberal-democratic political structure and a social market economy. The suggested measures are instruments for creating a reasonably equitable, forward-looking, educated society.

Positive regional developments and negative internal ones

One of the paradoxes of the current era is the positive impact regional developments have had on furthering national identity in Pakistan, although internal developments are causing severe strains. While regional developments have assisted in reinforcing national identity, domestic developments are, at present, leading to an implosion.

Two regional events, in particular, deserve mention. In themselves both events are tragic, but their impact on Pakistani society has been to create certain bonds.[5] The tearing down of the Babri mosque in India in 1992 had a profound impact on Pakistan's post-partition generation. Pakistan's demographic profile is such that the majority of the country's population has not lived in India.[6] The belief in Pakistan's rationale and legitimacy has been strengthened by the destruction of the Babri Mosque in particular and the rise of Hindu fundamentalism in general. The revival and persistence of communal tensions across the border have reinforced the empathy for the insecurity felt by Muslims as a minority in India. These tensions have helped mitigate the cynicism about the rationale for Pakistan's existence.

Second, events in Afghanistan and the Soviet Union have substantially reduced the possibility that the northern areas of Pakistan will merge with Afghanistan and Central Asia.[7] After Bangladesh, there were mounting fears that the NWFP and Balochistan would secede and merge with cultural identities in Central Asia and Iran, which are historically powerful. The mobile history of the region suggests that new nation-states could be created in several ways which are different from the existing boundaries. The threat of secession, however, has receded after the disintegration of Afghanistan and the Shia fundamentalist revolution in Iran. Pathan integration into Pakistan's power structure and economy is now extensive. No substantial group within Pakistan has an interest in seceding, nor the capacity to do so. Neighbouring governments and external powers also have an interest in a united Pakistan, since a further dismemberment would create major territorial uncertainties.[8]

In contrast to these external developments, domestic instability is testing unity and self-belief. There is a growing sense of anarchy and loss of control. The absence of direction and the non-resolution of simmering conflicts are undermining the viability of democratic institution-building.

Murtaza Bhutto's killing, at the hands of state agencies in September 1996, is illustrative of the deep malaise that now engulfs Pakistan's political system. The murder of the Prime Minister's brother, and the apparent inability of Benazir

Bhutto to take action against the culprits, contributed to the sense of impotence of her government. Murtaza's killing proved to be the final straw leading to the dismissal of Benazir Bhutto's much maligned second regime. It was also another painful reminder that the key to Pakistan's future economic and political security lies in Karachi. The city's disintegration has for too long been viewed as a provincial matter.

The sections below examine the short-term dynamics of the political system, and then analyse the underlying structural problems which have immobilized state institutions and led to an intractable paralysis of governance.

THE CURRENT INSTABILITY
ITS DYNAMICS AND EFFECTS

The current political system has incentives for anarchic, unstable government, not parliamentary democracy. It is thus the worst of all possible worlds. This distorted incentive comes from two simple facts: no elected civilian government has ever transferred power to another civilian government in Pakistan; all have been replaced through non-electoral instruments. On average, military regimes have tended to last for a decade, while civilian regimes have a tenure of three years.

Because of the distorted incentive, the opposition has an interest in destabilizing the country rather than helping to build democratic institutions. Their governments were removed in a similar way, and therefore they will test the will of those who hold ultimate power, which does not reside in parliament. Previous dismissals have made it clear that ultimate power still resides with the military. This power is frequently exercised through what has become, in effect, a presidential system, although he is not elected through a popular vote.[9] Thus, a major problem in the political system prevalent since 1988 is the incentive to destabilize rather than act as a 'responsible' opposition.

This instability would not be quite as serious if the economy could be insulated from it. This is largely the case in countries such as Italy and Korea, where many political upheavals have coexisted with a robust economic performance. Unfortunately, this is not the case in Pakistan and the economy has suffered. The country needs to grow by at least 6% per annum, just to keep unemployment pressures from mounting. Growth in the region of 7 to 8% is desirable and achievable under a stable policy regime.

The principal political reason for the poor performance[10] is the rural-urban split in political alliances, frequent policy shifts, and politically-determined uncertainties on private capital. This leads to a haemorrhage of private investment. PPP is almost an entirely rural party[11] and the opposition consists of industrialists and traders, whose enterprises become the subject of victimization. This leads to an investment 'strike' and protests. The incentive to bring a government down through mass protest was noted earlier. When those involved in the process are urban businessmen and trading groups, both political and economic systems suffer.

There are many economic reasons for the slowdown in growth, which have much to do with the macroeconomic unsustainability of the growth path pursued in the 1980s. But this slowdown in growth has been compounded by political divisions affecting policies and stability. These have accentuated the economic causes of the slowdown.

When you compound the above with the escalating violent ethnic conflict in Karachi, you get a situation in which the civilian political system appears as an impediment to the next stage of economic development in Pakistan—labour-intensive exports. For the Pakistani economy, the opportunities provided by labour-intensive exports to the booming East Asian economies are the key to employment generation. Upgrading quality and increasing value added in manufacturing activities—such as leather products, garments, and textiles—are crucial if the country is to absorb the growing labour force productively.

Such employment generation would diffuse some of Karachi's problems as well. Too frequently, the protagonists in Karachi have focused on the job quota policy in the public sector, which is a form of positive discrimination. However, this is more a symbolic than a real debate, since there are virtually no jobs in the public sector. The critical issue is the pace of employment generation in the private sector, which would be influenced considerably by the success of a manufacturing export drive. Thus, Pakistan and Karachi are caught in a vicious circle. Conflict in the principal commercial city has undermined a manufacturing export drive and deterred foreign direct investment.

One of the major economic costs of Karachi has been the failure of Pakistan to benefit from globalization. Between 1986-90, foreign direct investment (FDI) grew exponentially, at annual rates of 28% across the world. Much of the FDI came into Asia, but generally shied away from Pakistan, largely due to the conditions in Karachi.

In brief, the dynamics of the current system are pushing the country into persistent political instability and economic stagnation. Underlying these short-term dynamics are a number of unresolved structural factors which are, as noted earlier, leading to a paralysis of governance.

THE STRUCTURAL PARALYSIS OF GOVERNANCE

As it approaches its Golden Jubilee celebrations, it is widely acknowledged that the country has lost direction, its institutions are not working, and its elite is above the law. These are symptoms of a political system that has aggravated rather than resolved or accommodated the four competing claims and sources of conflict evident since independence. The Pakistan movement contained the dynamics of four distinct groups, whose subsequent conflicts have shaped the country's political economy:[12]

- The **Muhajir elite**, who were the descendants of the Muslim leadership who had governed India since the 13th century. They led the Pakistan movement politically and provided the core of the initial entrepreneurial class. They had no physical base in the country that was created, somewhat similar to the situation in Taiwan.

- The **religious ulema** who, ironically, did not support the movement for a separate Muslim state in South Asia and were not in the forefront of a movement which was led by liberal constitutionalists.

- The northern **landlord-military** elite, which had provided substantial manpower to the British colonial army. Such recruitment was based on notions of 'martial races'. The relationship between the northern landlord-military elite and the Muhajir leadership was fraught with friction.

- The **mass-base** of the Pakistan movement, which had great expectations regarding the equity principle that would guide the new nation-state. To its followers, the Pakistan movement was about improving the lives and the standard of living of South Asian Muslims and not just the elite groups.

After partition, all four components exerted mutually incompatible demands on the political system. Instead of a firm direction and the resolution of conflicting demands, the state has become the repository of fundamentally incompatible conflicts.

1. The Muhajir Elite

The Muhajirs have lost power and are embroiled in a debilitating ethnic conflict with the group that ironically accepted them at partition but have since felt marginalized in their own province. As leaders of Indian Muslims, the Muhajirs tended to disapprove of ethnic identities, emphasizing the larger communal similarity. Subsequently, the Muhajirs have moved from an anti-ethnic force to one which insists on being recognized as a fifth nationality within Pakistan. It is not surprising that in a country where ethnicity has played such a major role in shaping identities, this fifth 'imagined community' has surfaced. The political system has not yet produced a stable equilibrium as far as the struggle between ethnic groups is concerned. Accommodation amongst ethnic groups is far from settled, and conflict is most acute in Sindh, although prevalent in other regions as well.[13]

2. The Religious Ulema

For the first two decades the religious leadership had no share in power.[14] As mentioned earlier, many of them had opposed Pakistan. Thus, they played a far less influential role than the religious groups in Israel, the only other modern nation-state created exclusively on the basis of religion.

The religious groups were mainly involved in sectarian conflicts in the early post-independence years. This was evident in the Qadiani movement in the early 1950s, when religious parties used street power to try and have a sect declared as being beyond the pale of Islam. But these groups were supplicants to a generally more 'westernized' elite, a hybrid generation created by colonialism. Religious parties were largely marginal to the policy issues, and Pakistani elite secularism was in many ways very similar to that in India.

But the influence of the religious leaders has increased substantially since the early years. They received a strong boost after the 'oil boom' in the Middle East and the increasing wealth and influence of conservative governments in the region. Resurgent pan-Islamism, along with financial resources, provided external support to the religious parties. Domestically, their major ally came in the form of General Ziaul Haq. Under him, they got their first taste of power, as the Jamaat-i-Islami got four posts in the Cabinet;[15] ironically, at a time when this religious party's popular support was wiped out in its erstwhile stronghold, Karachi.

As a consequence, Pakistan got a theocracy from the top during the 1980s; this was very different from the mass-based Iranian revolution, but none the less had far-reaching institutional implications, which have compounded the paralysis of governance. The reforms undertaken at this time have affected the basic institutional structure. There was ambiguity about which law was supreme: the precise pronouncements of the Shariat Courts, or civil law. The validity of existing finance laws was, for example, challenged on grounds of incompatibility with religious injunctions relating to interest. Matters came to a head in 1991, when all interest-based financial laws were to be abrogated; the issue was not clarified but handled by default. The government referred the issue to the court, where it lies dormant in the expectation that it will be forgotten.

The legal system, the social system, and the constitution underwent radical change during this half-baked theocracy. The social change involved particularly harsh legal measures against women—at a time when much of East and South East Asia were enacting progressive measures which were advancing women's role in society.

The religious leadership had reshaped a Pakistan from whose creation they had largely been excluded. The 1980s created a comprehensive institutional mess at the level of the state; with the revival of liberal democracy, many of these fundamentally contradictory institutional changes remained in place. They were not abrogated and their legal protection, through the Eighth Amendment, paralysed government institutions.

The revival of civilian government has occurred under a confused institutional umbrella. Previously enacted regressive measures against women are difficult to repeal. Similarly, ordinances which effectively introduced a presidential system could not be repealed without a two-thirds majority in parliament.* In a political system providing an incentive for the opposition to topple a government through street power, such structural reform is postponed. The paralysis of governance is compounded since you cannot pursue theocracy and liberal democracy at the same time.

In brief, the political system has not clearly resolved the precise role to be played by religion. Legal and institutional changes undertaken during the 1980s have left an ambiguous legacy, which has not been resolved after the revival of parliamentary democracy. Clerical parties are not likely to come to power but they have already shaped the institutional and cultural environment.

3. The Military-Landlord Elite

The political system is further compounded by the inability to resolve the question of the supremacy of civilian or military rule. Competitive tensions between the northern military-landlord elite and the civilian political leadership from other provinces surfaced soon after partition.[16] These were compounded by the mysterious assassination of Liaquat Ali

---

* While this book was in production, in April 1997, through the 14th Amendment to the constitution, the powers with regard to dismissal of national assembly and appointments of chiefs of armed forces were withdrawn from the President.

Khan, who was the last civilian political leader from amongst the refugees from India to have exercised power. The civilian leadership of the majority province, Bengal, was largely left out of substantive policy-making power.

The troublesome issue is not that there was conflict about the supremacy of military and civilian rule. This debate has occurred in all the countries liberated from colonialism and engaged in subsequent overwhelming social change. What is contributing to the paralysis of governance is the fact that the issue remains unresolved after 50 years. The country has produced fragile and temporary democratic institutions which are replaced periodically with martial law. The process has been somewhat similar to the one in Thailand, which has also witnessed a constant see-saw between military and civilian supremacy.

Until recently, a non-elected president had supreme authority over an elected prime minister, adding to the confusion over the distribution of state power. This was the result of a military president wishing to exercise control over the civilian leadership. But unlike General Pinochet in Chile, who withdrew in a manner which has allowed democratic politics to revive, General Zia's ordinances had created a paralysis of authority. It is difficult for a civilian government to establish a direction for the country and to pursue it, if it is always under threat of arbitrary removal. Time which should be utilized in governing with authority and strength is wasted in institutional bargaining and internal compromise to retain power. The insecurity is compounded by the fact that not a single elected government has transferred power to another.

Thus, martial law, theocratic institutions, and a liberal democracy make a strange cocktail and create an unworkable institutional hybrid. Unresolved questions about the military, civilian, or theological roots of the institutions of state have contributed to the paralysis of governance.

4. Mass Equity Expectations

Finally, the Pakistan movement embodied expectations of economic equity. For ordinary citizens, the rationale of the new nation-state lay in the opportunities it provided for South Asian Muslims. Policies which laid the base for private sector led development were sensible and have contributed to a respectable growth performance. But in many other crucial areas, the state moved strongly against an equity principle being embodied in policies. There were no land reforms, and the landed elite continue to be exempt from direct taxation. It is estimated that the landed aristocracy receives between 6 to 10% of the national income but pays virtually no direct taxes.[17]

By the mid-1990s, the income distribution was the worst in the country's history since independence. Unlike Eastern Asia, basic education and health investments have been neglected, making Pakistan one of the least literate countries in the world.

Allied to these causes of inequity is the total lack of accountability of the elite under law. There is a virtual impunity against illegal actions. Laws are openly flouted by the powerful. Political protection is frequently and visibly granted to criminals. The absence of any serious attempts to address equity has created two nations.

The result of these four sources of conflict being intensified through the political system, rather than resolved or mitigated, has led to an overwhelming sense of paralysis and *Angst*. A confused institutional structure and the lack of direction creates a splintering of the state. Institutions appear to be pursuing separate agendas without any overall direction or control. While the state seems paralysed and unable to give direction, employment pressures and social explosion mount. The tensions are intensified, as safety valves such as labour migration to the Middle East dry up.

STEPS TOWARDS RESOLUTION

Does this bleak picture imply an implosion and a descent into further internal chaos? Or will Pakistan pull back from the brink and demonstrate a resilience that has been evident in the past? An implosion is possible if no corrective measures are taken and the country slides into greater anarchy. But there is nothing inevitable about the process. There is an intense national debate on what needs to be done and the scale on which it needs to be enacted.[18] Future trends will be determined by the pace and direction of the response to the current paralysis.

Three scenarios are suggested below. The first contains measures required to address the fundamental dilemmas confronting the political economy of Pakistan. The direction of reforms suggested is aimed at creating a tolerably harmonious liberal democracy and a reasonably equitable economy.

The other extreme is the third scenario which is the likely drift towards an implosion that is an inherent danger in the arrangements prevailing in the mid-1990s. The middle ground, and second scenario, rests on the ability to undertake some but not all of the reforms suggested in the policy agenda outlined below. The 10-issue agenda for an optimum reform scenario consists of a mix of critical political, administrative, and socio-economic reforms:

Political

1) Since military intervention takes place in a vacuum of power, civilian institutions should be strengthened through constitutional arrangements .so that such a situation does not come to pass. Political parties should practise politics of tolerance and learn to live under opposing regimes without resorting to efforts which will destabilize the government. There should be no ambiguity and no going back on this issue; it will simply compound the current institutional crisis. Too many governments have been replaced in the recent past. None of the summary dismissals have arrested the political decline and corruption, which they were supposed to do. Benazir Bhutto's second dismissal has also compounded rather than resolved the problem. A serious commitment to addressing corruption requires the creation of a genuinely independent judicial and law enforcement system. Arbitrary presidential removals, even of patently unsavoury and incompetent regimes, do little to resolve the underlying institutional confusion. The principle of elected civilian governments transferring power must be allowed to be embedded.

2) The Muhajir-Sindhi conflict is the most serious political problem confronting Pakistan. Its resolution is required, not only for more harmonious ethnic relations but for sustained economic growth. Outward-oriented labour-intensive manufacturing is critical for income and employment generation. Such a sizeable and sustained increase in exports is not possible until Karachi becomes calm, and investment is made in the modern infrastructure necessary for exports. Economic measures in support of political initiatives should include the encouragement of Sindhi entrepreneurs,[19] through directed credit schemes, to establish export-oriented firms. Such interventions have been used effectively to support the Bumiputras in Malaysia[20] within a disciplined market framework. Export-orientation will provide that discipline. Karachi is not a regional problem. It is an issue which is central to Pakistan's economic and political progress. A workable accommodation between Muhajirs and Sindhis will require a Herculean effort to rise above the accumulating bitterness. None the less, Pakistan's continuing nation-building struggle requires a concerted attempt to thrash out a power-sharing agreement. Previous failures to do so between the MQM and PPP ought not to be the excuse for giving up the ghost. The MQM remains a representative force and needs to be given a say in the urban local government, at the very least. Its armed militant activities have to be crushed as part of the process of removing weapons from civilians. Social measures in support of political reconciliation should include the encouragement given in schools. But the approach should be based on incentives, not threats. Muhajir children should be encouraged to have a basic conversational competence in Sindhi, but without the threat of linguistic job quotas. People cannot be expected to be fluent in all three, but citizens of Sindh should be able to communicate in English, Urdu, and Sindhi. Measures such as these would be a small investment—but with potentially big returns—for social cohesion.

3) Theocratic laws, which discriminate against women and are therefore in violation of the 1973 constitution, must

be repealed. The present regime can put its overwhelming majority to good use and take initiatives aimed at the dismantling of gender discriminatory legislation.

Socio-economic

4) Mandatory primary education must be introduced gradually over the next decade. This should initially cover the first five years of schooling only. This is a key social investment, with huge externalities. Women must get basic education to assist in the change of their subservient role. This is also the most effective way of ending child labour and associated ills. Mandatory primary education helps raise the cost of rearing children and, thereby, puts pressure on reducing the fertility rate. Child labour provides the reverse incentive for fertility behaviour. Primary education and health investments are critical for reducing population growth.

5) The privatization of state and financial sector institutions, ruined through patrimonial influences, should continue. Politically motivated debt write-offs, land grants, and such corrupt activities have increased the returns from rent-seeking behaviour rather than from building efficient and internationally competitive business enterprises. A significant part of the proceeds from the sale of public units should go into writing-off domestic debt. As discussed earlier in the text, budget deficits in the 1980s were financed through domestic debt accumulated at high interest rates. One of the ironies of the situation is that a number of large landholders have invested their savings in these bonds, thus earning high returns due to a budget deficit which they helped create.[21] This debt is imposing a huge burden on this as well as future generations. Debt servicing has become the single largest item of public expenditure, higher than defence spending. A critical immediate opportunity for addressing this problem is to use privatization revenues to retire domestic debt. This will simultaneously release resources for needed expenditures on human development by reducing the largest claim on public resources.

6) Raising the level of savings in Pakistan is critical for sustaining a high level of growth. At present, the country's savings rate is in the region of 14% of GNP. This compares with savings rates of 30 to 40% in Eastern Asia. It is true that East Asian high savings are part of a virtuous circle of high growth and higher savings. None the less, their savings rate was higher even when they were at a stage comparable to that of Pakistan. Further, they undertook several measures to raise the volume of savings, thereby becoming more self-reliant. Sustaining growth and reducing aid dependence requires that Pakistan urgently undertake measures to raise the savings rate by around 6 to 8% of GNP. Past efforts have tended to be oriented more towards curbing the conspicuous consumption ethos through indirect taxation of luxuries. More concerted efforts need to be channelled towards better savings mobilization. Clearly, the privatization of financial institutions is a move in the right direction. It needs to be supplemented by other measures. The use of the postal system, for example, has been extremely effective as a source of savings in Eastern Asia. Indeed, this has been far more substantial as a source of savings, than other mechanisms which have attracted more attention, such as the Grameen Bank in Bangladesh. In sum, saving mobilization efforts have to combine a mix of privatization, an examination of the potential of postal savings institutions, and micro-credit schemes, such as Grameen.

7) Policy reforms under way to create better incentives for exports should be sustained. Exchange rate management to maintain competitiveness has to be accompanied by supply side measures. Inadequate communications and physical infrastructure, as well as shortages of skilled manpower, are serious bottlenecks to a growth in higher quality exports.[22] These include the need for public investment in physical infrastructure and training. Investments in physical infrastructure could be aided by higher savings mobilization and FDI. Skill training could be enhanced by joint ventures and training institutes which could be funded by public resources, but should have a strong management involvement by private firms.

Policy reform in sectors such as textiles and leather must be made to increase fiscal incentives to export higher value added items. Political stability in the port city of Karachi is also essential, as mentioned earlier, for a sustained export drive.

8) Ideally, land reforms should be enacted to reduce the political power of the landed elite and to improve economic equity. However, in the current circumstances, land reforms would be half-baked and would make matters worse by increasing insecurity and reducing investment. The rural equity issue should be addressed through two measures. First, the introduction of direct taxation on agricultural income, which should be used to finance: mandatory primary education; targeted credit for export-oriented units established by Sindhi entrepreneurs, and building the infrastructure required for export promotion. Formally, the agricultural income tax is likely to have been passed by the time this book is published. However, what is important is not only that substantial resources are raised but also that the proceeds are seen to be linked to equity-enhancing measures. If the impression is created that landlords are being taxed to finance debt servicing and defence, popular enthusiasm will wane. Linking the tax reform to specific equity changes will cement social cohesion. The second element for reducing landlord influence on politics is to insist on the holding of an honest census. This is required for obvious reasons, but the simple truth it is likely to reveal may have more far-reaching political impact than a half-baked land reform.[23]

Institutional

9) Administrative reforms are crucial. No civil service can perform effectively in the conditions which affect Pakistan's bureaucrats. Only 5% of jobs in the civil service are now given on merit; the rest are given on quotas. Pakistan's debate on the civil service too often focuses on its political role. The civil service needs to become an efficient and professional management agency. The task of managing a society of 130 million is extremely

challenging and requires professional competence. Lateral entries and arbitrary dismissals should be terminated. Professionalism and morale could be boosted by sound entry procedures through the revival of an independent Public Service Commission.[24]

10) An independent and non-theocratic judiciary is needed. While the broader principle of laws remaining consistent with Islam could be maintained, as it was in the 1950s, the Shariat Courts should be disbanded. The appointment of judges needs to be protected from the current level of politicization. A number of proposals have been made in this regard which require implementation.[25] Judicial scrutiny of executive actions is required through more effective local tribunals and ombudsmen. The momentum to create an independent judiciary, as envisaged in the 1973 constitution, needs to be sustained. Along with the civil service reforms referred to above, these would improve accountability of the executive, provided there is civilian rule. As with many policy areas in Pakistan, the details of the reforms required to create an independent judiciary have been well-documented.

THE THREE SCENARIOS

The above set of measures represents a suggested optimum scenario. If these reforms are undertaken, many aspects of political fragmentation and inequity would be arrested. Many of the suggested reforms are not new and involve implementation of the 1973 constitution. Some of the social policy and economic reforms build on the success of Eastern Asia. While it is relatively easy to identify the changes required, the agency of change is not self-evident. But the ferment within urban groups and the frustration with the existing order is likely to see the emergence of political forces with such an agenda.

The second would be the medium or reasonable scenario. Not all of the conflicts are resolved but some of the key ones are, in order for the country to establish a clearer economic and political direction. Not all the reforms are undertaken, such as land reform, and not all the laws that need to be repealed are replaced, but they are ignored in implementation. However, an agreement on civilian rule is reached; Karachi stabilizes and export-led growth picks up.

Finally, there is the worst case of the implosion scenario. Pakistan is unable to resolve its increasingly complex crisis of governance. It implodes internally, with a number of conflicts—ethnic, sectarian, and criminal. The state is unable to control light weapon proliferation, the economy declines to negative per capita growth, a debt crisis looms, and inflation accelerates. Unfortunately, Pakistan appears to be heading in this direction.

The recently elected Nawaz Sharif government has the political space and the support of business to give Pakistan a sense of economic direction. Early moves suggest a promising start. Much depends on the outcome of this historic opportunity for Nawaz Sharif, perhaps even greater than the opportunity that Z.A. Bhutto had in 1972.

Pakistan is situated at the crossroads of the West and the East. It has tended to look westwards—either to the West or to the Muslim Middle East. Only some technocrats, particularly economists, have been fond of looking East.[26] It is time Pakistan went beyond its security alliances with China as its main interest in the East. It needs to learn, participate, and take advantage. A new world is being created within Asia. It must not let the opportunity slip. An imploding Pakistan is likely to rediscover, as Africa has done, that the world carries on without undue worries about the marginalized.

NOTES

1. Title of UNDP report on Pakistan's development, 1995. The author was a member of the report preparation team.

2. For details of the political background to Pakistan's break-up see Zaheer, H : *The Separation of East Pakistan,* (Oxford University Press, Karachi, 1995).

3. Even a casual review of newspapers, journals, magazines from Pakistan, and outsiders' articles on the country, demonstrates a virtually universal mood of *Angst* and pessimism.

4. Nawaz Sharif's Muslim League and the MQM are both largely urban parties.

5. Whether these bonds are temporary, as is frequently the case with unity during war, is difficult to judge.

6. Indeed, over half the population is under 25, which means they were not alive at the time of the last conflict with India (1971).

7. Afghanistan was the only country to vote against Pakistan's admission to the UN.

8. This was not the case in Bangladesh, where the former East Pakistan became a new nation-state. A balkanization of the current Pakistan would create major difficulties for neighbours, even if it were to happen, which is most unlikely.

9. Under General Zia's martial law regime (1977-85) the 1973 constitution was neither abrogated nor retained—it was held in 'abeyance'. In 1985, 8th Amendment Act was passed by the parliament which, in effect, tilted the balance of power strongly in favour of the President and away from the Prime Minister.

10. These economic factors were examined in Chapter 7.

11. Except in the NWFP, where its good showing in Peshawar and Mardan, in the 1993 election, consolidated the PPP's urban vote in the numerically smaller province.

12. The term 'political economy' is being used in the sense of how the exercise of power, and conflicts over the distribution of power, affect economic development. The choice of policy instruments is influenced by the struggles over power, rather than as simple outcomes of a technical debate over policy choices.

13. Many of these ethnic tensions lay buried under the surface until the break-up of Pakistan, which was also along ethnic lines. But until 1971, the tensions were between the Bengalis of East Pakistan and the unified West Pakistan. The ethnic diversity of the latter surfaced more clearly after 1971.

14. Their first taste of power came when the Jamaat-i-Islami was used by the army in East Pakistan as a vigilante force against Bengali nationalists.

15. In 1979, they got the important portfolios of Information and Broadcasting, Production, Water and Power, and Planning.

16. These differences had been evident earlier in a somewhat different context. The formation of the landlord-based Unionist Party in the Punjab, during the 1930s, was partially due to their distrust of the Muslim League leadership which consisted of the

more urbanized groups of northern India.

17. For details see, Mahbubul Haq: *A New Vision of Economic and Social Justice,* (Progressive Publishers, Lahore, 1995).

18. The entry of figures such as former cricketer Imran Khan reflects this sense of urgency regarding wholesale changes. Imran, amongst others, has emphasized the need for structural reform rather than marginal changes.

19. In some export activities, Sindhi entrepreneurs have already emerged. Pakistan's most successful and sophisticated mango exporter is a Sindhi farmer.

20. Malaysia has had comprehensive positive discrimination policies, including preference to Bumiputra owners relative to Chinese, in the privatization of some public enterprises.

21. Landlords are by no means the only category of tax avoiders. But they contributed to the deficit by obstructing proposals for the direct taxation of agricultural incomes.

22. Pakistan's exports are still heavily concentrated in simple low value added products in textile and leather.

23. Farming, however, should not be nationalized or collectivized under any circumstances.

24. For details on administrative reform proposals see, *inter alia, The Economy Commission Report of the Government of Pakistan,* (Islamabad, 1992) and the UNDP/GOP: *Management Development and Administrative Reforms In Pakistan,* (Islamabad, 1994).

25. The Human Rights Commission of Pakistan, for example, has been active in proposing specific reform measures for greater judicial independence.

26. In the South Asian contexts, there is an obvious need to reduce Indo-Pak tensions, particularly as the region is undergoing substantial increases in military spending. The measures required to build trade links, use SAARC effectively, and move on more delicate issues such as Kashmir, are an important dimension but these issues, which have received intense attention, are not dealt with in this book.

Index